An Anthology of Educational Thinkers

by Sally Featherstone

B L O O M S B U R Y

LONDON · OXFORD · NEW YORK · NEW DELHI · SYDNEY

Featherstone Education
An imprint of Bloomsbury Publishing Plc

50 Bedford Square	1385 Broadway
London	New York
WC1B 3DP	NY 10018
UK	USA

www.bloomsbury.com

Bloomsbury is a registered trademark of Bloomsbury Publishing Plc

First published 2016

British Library Cataloguing-in-Publication Data
A catalogue record for this book is available from the British Library.

ISBN:
PB 978–1–4729–3471-0
ePub 978–1–4729–3469-7
ePDF 978–1–4729–3468-0

Library of Congress Cataloging-in-Publication Data
A catalog record for this book is available from the Library of Congress.

10 9 8 7 6 5 4 3 2 1

Typeset by Newgen Knowledge Works (P) Ltd., Chennai, India
Printed and bound in India by Replika Pvt. Ltd.

This book is produced using paper that is made from wood grown in managed, sustainable forests. It is natural, renewable and recyclable. The logging and manufacturing processes conform to the environmental regulations of the country of origin.

To view more of our titles please visit www.bloomsbury.com

Contents

Introduction

Knowing what we must do is neither fundamental nor difficult, but to comprehend which presumptions and vain prejudices we must rid ourselves of in order to educate our children is most difficult.

Maria Montessori

Have you ever wondered why we do some of the things we consider good practice in the early years?

- What makes us so sure that play is essential for children under seven?
- Who said that access to the outdoors, in a garden or outdoor area should be an entitlement?
- Why is attachment so important – is that where the Key Person idea came from?
- We assume that talk is essential to children's development, and we do so much of it, but where is the research?
- Does child-sized furniture, and easy access to resources and equipment really make children more independent?
- Are young boys naturally more aggressive than young girls? Where is the research?
- Who started the conversation about nature and nurture? Is it genes or upbringing that makes kids like they are?
- Who decided what constitutes 'outstanding practice in early years'?

To help you make sense of the history of early education, you will find in this book the triangulated links between our practice (what we do in our settings), the theorists who have untangled how children's brains, bodies and imaginations work, and the documentation that supports us in hopefully getting it right for inspectors, managers and most importantly for the children.

This anthology is idiosyncratic, and it is interesting in a sector overwhelmingly populated by women, that of the 33 theorists in this collection, only seven are female. I have included people whose work makes sense to me, and mostly these are psychologists, who study the human mind and human behaviour in the real world, rather than philosophers who study the nature of reality, existence, knowledge, values, reason, mind and language in the abstract. However, some people are both philosophers and psychologists, so I have had to be accommodating in my selection.

In writing about Montessori, Vygotsky, Piaget and other educational thinkers, I wanted to make a collection of theorists and practitioners who have concentrated on practical strategies, either based on the observation of children, or by working directly with them. I also wanted to extract the parts of their work that have had an influence on current early years practice across the world, so you won't find every detail about the life of every theorist in the list. For this you will have to return to the original sources, where you will find the details of everything they ever researched or considered (further reading details are listed in the bibliography p 307). I have just focused on early education.

Even so, my list of 33 influential figures in early education has resulted in a significant volume of pages, ranging in time from the 17th century to the 21st and including:

- The revolutionary Comenius, working in the 17th Century;
- Rousseau, Pestalozzi and Fröebel in the 18th and 19th centuries;
- Binet, Gessel, Pavlov, Dewey and others in the late 19th and early 20th centuries;
- The time of the famous woman educators, among them Montessori, the McMillan sisters and Isaacs, working to promote nursery education in the early 20th century followed by Bruner, Bronfenbrenner, Bowlby and Bloom in the mid- to late 20th century;
- The idealists of the mid- to late-20th century: Malaguzzi, Friere and the ground-breaking influence of Vygotsky;
- And still working, the gurus of the turn of the century, Goleman, Gardner, Csikszentmihalyi, Dweck and others, taking us forward into the 21st century.

My criteria for selection, and the complex nature of some research has resulted in entries of different lengths, and some people who are giants in the field of psychology in general may appear relatively short. This is because the part of their work that relates to early learning is only a small part of their entire life's effort.

The 33 sections of the book are arranged alphabetically by name, and for each individual I have included:

- An overview of their life, love, theory and research;
- Their legacy, and the influence of their work on others;
- How their work has shaped, and relates to the current policies and curriculum guidance across the four countries of the UK;
- Some discussion points to spark your own thinking, and conversation with your colleagues.

In collecting and organising this information, it became clear that I would not be able to include lengthy sections about every well-known name in education history, particularly those whose work has been published most recently. 16 additional names are included as Appendix 1 (p 290), and half of these are women, giving a reassuring message about the experts that will be influencing this sector in future. It also became obvious that a useful addition might be some of the distinctive pre-school and early years systems, such as Forest Schools, and short descriptions of these are included in Appendix 2 (p 297).

Jane Addams

Full name: Jane Addams

Born: 1860

Died: 1935

Place of birth: Cedarville, Illinois, United States

Countries of residence: United States

What she did: Jane Addams worked to improve the living conditions, health and education of immigrant families in Chicago in the early 1900s. She wrote about how immigrant children became 'Americanised' and the consequent loss of connection with their families and cultures.

Influences on education today: Provision in schools to support immigrant children and their families, including those whose first language is not English, to value and preserve their own cultures while adapting to life in a new country.

Theories and areas of work: Socio-behaviourist, American pragmatist

Key influencers and followers: John Stuart Mill; John Dewey

Key works: *The Public School and the Immigrant Child* (1908), *The Spirit of Youth and the City Streets* (1909), *Twenty Years at Hull House* (2004)

With all the efforts made by modern society to nurture and educate the young, how stupid it is to permit the mothers of young children to spend themselves in the coarser work of the world!

Jane Addams

Life, love, theory and research

Jane Addams was born in 1860, in Cedarville, Illinois, the eighth child in a prosperous family. However prosperous, her family appears to have suffered the sorrows common to many families at the time – her mother died when Jane was two years old, three of her siblings died in infancy and another died at the age of 16. This left Jane with much more free time and less supervision than many of her friends; she spent her time playing out of doors, reading and attending Sunday school. When she was four she contracted tuberculosis of the spine, leaving her with curvature of the spine, recurring ill health and loneliness; she was unable to play and run with other children and they often teased her.

She soon became conscious of her appearance, reluctant even to walk to church with her father, an agricultural businessman who she adored.

By the time she reached her teens Addams wanted to make a contribution to her country. She had dreams of working with the poor and decided to become a doctor. She wanted to study at the newly opened college for women in Massachusetts, but her father insisted that she should be nearer home, so she entered the Rockford Female Seminary in Illinois, where she gained a college certificate in medicine in 1881 even though this was not the degree that she really wanted.

The sudden death of her father and the inheritance of a large sum of money changed her life; she moved with her family, including her stepmother, to Philadelphia where she, her brother and her sister, began to study for their degrees in medicine. Further illness, a spinal operation and eventually a nervous breakdown meant that Addams never completed her studies.

The family later returned to Cedarville where Addams' stepbrother operated once more on her back, advising her not to finish her studies, but to take a two year travelling tour of Europe with her stepmother, leaving in 1883. The tour did nothing to improve Jane's mental state and she returned home to another period of depression, during which she read widely about religion and social justice, and decided that she didn't need a degree to be able to help the poor. At this time she also read some of the work of John Stuart Mill, and a magazine article, which was to change her life.

The article described a new charitable idea: the establishment of settlement houses, where mixed social groups and families lived in houses intended to bridge the gap between people from all social and financial backgrounds, working towards a future without poverty or a class structure. This idea inspired Addams to go to England in 1887 with a few friends to visit the first settlement house, Toynbee Hall, in Tower Hamlets, London – housing that still exists today with the same charitable intentions. There they met followers of the settlement movement who were dedicated to blurring the lines between rich and poor by living together, with each group continuing their lives as before, while learning about their fellow residents – creating a neutral space where different communities and ideologies could learn from each other and seek common ground for collective action. She said of the Toynbee Hall settlement:

> … [they] have their recreation clubs and society all among the poor people… in the same style in which they would live in their own circle… so unaffectedly sincere and so productive of good results… it seems perfectly ideal.

> (Knight, 2010)

Addams could have remained a generous rich woman who shared her wealth with poor people by occasional good deeds. However, she decided that even if she couldn't become a doctor, she could still devote her life to making what changes she could, and so she joined the settlement movement. In 1889, with her friend Ellen Gates, Addams founded the settlement Hull House in Chicago, partly funded by Addams herself, and partly by donations. Addams and Gates were the first residents, and the house gradually filled until there were about 25 women, some with children. Hull House was a centre for research, study and debate, including studies of housing, midwifery, infectious diseases, the dangers of poor social health, drug misuse, overcrowding, children's reading, the fate of newsboys, infant mortality, midwifery and truancy. The house provided a place where women from different backgrounds could live together. There was a night school, after-school clubs for children and other facilities for the local residents, many of them immigrants. At its height, Hull House had some 2,000 visitors joining its activities every week, mostly people from the local area.

Addams also saw art as a way to release people from the drudgery of work and to think and act independently, so she opened an art studio and a gallery. Children were welcomed to art sessions here, to work alongside artists, visit local museums and to paint and draw out of doors.

Addams became interested in the problems faced by families immigrating to the United States from other countries, including Europe. The local immigrant mix included Jews, Germans, Italians, Greeks, Canadian French and Irish. These people were mostly impoverished and often neglected their children as they worked long hours for little pay. Addams became very aware that immigrants were in danger of losing their cultural identities after they came to Chicago, losing touch with their culture, language and customs. She began to look at the fate of the children of immigrants, and how they became 'Americanised', losing their cultural identity too. She observed the way that many children had nowhere else to play except the streets, and her book, *The Spirit of Youth and the City Streets* (1909), supported the establishment of play centres and recreation programmes to counteract the erosion of children's spirits when they lived in cities. Hull House also provided many facilities for children, including a kindergarten, reading groups and college extension courses, alongside a playground where children could play safely, off the streets. Her pioneering work in this area accelerated the play movement and provision of play facilities throughout the city of Chicago.

The original purposes of Hull House became focused on educational and social support, including childcare, educational opportunities and the provision of large meeting spaces. Addams gradually expanded her personal influence to include enhancing the role of women. She supported the suffrage movement and encouraged both men and women to consider the future role of women in society, not just as housekeepers and child-rearers. One example of her later social work was her struggle to improve refuse and garbage collection, which she knew were causes of disease in the city, and as a result of this, she was the first woman appointed as sanitary inspector of Chicago's 19th Ward. A Because of her work, death and the diseases associated with street cleanliness were greatly reduced.

Addams was the first American woman to be awarded the Nobel Peace Prize (1931), and is recognised as the founder of the social work profession in the United States. She died of cancer in Chicago in 1935, aged 74.

Although Addams' lifetime of work might be referred to as social work, her interest in the backgrounds and the 'Americanisation' of the children of immigrant families gives her the right to a place in a book of educational theorists. Hull House had high educational ambitions and provided for children throughout their young lives, from kindergarten to postgraduate level, and she was committed to helping immigrant children to preserve their heritage and background as they gradually became assimilated into American life.

Addams' work in the USA at the beginning of the 20th century gives us a clear warning as we reflect on how well we have integrated our own immigrant population of the past hundred years, and how we should respond as we await the arrival of a new wave of immigrants from Africa and the Middle East.

Legacy and impact

Many of Addams' progressive ideas have contributed to the welfare of children and to society in general throughout the United States, where her fight for clean water and for local and national government spending on the health and well-being of poor families and immigrants can be measured against social progress. The educational aims she had are less easy to track, and whether immigrants to the United States in the early 20th century thought that she did preserve their feelings of cultural identity, it is difficult to know. In many ways we have not come far from her times, when she said to a teaching conference in Chicago:

> At present, the Italian child goes back to his Italian home more or less disturbed and distracted by the contrast between the school and the home. If he throws off the control of the home because it does not represent the things he has been taught to value, he takes the first step towards the Juvenile Court.

> (Addams, 1908)

In the mobile society of 2016, with refugees and migrants entering Europe in huge numbers, unknown since the end of the Second World War, teachers have the same concerns. Refugee and migrant children are losing their heritage, but feeling unwelcome in European communities. In school, there is little recognition of their culture or language, and after school, migrant children drift, with little sense of community. Is it any wonder that some become radicalised, and others enter the world of petty or more serious crime?

> …perhaps the schools ought to do more to connect these children with the best things of the past, to make them realise something of the beauty and charm of the language, the history and the traditions which their parents represent.

> (Addams, 1908)

By 2012, one in ten people in the EU was born abroad, increasing more than 30% since 2010. A 2015 OECD report entitled: 'Indicators of Immigrant Integration' reports that:

> The active participation of immigrant families and their children in the labour market and more generally, in public life, is vital for ensuring social cohesion, in the host country and the ability of migrants to function as autonomous, productive and successful self-realised citizens..
>
> (OECD/EU, 2015)

However, immigrant children in the UK still have less chance of getting a good job, are more likely to live in poverty, and are more likely to want a job but not be able to get one. It's even worse for those born in countries outside the EU. Immigrant children are also less likely to attend early childhood education, resulting in those that don't being up to two years behind in reading at age 15.

Some countries have made efforts to improve the chances of immigrant children, and examples vary, ranging from those with a commitment to complete integration, to short-lived experiments, doomed almost from the start. For example:

- The Te Whariki curriculum in New Zealand and the curriculum for the Foundation Phase in Wales are two examples which, through bilingualism and cultural inclusion, attempt to value the cultures of both the minority indigenous population and the majority, usually English speakers.
- In the United States, the No Child Left Behind initiative has laudable aims, but has sunk into a pit of underfunding and disagreement.

In the UK, although each of the four countries has significant elements of disadvantage particularly in big cities, each one has addressed the issue of immigration from new cultures in different ways, some more successfully than others.

In the last decades of the 20th century the UK government followed a policy of integrating children, many of whom were from the Commonwealth, including previous colonies and protectorates where independence had resulted in persecution for some religious or ethnic groups, by providing dual-language teaching in the early years. Bilingual teaching assistants and teachers worked with the children in school, resources and objects of faith from different cultures and religions were provided, and even schools where there were no immigrant children were expected to acknowledge a growing multiculturalism by celebrating special days and festivals. Books and stories that aimed to educate white English children about religions and cultures other than their own were provided.

This focus on the children and the schools often left parents out of the equation and we now appear to be back in the situation Addams was faced with where parents, and especially some mothers, even after living for decades in the UK, are trapped at home still unable to speak English or to participate in the society they live in or the education of their children. This situation provides a potential problem for their children and for society as a whole. Children are again living in two societies – home and school – with their friends in a sort of limbo in the middle. Muslim children from Asian countries and refugees from Kenya are not the only ones to experience this tension between home and school; it applies to a significant number of children migrating into the UK from the EU, and particularly from countries that were formerly behind the Iron Curtain. This issue must be addressed before we embark on welcoming, integrating and educating the children of the current wave of immigrants, scattered from their homes in Syria, Somalia, Iraq and many other countries in Africa and the Middle East. These children will be failed by our education system if we cannot respond appropriately to both their cultures and them as individuals.

The number of immigrant children entering England in the last few years has increased dramatically. Reading the following quotes from a report published in 2015 (but using figures from 2013) it is obvious that the expected influx of immigrants from the Middle East and Africa can only exacerbate the need to prepare schools and settings to accommodate and support these families and the young children who travel with them. A recent report by Oxford University identifies the following issues for the government and for schools, particularly those working with younger children:

> At the end of Reception (5yrs) only 44% of pupils recorded as having English as an Additional Language (EAL) achieve a good level of development (GLD), compared to 54% of pupils recorded as FLE (first language English).

> (Strand, 2015)

Early in the 20th century Addams was concerned that insufficient attention was being paid to supporting the families of immigrants, and particularly to their children. This issue is set to rise to the surface again in the 21st century, and practitioners will need guidance on how to manage the challenge it will present.

Influence on early years practice in the UK

The curriculum frameworks in the UK reflect a long-standing commitment to supporting children who are learning English as an additional language (EAL). However, the emphasis on encouraging the use of a child's home language and in involving parents has changed, and there is much more focus on a collaborative and inclusive approach.

England

- The 'Statutory Framework for the Early Years Foundation Stage' still emphasises the preparation of children for the next stage of learning by ensuring that they are fluent in English by the time they are five.

- There is also a requirement that practitioners should be able to offer a good model of spoken English for children to hear and copy.
- For children whose home language is not English, providers must 'take reasonable steps to provide opportunities for children to develop and use their home language in play and learning, supporting their language development at home'

(DfE, 2014).

Scotland

- In 2009, the government inspectorate in Scotland produced a report about immigrant families and the impact they and their children are making on schools, entitled 'Count Us In: Meeting the needs of children and young people newly arrived in Scotland'. It includes statistics on the number of immigrants entering Scotland and analyses how well these immigrants are being supported, as well as specifying what improvements still need to be made. Recommendations include making sure students needs are assessed appropriately and ensuring every student receives appropriate support and challenge in order to progress.
- The curriculum in Scotland is bilingual, being presented and delivered in both English and Gàidhlig (Gaelic), but there is also an understanding that some children may use additional languages, as specified in 'Creating a Curriculum of Excellence Part 1: 3–18 Curriculum.'

Wales

- The curriculum in Wales is also delivered as a bilingual programme. In some areas, the Welsh language is taught as an additional language throughout the Foundation Phase (3–7), and in Welsh-medium schools, Welsh is the medium for both teaching and learning.
- In the 'Foundation Phrase Framework' documentation, there is a commitment which may prove difficult to fulfil, as it states that children should learn both English and Welsh, and be encouraged to use their home language for learning.
- In the document relating to inclusion, the Welsh government recognises the isolation the ethnic minority children can feel when they don't have other children from their own culture to relate to.
- There is also recognition of the risk that children will face without proficiency in either their home language or in English or Welsh.

Northern Ireland

- The number of immigrant children in schools in Northern Ireland has similarly risen. A large number of these children are from Roma and Somali families, and many have had 'interrupted education' or disturbing experiences. Details of this were provided in a research report entitled 'The integration of newcomer children with interrupted education into Northern Ireland schools'.

- In the same report, schools found that assessing children's levels of competence in a range of subjects was almost impossible because of individual children's experiences. These meant that using standard assessment processes, such as the Common European Framework of Reference (CEFR), was very difficult because the children's level of learning was so restricted, and they either had no previous school experience, or had made multiple moves from school to school, sometimes across several countries. Obviously there is a need for 'a tool, which assesses literacy and numeracy levels of the child in his/her mother tongue thus helping to build a more complete picture of the child's academic ability.' (Northern Ireland Strategic Migration Partnership, 2014). Parents interviewed during the research were appreciative of the work that schools have done, particularly in the small number of schools where this work has encouraged a mutual respect and understanding by providing home-liaison services.

The integration of children from migrant, immigrant, and ethnic minority backgrounds has changed only a little since Addams was working in Chicago. At that time, she could not have imagined how different life would be for immigrant children in the 21st century, and how early education would contribute, even though we still have a way to go until genuine cultural respect flows from family to school and vice versa.

Key guidance documents for countries in the UK

DfE, (2014) 'Statutory Framework for the Early Years Foundation Stage'.
HMIE, (2009) 'Counting us in: meeting the needs of children and young people newly arrived in Scotland'.
Welsh Assembly Government, (2015) 'Foundation Phase Framework'.
Northern Ireland Strategic Migration Partnership, (2014) 'The integration of newcomer children with interrupted education into Northern Ireland schools'.

Things to think about

- What do you think would be the best way to build mutual respect and trust between early years settings and the families of immigrant/migrant children?
- Some children of immigrant/migrant families have very poor levels of language which can frustrate them and other children. What can we do to help?

- What are the best techniques you have used for making a new child feel welcome in your group?

- It would be impossible to provide bilingual support for every language and every immigrant/migrant child. What is the solution?

- How would you manage a home visit to a family who have just arrived in your catchment area with a child who is about to enter your setting?

- How would you find out about the backgrounds of the children in your class during your first week working in a new school?

Albert Bandura

Full name: Albert Bandura
Born: 1925 (still living)
Place of birth: Mundare, Canada
Countries of residence: United Sates, Canada
What he did: Developed the social learning theory: that humans learn to behave by watching each other. Carried out the Bobo doll experiments exploring aggression in young children and whether or not they are influenced by seeing adults modelling aggressive behaviour.
Influences on education today: Practitioners are still very conscious of the effect of adult behaviour on young children. TV often makes this problem worse, and practitioners feel a responsibility to attempt to help children to understand and manage their own aggressive instincts.
Theories and areas of work: Socio-behaviourism, psychology
Key influencers and followers: Robert Sears, Richard Walters
Key works: *Adolescent Aggression* (1959), *Aggression: A Social Learning Analysis* (1973)

Psychology cannot tell people how they ought to live their lives. It can however, provide them with the means for effecting personal and social change.
Albert Bandura , Social Learning Theory, 1976

Life, love, theory and research

Albert Bandura is a Canadian and the youngest child and only son of a family of six of Ukrainian descent. He lived in a remote village and as a child had to become independent and self-motivated in learning. His parents were influential in encouraging him to explore the world beyond the small hamlet where he lived.

In 1949 Bandura moved to the United States where he became a citizen in 1956. He obtained his first qualification in psychology from a distance-learning course and went on to work in universities in the United States where he became famous for work in behavioural psychology. He married in 1952 and has two daughters.

Bandura has become one of the most frequently cited psychologists and has been described as one of the most influential psychologists of all time. He is mainly valued for his work in developing the social learning theory which he believes shapes our lives. The theory states that we learn social behaviours by watching other humans and by copying what we see, reinforcing the learning as we imitate others who we want to be like.

Children are surrounded by adult models of behaviour, both within and outside their families, and young children are spending more and more time with adults outside their homes, watching adults who they may or may not know very well. Young children, particularly boys, will often model their behaviour on superheroes and other characters from film and TV, and many children model the behaviours of their parents and other family members when playing in home corners or other role-play areas. Practitioners are also used as models by the children they work with and can sometimes see their own characteristic behaviours carefully and accurately copied by children in their social play!

Bandura found that the people around the child would respond to their emerging behaviours with either reinforcement (praise and even amusement) or punishment (criticism or facial expressions of disapproval). Of course, positive reinforcement will encourage the child to continue the behaviour so if, for instance, a child is praised for consoling their soft toy in the way he has seen his parents consoling him, he will repeat this behaviour.

Bandura used observation methods to collect information in support of his theories. The most well known of these is the series of experiments called the Bobo doll experiments (carried out in 1961 and 1963), where, under lab conditions, children were exposed to aggressive adult models of behaviour and their subsequent behaviour was observed. Bandura's theory was that neither classical conditioning (see Pavlov p 225) nor operant conditioning (a theory of Skinner, see Appendix 1 p 296) are adequate models to explain human behaviour and that much of our behaviour is learned from other humans. He took behaviourism into the social world, suggesting that reinforcement of learning occurs as we imitate or model ourselves on others we want to be like. He acknowledged the role of mental processes, recognising that learning can occur even though reward or reinforcement may not be immediate or obvious.

The Bobo doll experiment

In 1961, Bandura conducted a study to find out if social behaviours, such as aggression, can be acquired by observing and imitating others, even adults that the child does not know. He and his team carried out tests with 36 boys and 36 girls aged between three and six years old who were attending the Stanford University nursery school in the United States.

First, the children were observed in their nursery school before the experiment to establish how aggressive they were by nature.

Method

The experiment was carried out in a psychology lab to ensure consistent resources, environment and data. The three groups were initially exposed to identical conditions but after the introduction:

- the first group experienced a very aggressive role model;
- the second group experienced a non-aggressive role model;
- the final group was a control: they were observed in the lab but had no adult model.

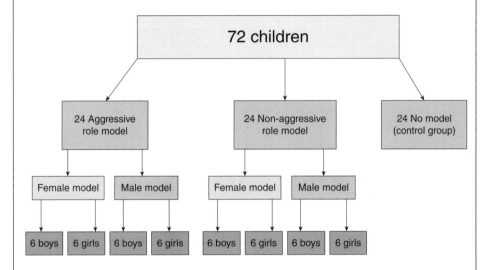

Stage 1: Modelling

In the experimental conditions, the children were individually shown into a room containing toys, potato printing and drawing materials on a table in one corner. They were encouraged to get involved in the play materials, then left for 10 minutes during which different groups had different experiences:

1. The first two groups (the aggressive role model groups) experienced a male or female adult in the room behaving aggressively towards a toy called a 'Bobo doll'. The Bobo doll is a large inflatable clown, with a smiling face. The adults attacked the Bobo doll in a distinctive manner – they used a hammer in some cases and in others threw the doll in the air and shouted 'Pow, Boom'.

2. The second two groups experienced a male or female adult in the room behaving in a non-aggressive way, playing in a quiet and subdued manner for 10 minutes with a construction set and ignoring the Bobo doll.

Albert Bandura

3 The final groups of 24 children were used as a control group and not exposed to any adult model at all.

Stage 2: Aggression arousal

In order to arouse the aggressive behaviour needed for the next part of the test, all the children, including the control group were subjected to 'mild aggression arousal'. Each child was separately taken to a room containing relatively attractive toys. As soon as the child started to play with the toys the experimenter told the child that these were the experimenter's very best toys and she had decided to keep them for the other children and they couldn't play with them. The adult's behaviour was intended to arouse aggression in the child. The experimenter then took the child into another room.

Stage 3: Test for delayed imitation

The next room contained some aggressive toys and some non-aggressive toys. The non-aggressive toys included a tea set, crayons, three bears and plastic farm animals. The aggressive toys included a mallet and peg-board, dart guns and a three-foot Bobo doll.

Each child was in this room for 20 minutes and their behaviour was observed and rated using a one-way mirror. Observations were made at five-second intervals, giving 240 response units for each child.

Behaviours that didn't imitate that of the model were also recorded, for example, punching the Bobo doll on the nose.

Results

- Children who observed the aggressive model made far more imitative aggressive responses than those who were in the non-aggressive or control groups.

- There was more partial and non-imitative aggression among those children who had observed aggressive behaviour, although the difference for non-imitative aggression was small.

- The girls in the aggressive model condition also showed more physical aggressive responses if the model was male, but more verbal aggressive responses if the model was female. However, the exception to this general pattern was the observation of how often they punched the Bobo doll, and in this case the effects of gender were reversed.

- Boys were more likely to imitate same-sex models than girls. The evidence for girls imitating same-sex models is not strong.

- Boys imitated more physically aggressive acts than girls.

- There was little difference in the verbal aggression between boys and girls.

Bandura used these results to support his social learning theory, a theory that children learn social behaviour (such as aggression) by watching the behaviour of others. Since the reports of this study made in 1970, many researchers and commentators have used his theory to support their own views on the effects of violence in the media on children's behaviour.

Experimental methods such as the Bobo doll experiment are useful because:

- The findings appeared to show that adult models did have an effect on the children's behaviour, because all the distracting variables had been removed. They are the only means by which cause and effect can be established.

- Variables in these experiments, such as gender, the time of observations and the behaviour of the models could be carefully controlled by scientists.

- The use of standardised procedures makes these experiments relatively easy to replicate.

Limitations of the procedure include:

- There is no social interaction between the child and the adult model during the experiment, and this meant the child could have no effect on the behaviour of the adult (this way of conducting an experiment is called ecological validity).

- The model and the child are strangers, unlike most behaviour observed by children which takes place within the family.

- Some of the children were already familiar with the Bobo doll and these children were much less likely to be aggressive towards it than children who were new to the doll. Possibly the novelty of the doll made it more likely to spark aggressive behaviour.

- The experiment covered a very short period in a child's life and results were measured almost immediately. Snap-shot studies such as this should not be used on their own to confirm long-term effects.

- Some commentators have implied that the study was unethical, as no check was made on whether individual children included in the study suffered any long-term effects from experiencing the adult aggression.

- The children were all white and all had university student parents, so were not a representative sample.

- Bobo dolls are made to be punched, so some children may be confused into thinking that the adults wanted them to copy the real or video model.

Legacy and impact

Bandura followed up this experiment in 1963, when the procedure was repeated. However, this time the children watched video film of an adult model acting aggressively to the

Bobo doll. Different groups of children saw this behaviour either rewarded with sweets, followed by a 'Don't do it again' warning or with the film ending right after the aggression.

The experimenter did not find differences in the children's subsequent behaviour towards the Bobo doll, based on which film they had watched, indicating that rewards and punishments don't appear to influence learning or remembering information, they just influence whether the behaviour is copied or not. Further research used film and real models with different groups, finding that children who had seen either model of aggressive behaviour were twice as aggressive as the control group, and boys exhibited more overall aggression than girls.

There is some evidence that Bandura's research has affected our views of the impact of violence on children's behaviour. Over the years there have been many research projects and reports on the effect of violence on TV, film and computer games on children's perceptions and imitation of violent behaviour. The television watershed, now entirely undermined by free access to material by computer streaming, and the proliferation of violent computer games and films, continue to concern adults all over the world but no-one has come up with convincing evidence that the increase in violence in society has a direct effect on children. Even the high school shootings in America, terrorist attacks worldwide and stories of teenagers tempted into horrific situations through computer gaming have not seemingly given us enough evidence to indicate that violence breeds more violence.

Influence on early years practice in the UK

Much of the influence of Bandura's work on aggression and violence in young children has been in the area of behaviour management and support for children with special educational needs. Practitioners who work with the youngest children are familiar with the normal tantrums and minor differences among children who may not have had to compromise, share or wait their turn within a large group. This low-level aggression and lack of self-control is managed in early years settings in the following ways:

- Through planned curriculum activities in Personal, Social and Emotional Development, which are undertaken every day and reinforced throughout the day by practitioners: These include circle time, work with puppets and soft toys, stories which focus on feelings and relationships and playing games which encourage children to take turns, work with another child or contribute to a group task.

- Some children find the experience of being away from home, and adjusting to life in an early years setting really difficult and need additional support, particularly in activities that require concentration and sitting still. Teaching assistants or additional practitioners are often the answer as they can provide the sensitive support that children need as they adjust to a new situation.

- The behaviour of a small number of children is of such great concern to practitioners, their managers and the child's parents, that external support from specialists is sought. In these cases, a psychologist or member of a specialist support team is asked to observe the child and give advice about the next steps in helping them to manage their own behaviour in the hope that improvements can be made before the child enters full-time schooling.

- In rare cases, a very young child may be admitted to a specialist school or unit which caters specifically for children with behaviour difficulties. Early admission to this type of provision where intensive support can be given by practitioners who are experienced in managing behaviour disorders is always provided with the expectation that the child will be readmitted to mainstream education.

Early intervention is seen as a crucial element in managing children's behaviour so the responses of practitioners in early years settings can be vital in identifying which children are having difficulties, beginning the process of support and involving the parents in any behaviour management programmes that may be used. The advice and guidance given to practitioners when they are concerned about a child's behaviour differs across the four countries of the UK but the underlying message is the same. What follows is just a small taste of this advice which is usually produced by the relevant special needs team, and can be found on the websites of the government departments of each country.

Scotland

- Guidance to support practitioners working in Scotland reflects the most recent research into behaviour in schools and settings, research that has continued ever since Bandura's original Bobo doll experiments. It gives consistent messages to practitioners and teachers working across the whole 3–18 age range about early intervention, involving families and helping children to fulfill their potential.

- A report entitled 'Framework pre-birth to three' explains that difficult and unexpected changes in a child's life help them to learn how to deal with their emotions and stress effectively, 'and develop the social, behavioural, and cognitive skills needed to overcome obstacles.' (Talge, Neal and Glover, 2010).

- The Early Years Framework for Scotland suggests that early intervention can prevent children from falling into a cycle of deprivation, antisocial behaviour and poverty, and can save thousands of pounds now and in the longer term.

(The Early Years Framework, Scottish Government, 2008).

Albert Bandura

Wales

- In Wales, the guidance again starts with the youngest children, giving a consistent approach and practical, down to earth advice that practitioners and teachers in the Foundation Phase can implement immediately in their settings and schools.

- There are references to recent studies of brain development and how stress can affect the way that children react.

England

- In England, guidance also recognises that early brain development, social conditions, upbringing and genetic factors can all affect children's behaviour. Stress triggers the production of cortisol in the brain and body, and cortisol in turn affects how children behave, making them much more likely to be over-active, aggressive and difficult to reason with.

- The 'Special educational needs and disability' documentation emphasises how important it is that special educational needs are identified and provided for as early as possible: 'Early action to address identified needs is critical to the future progress and improved outcomes that are essential in helping the child to prepare for adult life.'

  (DfE/DoH, 2015).

Northern Ireland

- As in Scotland and Wales, the guidance to practitioners in Northern Ireland gives practical strategies and background information from neuroscience to help practitioners to feel they have the tools to make real changes in children's behaviour by helping them to manage the behaviours themselves.

- The 'Extended early years special educational needs (SEN) supplement, 2012' is particularly helpful in the management of special needs in very young children. It gives a step-by-step approach which includes examples and a range of simple strategies for managing behaviour including aggression.

Aggressive and antisocial behaviour is one of the most worrying issues for individual practitioners and for settings and schools, and appears to be a continuing feature in most settings and a serious feature in others. Stress, marital breakdown, poverty, and overcrowding are some of the causal factors, and these may be further worsened by watching violent screen images, lack of family cohesion, social media and the over-reporting of violence in media and TV. We know that children need security and stability which early years practitioners try to provide for all children, but for some, safe haven in a setting is not enough to counteract what happens when children leave it.

In a time when special needs support has suffered from funding cuts, it is useful for practitioners to have such detailed guidance.

Key guidance documents for countries in the UK

Talge, Neal and Glover, (2010) 'Framework pre-birth to three: Learning and teaching Scotland'.

The Scottish Government, (2008) 'The Early Years Framework'.

Welsh Assembly Government, (2012) 'Practical approaches to behaviour management in the classroom: a handbook for classroom teachers in primary schools'.

DfE, (2010) 'Inclusion Development Programme: Supporting children with Behavioural, Emotional and Social Difficulties – Guidance for practitioners in the Early Years Foundation Stage'.

DfE/DoH, (2015) 'Special Educational Needs and Disabilities: Code of Practice.'

Northern Ireland Department of Education, (2012) 'Extended early years special educational needs (SEN) supplement'.

Things to think about

- Do you think children's behaviour has become worse in the last few years? Why do you think this might be?

- Which sorts of behaviour do you find most challenging in your setting?

- Do you feel you have enough support in handling disruptive behaviour?

- Do you think children are in schools and settings too young or for too long, away from their mothers and the security they can bring? Or is it a good development that helps with early diagnosis and intervention?

- What is the best way to involve parents in helping to manage their children's behaviour?

- How much information do you have about how to handle behaviour difficulties, particularly when you first start working as a practitioner?

Albert Bandura

Alfred Binet

Full name: Alfred Binet

Born: 1857

Died: 1911

Place of birth: Nice, France

Countries of residence: France

What he did: Binet constructed the Binet-Simon intelligence test, later called the Stanford-Binet intelligence test.

Influences on education today: The Stanford-Binet test is among those used to identify additional needs and learning difficulties. Standardised assessments are now becoming much more common in early years education throughout the UK, and are used for identifying levels of development on entry and at the end of the early years to establish starting points for Primary school.

Theories and areas of work: Psychology, Psychometric testing

Key influencers and followers: John Stuart Mill, Jean Piaget

Key works: *Article entitled: L'Etude experimentale de l'intelligence (Experimental Studies of Intelligence)* (1903).

Our purpose is to be able to measure the intellectual capacity of a child who is brought to us in order to know whether he is normal or retarded. … We do not attempt to establish or prepare a prognosis and we leave unanswered the question of whether this retardation is curable, or even improveable.

Alfred Binet

Life, love, theory and research

Alfred Binet was born in Nice, the only child of a doctor and an artist. His parents separated when he was very young, leaving him with his mother who raised him until he was 15 when he went to Paris to study. He qualified in law in 1878 but went on to study medicine, where an introduction to psychology caused him to lose interest in medical studies. He was a self-taught psychologist and found that studying alone was very much suited to his introverted nature.

Binet was one of the psychologists who, at the turn of the 20th century, moved away from looking at children with problems and disabilities to examining what a normal child could do. He was particularly interested in how children think and reason, not in how much they knew of a particular subject. Binet lived and worked for his whole life in France, where at the end of the 19th century a law was passed making it mandatory for children from 6 to 14 to attend school, and it soon became evident that some were falling behind their peers and would need additional help in school.

Binet was already studying the difference between 'normal' children and those described at the times as 'abnormal', and during this time he was approached by the government to develop a test which would establish 'normal' ability. Binet and his research assistant Theodore Simon began work and in 1905, produced a new test for measuring intelligence, which was introduced and called the Binet-Simon scale. In 1908, they revised the scale, dropping, modifying and adding tests and also arranging them according to age levels from three to thirteen.

The purpose of using this scale of normal functioning was to reliably compare children's mental abilities to those of their peers. The test involved children following instructions, copying patterns, naming objects and putting things in a particular order – a variety of tasks Binet thought were representative of typical children's abilities at various ages. Binet and his team had based the tasks on many years of observing children in natural settings and what children of each age could be expected to know and be able to do.

The test consisted of a single series of 30 tasks of increasing difficulty, and was to be administered in a one-to-one situation, by a trained person, initially taking up to two hours to complete. The easiest test items included describing the use of a fork, the hardest items included asking children to repeat back seven random digits, find three rhymes for the French word 'obéisance' and to answer questions such as 'My neighbour has been receiving strange visitors. He has received in turn a doctor, a lawyer, and then a priest. What is taking place?' The team conducted a test trial on a sample of 50 children, ten children for each of five age groups selected for the study by their teachers as being average for their age.

The Binet-Simon test produces an age-related score, called the child's mental age, reflecting the level the child achieved on the test. For instance, if the child could answer the questions intended for the average 13 year old, they would score a mental age of 13, regardless of their actual (chronological) age. If a child of 10 scored at a 13 year old level, they would be deemed 'advanced' or 'gifted'. If they scored at a nine year old level they would be deemed 'retarded', a description used at the time for children who were not reaching the average level for their age. If the child's mental age was found to be the same as their chronological age, they were deemed 'normal'.

Binet was honest about the limitations of the information resulting from his scales of results. He stressed the fact that children developed at different rates and were often influenced by the environment in which they lived and were brought up. He realised that the tests resulted in quantitative rather than qualitative measures and that numbers alone could not really represent the whole child. Intelligence should not be based just on genetics and the only consistent measure would be to test children with exactly the same background and upbringing, which of course was impossible. Binet feared, and his fear was rooted in fact, that intelligence testing might be used for negative reasons such as evaluating immigrants or even to support theories of eugenics – the science of improving a population by controlled breeding to increase the occurrence of desirable heritable characteristics.

In 1916, Lewis Terman of Stanford University translated the Binet-Simon test into English, adapted it to the American culture and school curriculum and renamed it the Stanford-Binet test. This test is still in use today although it has undergone periodic revisions over the years, the last one a significant revision based on a new model of intelligence.

Initially the scores were reported in a simple score of a mental age, just as in the original, but later, mental age and chronological age were used to compute a new metric called the Intelligence Quotient or IQ. This was computed using what is now called the ratio method which involves putting the raw results into this formula: *divide a person's mental age by their actual age and multiply it by 100. For example a five year old with a mental age of 10 would have an IQ of 200 (10/5 x 100).*

Despite his other extensive research achievements and wide breadth of publications, Binet is most widely known today for his contributions to intelligence testing. He was a significant individual in his own right and should be recognised as having made a major contribution to our thinking about early years education, despite never being affiliated to a major university, having no formalised qualifications in psychology and never holding a professorship with a institution with significant numbers of students, where funds would be available to support his work.

Since Binet's death, he has been honoured in many ways, including the renaming of the Free Society for the Psychological Study of the Child to La Société Alfred Binet, and long after his death, an appearance in the journal *Science 84* when the periodical included the Binet-Simon scale in their list of the 20 most significant developments or discoveries of the 20th century.

Legacy and impact

Binet's mental scale was never used by the government of his own country during his lifetime, finding its fame after his death when it became popular across the world, giving the basis for a huge fund of literature and research. It has been used widely because of both the simplicity of the scoring, and how easy it is to administer. However, the simple age-related scores of these older tests have now been overtaken by more subtle methods of testing, particularly those that translate the scores into useful information for professionals and the general public. The currently favoured methods include using a curve of distribution rather than simple age-related norms. The curve of normal distribution, also known as the bell curve, shows scores against a whole population in a much more detailed and non-judgemental way. The scores of the whole population can be entered against a hundred-point graph with relatively few scores appearing at the ends of the curve and a large number around the mid-point. This method gives us a percentile rank for the individual; for example, a person scoring an IQ level of 115 on a particular test would fall at the 84th percentile, having outscored 84% of the population on that IQ test.

Psychologists and their publishers have worked to produce a range of intelligence tests, all assuring the user or purchaser that their test has been rigorously standardised across huge numbers of children. These tests are extensively used in schools to establish intellectual potential among cohorts of children and increasingly in industry to expand interview information in adult appointment processes.

The use of standardised tests to identify learning difficulties and needs has been a continuous thread since the days of Binet, and their use is a key element in judgements about specific learning and physical needs, some of which will attract additional staffing or funding. Educational psychologists, either centrally funded or employed by settings and schools (and sometimes by parents), work to locate these needs and may use standardised tests from a very early age to identify and track the development of the child. New tests have been developed for use with very young children, and to help with the identification of well recognised and more complex needs.

The current interest in raising standards has resulted in a battery of national government tests for school children including the SATs and phonics screenings, and are used to provide evidence of closing the gap between children from low-income families and those from more affluent homes. Screenings of every child at frequent intervals from the moment they enter an early years setting has become the norm and early years practitioners are being asked to contribute to the process by training to administer these screenings or providing information about the child gained through observation. Psychologists and many politicians are now much more aware of the disadvantages of relying solely on the results of standardised tests and therefore a wider picture of the child is usually collected, including information from the child's setting or school, their family circumstances and history and observations of the child at home and school.

Influence on early years practice in the UK

The most powerful impact of the work of Binet on the work of practitioners and the experience of children has been felt in the last 20 years. During most of the 20th century, standardised tests or tasks were generally not used with children under about seven years of age, unless they were thought to need special school education. This reluctance was partly because the interest in child development was not a key feature of government or educational policy and partly because tests for children of these young ages were limited and their results were thought to be unreliable. Of course there was also a fear that children might be 'labelled' at an unsuitably young age. Nursery schools and classes, and providers outside the maintained system were seen as suitable places for most children, perpetuating the philosophy that the great majority of children flourished better at 'their mother's knee' or at the knee of people outside the family who provided the same support.

However, the massive growth in funded childcare, combined with the introduction of national, age-related curriculum requirements across all the countries of the UK, has triggered an interest in children under school age. An imperative to get more women back into the workforce, a desire to raise standards of attainment at the end of schooling and a need to track progress across the whole school age range has required schools to produce conclusive information about the 'gap between children from deprived homes and those from more affluent families' described above. This often does not close during a child's school lifetime and the worrying aspect is that for many children, the gap gets worse as they grow older. Children from lower-income backgrounds are still significantly less likely to do well at school, to get a good job or to make positive relationships with others aside from their peers from more affluent homes.

Children are spending more time in out-of-home care than ever before, and the focus has turned to improving the quality of teaching and learning both before statutory school age and after.

England

In England this has resulted in the implementation of baseline assessment, intended to identify needs at an early stage; both those associated with cognitive, language and physical needs and also to track those children deemed to be in need of additional support because of their family poverty. The 'Early years: guide to the 0 to 25 SEND Code of Practice' states:

> It is particularly important in the early years that there is no delay in making any necessary special educational provision. Delay at this stage can give rise to learning difficulty and subsequently to loss of self-esteem, frustration in learning and to behaviour difficulties.

> Where a child appears to be behind expected levels, or where a child's progress gives cause for concern, practitioners should consider all the information about the child's learning and development from within and beyond the setting, from formal checks, from practitioners' observations and from any more detailed assessment of the child's needs.

(DfE, 2014)

The report entitled 'Early years foundation stage assessment and reporting arrangements 2016' states:

> EYFS profile assessment data can be a source of information about levels of development within a school or setting. For example:
> - levels of learning and development in each of the areas of learning for individual pupils, classes and year groups
> - the attainment of pupils born in different months of the year
> - the attainment of different groups of pupils, for example boys and girls.
>
> (Standards and Testing Agency, 2015)

The latest version of the EYFS Profile (the assessment undertaken by practitioners at the end of the Foundation Stage) is an assessment against a series of age-related statements, where a practitioner makes a judgement on whether a child has not achieved/achieved/exceeded each statement. These judgements are translated into a score which can be compared with others in the group, cohort, local area and across the country once the national figures have been compiled. Unfortunately, the standardisation of the original statements in the EYFS handbook was insecure so the process can only be seen as undergoing some sort of continuing standardisation through regular moderation between practitioners. The disadvantage of this method is that no one checked the thoroughness or coverage of the original statements and any test can be open to dangers of 'testing what is easily test-able'.

Scotland

A report analysing the Performance Indicators in Primary Schools in Scotland reported that children's developmental levels are assessed at the start of school using a standardised test '…at the beginning of Primary 1 by a teacher working through a series of questions with each child on a one-to-one basis.' (University of York, 2016) This creates a baseline from which progress is assessed during the primary years.

Wales

In Wales, baseline assessment on entry to the Foundation Phase is carried out through teacher observation as part of the profile document and assessment at the end of the Foundation Phase, at seven, is based on teacher assessment against the Revised Outcome Statements in the Foundation Phase handbook. The use of these becomes a statutory requirement in 2017.

It is evident that there is a move across the UK to collecting standardised information, which gives comparative data about trends and improvements over time. This information, tracked throughout the child's school life, and using a mixture of standardised tests and teacher assessment will be used increasingly to justify past financial investment and identify future targets.

However, the assessment of very young children still attracts criticism from child development experts who say that, for many reasons it is difficult to make accurate assessments of children's ability at such a young age.

Key guidance documents for countries in the UK

DfE, (2014) 'Early years: guide to the 0 to 25 SEND Code of Practice; Advice for early years providers that are funded by the local authority'.

Standards and Testing Agency, (2015) 'Early years foundation stage assessment and reporting arrangements 2016 (ARA)'.

University of York (2016) 'Children's development at the start of school in Scotland and the progress made during their first school year: An analysis of PIPS baseline and follow-up assessment data'.

Welsh Assembly Government, (2015) 'Foundation Phase Framework'.

Things to think about

- What do you think about standardised tests for very young children? Is it too young to be making such final judgements about their ability when they are still developing so rapidly?

- Have you ever been trained to administer standardised teats? Why do you think you need training for this?

- How much notice do you think a receiving teacher takes of the assessments made by the previous practitioner? Why do you think this is?

- The results from standardised tests and screenings are used to compare schools and in some cases to decide teachers' and practitioners' pay. What are the dangers of this?

- How would you use standardised information such as baseline assessments to begin to match the work you give to individuals in a new class or group?

Alfred Binet

Benjamin Samuel Bloom

Full name: Benjamin Samuel Bloom

Born: 1913

Died: 1999

Place of birth: Lansford, Pennsylvania, United States

Countries of residence: United States

What he did: Developed Bloom's Taxonomy, a way of classifying and organising the elements of learning, particularly in the cognitive (knowledge) domain.

Influences on education today: Bloom's taxonomy has influenced teaching, particularly in secondary schools, where it is used to improve planning and delivery of lessons. His work on mastery has recently become a focus for education at all ages, particularly in the teaching of maths problem solving.

Theories and areas of work: Hierarchical, Education

Key influencers and followers: Abraham Maslow

Key works: *All Our Children Learning* (1980), *Bloom's Taxonomy of Educational Objectives* (1956).

Creativity follows mastery, so mastery of skills is the first priority for young talent.
Bloom, Benjamin S. Taxonomy of Educational Objectives (1956)

Life, love, theory and research

Benjamin Bloom was born, educated and worked all his life in the United States. As a child, he was a voracious reader and a thorough researcher. He read everything and remembered what he read. When he was a child in Lansford, Pennsylvania, the librarian did not believe that he had really read the books he had borrowed in the morning when he came back to change them in the afternoon. However, he was able to convince her by answering all her questions.

Bloom was an educational psychologist who developed many theories about learning, including studies of exceptional achievement and mastery learning. Mastery learning breaks subject matter and content into small chunks, each of which is tested before the learner moves on to the next chunk, ensuring that the new material is not embarked on before the previous chunk is mastered. This method appears to be most effective when learners work in groups.

However, Bloom is much more famous for Bloom's Taxonomy which carries his name although in fact he was the chair of a committee of educationists who devised the theory of a classification of the elements of learning. Bloom divided educational objectives into three domains: affective (feelings), psychomotor (physical skills) and cognitive (intellectual). However it was the cognitive domain that fascinated him, and for which he is best known.

In 1956 Bloom published this theory and it was illustrated by the following diagram known as 'knowing the facts', which is read starting at the bottom layer. The original diagram was updated in 2001 and a new diagram was produced, which has generally replaced the first.

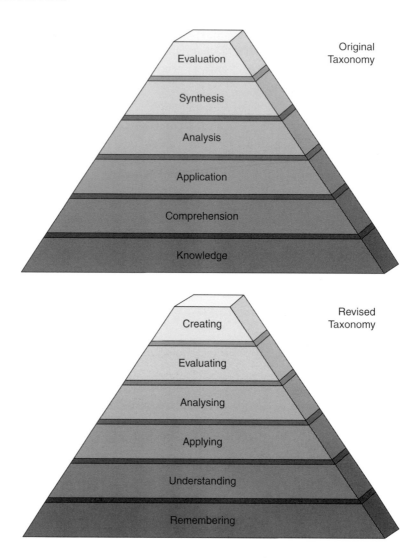

The revised taxonomy uses verbs to describe the domains, which has made it much easier for teachers to use in practice. The taxonomy has always been used more frequently in secondary and tertiary stages of education than in the early years and primary stages, therefore the components of the taxonomy are usually explained in examples constructed for older pupils. However, they all contain the same stages:

- *Remembering*
- *Understanding*
- *Applying*
- *Analysing*
- *Evaluating*
- *Creating.*

In this example, an early years practitioner is using the taxonomy to structure questions and activities for the young children in her group following a visit to the local park.

1. Recall knowledge or information.	2. Understand or interpret information in your own words.	3. Apply knowledge or generalise it to a new situation.
Example: *Tell me what the park was like. Draw and label a map of our park.*	**Example:** *Can you tell the rest of the children about your favourite thing at the park?*	**Example:** *Can you show us what the swans did when we threw the bread on the water?*
4. Analyse and break down knowledge into parts and show relationships among parts.	5. Synthesise or bring together parts of knowledge to form a whole and build relationships for new situations.	6. Evaluate or make a judgement on the basis of established criteria.
Example: *If that was the best part, what was the thing you didn't like?*	**Example:** *Can you use the blocks to make a model of the playground at the park?*	**Example:** *Do you think we should take everybody to the park? Why?*

The taxonomy was extended to other domains, including the affective domain (growth in feelings or emotional areas) and the psychomotor domain (action-based development). However, its overwhelming application has been in education, and teachers (mainly in secondary schools) have used it for many years to structure their lessons so children have opportunities to build their experiences over all the areas of the taxonomy.

There are differing views of the taxonomy and how it might apply to teaching and learning and some feel that the levels overlap, and/or are much more intertwined.

Some teachers only use the top three levels, seeing the lower levels as less relevant to their work. Others criticise the whole taxonomy as being a confusing presentation, with so many potential interpretations, that it is almost impossible to use.

Legacy and impact

Bloom's work was intended to help teachers to expand children's learning into higher forms of thinking such as analysing and evaluation rather than remembering facts or in rote learning. Curriculum design usually promotes the teaching and learning of knowledge, skills and attitudes, and the taxonomy is intended to remind teachers to go beyond the teaching of knowledge and skills into the realms of attitudes to learning.

Although it has been much more frequently used in secondary schools, it has been one of the significant influences on the inclusion of thinking skills and critical thinking throughout all years of schooling. There is now much more emphasis on having clear objectives in schools and the current practice is not only to have clear objectives for every lesson, including those in the early years, but to also ensure they are made clear to the children as well as the adults.

Influence on early years practice in the UK

England

A major development in the latest guidance for practitioners in the EYFS in England has been the inclusion of the 'Characteristics of Effective Learning', which emphasise the importance of *how* children learn not just *what* they learn. Including these characteristics in planning for the early years, and in reporting to parents, is now a statutory requirement as stated in the 'Statutory Framework for the EYFS': 'playing and exploring', 'active learning' and 'creating and thinking critically' (DfE, 2012).

In 'Development Matters', practitioners are advised to:

Use the language of thinking and learning: think, know, remember, forget, idea, makes sense, plan, learn, find out, confused, figure out, trying to do.

and

In planning activities, ask yourself: Is this an opportunity for children to find their own ways to represent and develop their own ideas? Avoid children just reproducing someone else's ideas.

(Early Education, 2012)

The emphasis on thinking skills and creativity, and the inclusion of these in reports to parents, has been welcomed by everyone working in the early years. However, there is always a tension between teaching those things that are easily assessed and those which are crucial to future learning but are time consuming to promote and ensure.

Northern Ireland

In Northern Ireland, the government has put a particular educational emphasis on Thinking Skills and Personal Capabilities, which links well with Bloom's work. In the Foundation Stage guidance 'Thinking skills and personal capabilities for Key Stages 1 and 2', practitioners are reminded that the key strands of Thinking Skills are 'Thinking, Problem Solving and Decision Making; Being Creative; Working with Others; and Self-Management' (CCEA; 2007). Practitioners are also reminded that development in a child's thinking is not just age related. Each strand is then examined to identify key skills and abilities, which resonate with the work of Bloom. For instance, in the Managing Information section:

Pupils should discover how to:

- *ask focused questions;*
- *plan and set goals and break a task into sub-tasks;*
- *use their own and others' ideas to locate sources of information;*
- *select, classify, compare and evaluate information;*
- *select the most appropriate method for a task;*
- *use a range of methods for collating, recording and representing information; and*
- *communicate with a sense of audience and purpose.*

(CCEA, 2007)

The advent of thinking skills in primary schools has focused our attention on the objectives of learning and whether these should be linked to what children are learning or how they are learning. Bloom's work has had a significant effect on this line of development.

Key guidance documents for countries in the UK

DfE, (2012) 'Statutory Framework for the EYFS'.
Early Education, (2012) 'Development Matters'.
CCEA, (2007) 'Thinking skills and personal capabilities for Key Stages 1 and 2'.

Benjamin Samuel Bloom

Things to think about

- What should a setting look like where critical thinking and creativity are really valued?

- How do you make sure that the children in your groups have time and resources to develop critical skills such as thinking, creativity, asking questions and finding things out for themselves?

- What is the ideal time balance in a day or a week between the teaching of knowledge and skills and opportunities for children to think, explore and find out for themselves?

- Which resources in your room encourage thinking skills? Which ones encourage physical skills?

- Thinking Skills and Personal Capabilities are central to the curriculum in Wales. How can newly qualified practitioners working in England ensure that the Characteristics of Effective Learning are at the heart of their practice?

John Bowlby

Full name: John Bowlby

Born: 1907

Died: 1990

Place of birth: London, England

Countries of residence: England

What he did: John Bowlby emphasised the importance of attachment between babies and young children and the adults who care for them.

Influences on education today: Central to practitioner guidance throughout the UK is an acknowledgement of Bowlby's attachment theory and the possible stress on very young children of attendance at out-of-home care. The key person approach is now a feature of all high quality settings.

Theories and areas of work: Psychology, Child development

Key influencers and followers: Donald Winnicott, Sigmund Freud, Konrad Lorenz, Harry Harlow

Key works: *Child Care and the Growth of Love* (1965), *Attachment and Loss, Volumes. 1, 2, 3* (1969, 1973, 1980).

If a community values its children, it must cherish its mothers.

John Bowlby, 1951 WHO Report

Life, love, theory and research

John Bowlby was born and brought up in London at a time when many upper-middle class English families hired nannies to look after their children. The nannies lived with the children in a separate part of the house, and the children rarely met their parents. In larger families like the Bowlby's, the nanny was helped by other servants and Bowlby, the fourth of six children, was almost entirely brought up by a nursemaid. It was thought at the time that too much attention from parents was likely to spoil children, so Bowlby only saw his mother after tea for a short time. He had no contact with his father, a surgeon, who was away for most of his childhood and youth. It is likely that the loss of his nursemaid, his original 'mother figure', as well as being sent to boarding school when he was ten, were what motivated him to become so interested in the attachment between children and their mothers or mother figures.

Bowlby studied at Trinity College, Cambridge University, originally following his father into medicine but swapping to psychology in his third year of study. During the rest of his time at Cambridge he worked at a school which he said influenced the direction of the rest of his life.

After Cambridge, Bowlby went to work with maladjusted children and then qualified in medicine in London. It was during this time that he began his interest in attachment and the problems of lack of attachment and this continued during and after the Second World War when he worked in London and Cambridge. His interest was in studying the effects of early separation of children from their key caregiver and the subsequent appearance of behavioural difficulties in these children. He began to believe that babies are biologically pre-programmed to make attachments with others and the first attachments are the most important.

He collected together the surprisingly sparse existing information on the attachment between babies and their principle caregiver – essentially their mothers or their mother substitute – and this included the research of animal behaviourist Konrad Lorenz from the 1930s on the imprinting of baby birds on their mother bird (particularly geese and ducklings). Lorenz found that baby birds would imprint on the first moving object they saw in the first hours after hatching. Working with geese, he investigated the principle of imprinting and even began to allow baby geese to imprint on him, following him around everywhere. Although Lorenz did not discover the topic, he became widely known for his descriptions of imprinting as an instinctive emotional bond. His work was filmed and subsequently viewed all over the world not just by psychologists but in general newscasts.

Working alongside James Robertson in 1952, Bowlby made many observations of young children experiencing intense distress when separated from their mothers, particularly in situations where there is threat or danger. Even in situations when other caregivers were present and attempted to comfort the baby, the child's anxiety was not diminished. Bowlby came to the conclusion that attachment was crucial in enhancing the survival chances of the baby, even today when there are far fewer dangers for small babies than there were in previous generations. He wrote about his research and observations in several books, one of the most widely read being *Child Care and the Growth of Love* (1965).

Bowlby believed that the removal of the key person in the child's life could result in serious harm to their emotional development, resulting in abnormal behaviour and erosion of emotional stability. He proposed that attachment and a fear of strangers can be understood within an evolutionary context in that the caregiver provides safety and security for the infant. Simply put, attachment enhances the infant's chance of survival. According to Bowlby, infants have a universal need to seek close proximity with their caregiver when under stress or when threatened. In fact, Bowlby felt that babies are born with the tendency to display certain innate behaviours which help ensure proximity and contact with the mother or attachment figure (for example, crying, smiling, crawling, etc.) which trigger caring responses from adults.

The primary caregiver is the safe base from which the secure and well-attached baby or toddler strikes out into the unknown, with the security of returning to base whenever they need to. This secure attachment is a prerequisite for stable relationships as an adult.

Bowlby's theory of attachment has key characteristics:

1 A child has an innate (inborn) need to attach to one main attachment figure (called monotropy). Even though a child may have more than one primary caregiver, the bond with the mother was seen to be key.
2 A child should receive the continuous care of this single most important attachment figure for approximately the first two years of life. If the attachment connection is broken or disrupted during the critical two-year period, the child will suffer irreversible long-term consequences of maternal deprivation and this risk continues until the age of five. Bowlby used the term maternal deprivation to refer to the separation or loss of the mother as well as failure to develop an attachment.
3 The long term consequences of maternal deprivation might include delinquency, aggression, depression or inability to show affection or concern for others.

Bowlby and his colleagues also constructed a three-stage explanation of the feelings associated with short-term separation from a secure attachment figure which leads to three progressive stages of distress. This is known as the PDD model:

1 **Protest**: The child cries, screams and protests angrily when the parent leaves. They will try to cling on to the parent to stop them leaving.
2 **Despair**: The child's protesting begins to stop and they appear to be calmer although still upset. The child refuses others' attempts for comfort and often seems withdrawn and uninterested in anything.
3 **Detachment**: If separation continues the child will start to engage with other people again. Some babies and young children may even reject the caregiver on their return and show strong signs of anger.

Around the age of three, these characteristics seem to become part of a child's personality (their internal working model) and thus affect their understanding of the world and future interactions with others. Bowlby was convinced that the primary caregiver acts as a prototype for future relationships via the internal working model.

There are three main features of the internal working model:

- a model of others as being trustworthy
- a model of the self as valuable
- a model of the self as effective when interacting with others.

This mental representation guides future social and emotional behaviour as the child's internal working model guides their responsiveness to others in general.

After many years of study Bowlby came to the conclusion that, '...the infant and young child should experience a warm, intimate, and continuous relationship with his mother (or permanent mother substitute) in which both find satisfaction and enjoyment' and that not to do so may have significant and irreversible mental health impacts on the development of the child.

Legacy and impact

Bowlby's ideas had a great influence on the way other researchers thought about attachment, and much of the discussion of his theory has focused on his belief in monotropy – the central place of the 'mother figure'. Bowlby never disputed that young children form multiple attachments, but he always affirmed that the attachment to the mother is unique in that it is the first to appear and remains the strongest of all.

In the 1950s and 1960s, Harry Harlow, an American psychologist made a series of experiments using rhesus monkeys to test whether the attachment theory was true in other animals. He thought that the young monkeys (as in young humans) merely wanted physical comfort and food and that there was nothing exceptional about this that could be identified as being any form of 'attachment'. He thought that attachment resulted from care and was not innate in the infant, so he devised two tests for two different groups of baby rhesus monkeys. The first group of monkeys were raised in complete isolation, having no contact with other monkeys or humans – they were fed by scientists but not handled; the second group were separated from their mothers and raised with a choice of two surrogate mothers.

He observed the monkeys for 165 days and collected the following evidence from the different groups:

- **The first group:** of these monkeys, some died and others were frightened and behaved in an abnormal manner. They could not interact with other monkeys even when they were older.

- **The second group:** Eight monkeys were placed in cages with access to two surrogate, inanimate mothers, one made of wire and one covered in soft terry towelling. Four of the monkeys could get milk from the wire mother and four from the cloth mother. Both groups of monkeys spent more time with the cloth mother (even if she had no milk). The infant would only go to the wire mother when hungry. Once fed it would return to the cloth mother for most of the day. If a frightening object was placed in the cage the infant took refuge with the cloth mother (its safe base). Even a fake 'mother' could give some comfort to the baby monkeys, supporting the view that attachment is about more than just providing food.

These experiments demonstrated that the surrogate monkeys became much more timid, found interaction with other monkeys difficult, were easily bullied and the females even became less effective mothers themselves.

Harlow concluded that for a monkey to develop normally she or he must have some interaction with an object to which they can cling during the first months of life (the critical period). Clinging is a natural response – in times of stress the monkey runs to the object to which it normally clings as if the clinging decreases the stress. Harlow assumed therefore that it was social deprivation rather than maternal deprivation that the young monkeys were suffering from. When he brought some other infant monkeys up on their own, with 20 minutes a day in a playroom with three other monkeys, he found they grew up to be quite normal emotionally and socially.

In 1964 Rudolph Schaffer and Peggy Emerson made a longitudinal study of 60 babies, observed in their own homes at monthly intervals for the first 18 months of life. Their behaviour and interactions with their carers were noted and their carers were interviewed. The mothers also kept diaries of their babies' behaviours.

This study established that there was a regular sequence of the development of attachment:

- **0 to 6 weeks: Asocial attachment**. Many kinds of stimuli, both social and non-social, produce a favourable reaction such as a smile.

- **6 weeks to 7 months: Indiscriminate attachments.** Infants indiscriminately enjoy human company and most babies respond equally to any caregiver. They get upset when an individual ceases to interact with them. From 3 months, infants smile more at familiar faces and can be easily comforted by a regular caregiver.

- **7 to 9 months: Specific attachment**. The baby has a special preference for a single attachment figure. The baby looks to particular people for security, comfort and protection, and shows stranger fear (fear of strangers) and separation anxiety (unhappiness when separated from a special person). This has usually developed by one year of age.

- **10 months and onwards: Multiple attachment.** The baby becomes increasingly independent and forms several attachments. By 18 months the majority of infants have formed multiple attachments.

One factor that affected attachment was the response of the adult to the babies' signals rather than the presence of the key caregiver, and this came to be known as 'responsiveness' or in some documentation this is called 'attunement'. Intensely attached infants had mothers who had responded quickly to their demands and interacted with their child. Infants who were weakly attached had mothers who often failed to interact.

By 10 months old, many babies have several attachments including mothers, fathers, grandparents, siblings and neighbours. The mother is the main attachment figure for

John Bowlby

about half of the children at 18 months old and the father for most of the others. The most important fact in forming attachments is not who feeds and changes the child but who plays and communicates with him or her. Therefore, responsiveness appeared to be the key to attachment.

'Attachment is a deep and enduring emotional bond that connects one person to another across time and space.'

(Ainsworth, 1973; Bowlby, 1969)

Influence on early years practice in the UK

Attachment theory has had a tremendous influence on childcare and early years education and those opposed to early childcare, particularly before the age of two, consistently quote Bowlby's research into the damage that can be done to very young children who are cared for by others rather than their mothers. The response to this concern from within early childcare has been both thoughtful and helpful to practitioners. The fact is that many more mothers are at work and many more babies and young children are in early childcare settings, so we all need to be both sensitive to children's needs and aware of the realities.

The guidance to practitioners in all four countries of the UK makes strenuous efforts to inform practitioners of the importance of the key person in the lives of babies and young children in early care. The key person is the replacement primary caregiver, and his or her own key person should be a stable and consistent feature of the setting for every child. She or he must know the child and their family well, and in settings for the youngest children, the key person plans the curriculum and manages the record keeping for her own key group.

In the national 'Statutory Framework for the Early Years Foundation Stage' attachment (and attunement) are seen as part of the role of the key person: 'Their role is to help ensure that every child's care is tailored to meet their individual needs, to help the child become familiar with the setting, offer a settled relationship for the child and build a relationship with their parents' (DfE, 2014).

In the 'Development Matters guidance, practitioners are encouraged to:

- *Ensure that the key person or buddy (a knowledgeable substitute) is available to greet a young baby at the beginning of the session, and to hand them over to parents at the end of a session, so the young baby is supported and communication with parents is maintained.*

- *Make sure the child can explore from the secure, close-by presence of their key person.*

- *Make sure the key person stays close by and provides a secure presence and a refuge at times a child may be feeling anxious.*

- *Support children who are anxious on separating from their parents by acknowledging their feelings and reassuring them.*

(Early Education, 2012)

Scotland

In Scotland, there is a real commitment to making the concept of the key person work for children and the key person approach is described in the following way in 'Framework pre-birth to three':

The key person meets the needs of every child in their care and responds sensitively to their feelings, ideas and behaviour. They offer security, reassurance and continuity, and are usually responsible for feeding, changing and comforting the child. The key person helps children to develop relationships with members of staff and other children. They skilfully observe children in their play, their relationships and in day-to-day activities, in order to inform future opportunities and experiences that best meet the needs and interests of children.

The key person approach is a way of working in settings in which the whole focus and organisation is aimed at enabling and supporting close attachments between individual children and individual staff. The key person approach is an involvement, an individual and reciprocal commitment between a member of staff and a family.

(Learning and Teaching Scotland, 2010)

The key person is at the heart of early years education, and has been ever since young children were first cared for away from their natural mothers. If we don't get this relationship right, we will spend the rest of a child's time in education trying to undo the damage made.

The 'Framework pre-birth to three' documents in Scotland emphasise the importance of both attachment and attunement (described as 'tuning in' to babies) and makes a clear difference between the two:

Attachment

Responsive and caring adults are essential for babies and young children to develop and thrive. If babies have a secure attachment to at least one person, they are more likely to develop strong relationships and skills to cope with challenges later in life. Having a secure attachment refers to the deep emotional connection that babies form with their primary caregiver, often the mother.

Attunement

Attunement is when the adult is able to tune in to babies' needs, perhaps by closely observing their sounds, expressions and body language in a responsive and empathetic way. The important process of attunement begins between mother and baby even before a baby is born with the care and attention they receive in the womb.

(Learning and Teaching Scotland, 2010)

John Bowlby

Things to think about

- What would you say are the positives and difficulties of being a key person?
- Given that Bowlby and others after him appear to be saying that at around 18 months children move beyond the stage of close attachment to a major caregiver, do older children really need a named key person?
- Do you think that some babies and children attend early years settings at too young an age and for too long during the day?
- What are the key skills that a key person needs? Are there any of these that are more difficult to learn than others?
- Schools and settings are now admitting two year olds to their early years settings. How prepared would you be to be involved in their care?

Urie Bronfenbrenner

Full name: Urie Bronfenbrenner
Born: 1917
Died: 2005
Place of birth: Moscow, Russia
Countries of residence: Russia (until 6 years old), United States
What he did: Bronfenbrenner clarified the thinking of the educational world in moving away from 'the educational vacuum' into a realisation that the environment has a significant influence on our lives and learning.
Influences on education today: There is a universal acknowledgement of the importance of children's home environment in ensuring effective learning. Settings and schools make great efforts to include parents, and many take real account of environmental factors beyond the child's home. Bronfenbrenner was co-founder of the Head Start Programme in America, which is focused on children and families living in poverty.
Theories and areas of work: Developmental psychology, Education
Key influencers and followers: Mamie Clark and Edward Zigler, co-founders of Head Start
Key works: *Two Worlds of Childhood: US and USSR* (1970), *Making Human Beings Human* (2005).

Children need people in order to become human…. It is primarily through observing, playing, and working with others older and younger than himself that a child discovers both what he can do and who he can become--that he develops both his ability and his identity.

Urie Bronfenbrenner, 'Two Worlds of Childhood': U.S. and U.S.S.R., preface (1973)

Life, love, theory and research

Urie Bronfenbrenner was born in Russia, but moved to the United States when he was six, and lived and worked there after that. He became interested in how our social relationship with the world around us affects each of us and particularly how it affects the development

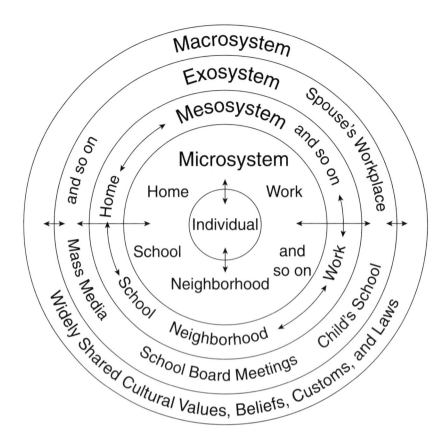

of children. He believed that human development and learning are deeply affected by the environment in which each person grows up and he called this ecological theory.

Every element in an environment affects a child's development and Bronfenbrenner divided these elements into five different levels, usually depicted as a series of concentric circles, with the child at the centre, starting with the environment closest to the individual:

1 **The microsystem**: the direct environment and the people closest to the child. Family, friends, teachers, caregivers and other adults such as neighbours; anyone who the child has direct contact with. They use their contact with these people to construct their personal environment. For a young child, the influences in the microsystem will include their parents and siblings, grandparents, and the practitioners and other children in an early years setting. How each individual relates to these people, and their responses in return, will affect close relationships.

2 **The mesosystem**: the next circle out is called the mesosystem and covers the relationships between each of the contacts in our microsystem. A distressed or neglected child may find it difficult to make stable relationships with practitioners and other children at nursery or school.

3 **The exosystem**: the next circle contains the effect of other people's microsystems on our own mesosystem. If one of a child's parent leaves or spends significant time working away from home, this may have an effect on a child's progress in an education setting and may tighten the bond between the child and the remaining parent. The exosystem consists of areas where we have little or no effect, but in turn affect us deeply.

4 **The macrosystem**: the macrosystem contains the culture within which the individual lives. This could include the socio-economic status of the individual (whether rich or poor), ethnicity, race or religion, gender or the educational expectations within their culture. Economic conditions or growing up in a third word country could also be included in an individual's macrosystem.

5 **The chronosystem**: The final circle, the chronosystem, covers the transitions, shifts and movements between other elements during an individual's lifespan. A divorce, a death in the family or a house move may have a significant effect on a child's behaviour and learning, setting them back by several months, after which they may or may not recover. Shifts in the chronosystem can delay physical, emotional and intellectual development, leaving a child struggling to catch up with their peer group.

Bronfenbrenner spoke to a government panel trying to establish a programme which would involve a child's family and community in an intervention effort aimed at raising the attainment of poor children. Bronfenbrenner's input made a significant difference to decisions made by this group and Head Start was born.

Legacy and impact

Bronfenbrenner's theory, published in 1979, was influential in making social and educational thinkers realise that we don't grow up in a personal vacuum; we are deeply affected at different levels, not only by the people we meet but by their interaction with each other. In turn, these relationships are affected by the political, economic and social environments in which we live. Bronfenbrenner has also influenced the way that many psychologists think about child development and the ecological systems theory has since become a foundation for other theorists' work.

Education practice has also been affected by the ecological theory and professionals working with young children (practitioners, teachers, managers and headteachers, policy makers and advisers) are now much more aware of the effects environmental factors have on the progress, attainment and personal development of young children.

Bronfenbrenner's research was used to underpin the Head Start programme adopted by the US government in 1964, focusing efforts on involving the child's family and community to create a more supportive environment for learning (see p 297 for more details of the Head Start programme).

Urie Bronfenbrenner

This awareness has also been reflected in the documentation and guidance for practitioners and parents across the UK, and practitioners have been increasingly involved in recognising the influence of parents, the community and wider aspects of culture on the development of children, particularly in their early years.

Influence on early years practice in the UK

Education thinking across the world has also been influenced by the ecological theory and the EYFS documentation recognises the importance of the family and community and how practitioners can manage the impact of events outside their control or the control of the child. The importance of involvement of, and information from parents, carers and other important people in the lives of children is recognised in documentation and advice across all countries in the UK.

England

The following quotes are from current documentation for the EYFS in England: 'Development Matters in the EYFS' and 'Statutory Framework for the Early Years Foundation Stage'. One of the goals for Personal, Social and Emotional Development at the end of the Foundation Stage recognises the need for children to be able to:

> ... talk about past and present events in their own lives and in the lives of family members. They know that other children don't always enjoy the same things, and are sensitive to this. They know about similarities and differences between themselves and others, and among families, communities and traditions.
>
> (Early Education, 2012).

> ... experiences respond to their individual needs and there is a strong partnership between practitioners and parents and/or carers.
>
> (DfE, 2014)

> For any assessment of development to be meaningful and useful, a complete picture of a child should be obtained. This will best be realised when parents, the child, and all practitioners and professionals who know or have involvement with the child, participate fully in the assessment process.
>
> (DfE, 2014)

The completion of the progress check at two emphasises the importance of involving parents, carers and others in recording and sharing information about individual children, and the documentation 'Know how: The progress check at age two' states:

> Parents and practitioners use this shared knowledge and understanding in order to plan together and think through ideas of how to move the child forward. Learning opportunities and

next steps can be planned for the setting and the home. This process builds on what parents know and do already with their child, and supports their confidence and knowledge in how to extend and strengthen the early home.

If there are any concerns about a child's development then practitioners and parents should consider all contextual information about a child before taking any further steps. For example, has the arrival of a new sibling in the family caused a child to regress to younger patterns of behaviour? Are there signs that the child is about to make a developmental leap in this area?

(DfE/NCB, 2012)

The guidance in Scotland, Northern Ireland and Wales also refers to the importance of the environments on children's learning, and it would be very unusual for a practitioner to dismiss this influence.

Key guidance documents for countries in the UK

Early Education (2012) 'Development Matters in the EYFS.'
DfE, (2014) 'Statutory Framework for the Early Years Foundation Stage'.
DfE/NCB, (2012) 'Know how – The progress check at age two'.

Things to think about

- What should you do if a child appears to be developing at a slower pace than expected in a particular area and you think that an element inside or outside their microsystem (the influences closest to the child) is contributing to this?

- How would you advise a colleague to respond where a child attends more than one setting or changes settings during the year or term?

- The EYFS allows practitioners to decide the timing of the progress check. How did your setting respond to this flexibility?

- As children grow older, it is often more difficult to keep track of the environmental factors affecting individuals in large groups. How could you collect and record this information for a large group of children who may be working with several different practitioners and whose parents may be working or otherwise difficult to contact?

- When a practitioner is inexperienced, it is easy to ignore or underestimate the effect of a child's home environment on their dispositions in a setting. How would you try to avoid this when you begin your career?

Jerome Bruner

Full name: Jerome Bruner

Born: 1915

Died: 2015

Place of birth: New York, United States

Countries of residence: United States, England

What he did: Bruner advanced educational thinking in learning to learn, observation in a natural environment, scaffolding (a term he invented) and the essential role of language in children's development.

Influences on education today: Scaffolding is a concept with which practitioners are now very familiar. Throughout the UK, the concept of scaffolding by supporting children as they explore and investigate the world, is at the heart of good practice.

Theories and areas of work: Constructivist, Cognitive psychology

Key influencers and followers: Lev Vygotsky, Loris Malaguzzi, Alison Gopnik

Key works: *Toward a Theory of Instruction* (1966), *Child's Talk: Learning to Use Language* (1983), *The Process of Education* (1960).

Thinking about thinking has to be a principle ingredient of any empowering practice of education.

Jerome Bruner, The Culture of Education, 1996

Life, love, theory and research

Born in New York, of Polish migrant parents, Jerome Bruner worked at Harvard University and at the University of Oxford. His latest work was undertaken at New York University, where he remained until his death in 2015, aged 100. Bruner studied the ways in which children learn and was convinced that a learner (even of a very young age) is capable of learning any material so long as the instruction is organised in the right way. Among other research and writing, he coined the term scaffolding, later used by Lev Vygotsky, and which is now widely used to describe the way we learn. By scaffolding, Bruner meant that social interaction plays a fundamental role in children's learning and development generally, helping them to build on what they already know in a sequential way, using language as a scaffold for their learning. This is particularly important when considering language development, as language appears to be integral to all learning. Bruner explored the way that children seem to simultaneously learn how to use language in order to communicate, and at the same time learn about how language works. Mastering the intricacies of conversation is a complex skill and one that children only perfect after continued practice.

Bruner also worked on the concept of the spiral curriculum where teachers and children revisit skills and knowledge at ever more advanced levels. This concept has been adopted by many teachers as it makes good sense to return to topics at a later stage as long as the challenge is continued. However, the spiral curriculum was criticised by conservative educators in America, where there are strict rules about the order in which concepts are taught, often without opportunities to revisit these concepts to expand and consolidate. Such revisiting is an essential feature of effective learning and is exemplified in the spiral curriculum model.

While working at the University of Oxford, Bruner collaborated with British psychologists and, for the first time, he went to children's own homes where he used videotape to capture the ways that children interacted with their parents. Bruner took the practice of observing children away from the laboratory and into the real lives of children. This way of observing was a new and unorthodox way to research, often criticised by his contemporaries, because it was thought to be less consistent than previous methods of observation and testing in laboratory conditions.

When he analysed his findings, Bruner began to construct a theory, which came to be referred to as an interactionist approach to children's language development, particularly evident in children who regularly conversed with adults and older children. He identified the ways in which parents interacted with their children through conversation, during which the two sides were able to create meaning together in a way that neither side could achieve alone. During these shared times the more experienced conversationalists were able to extend the child's understanding by drawing their attention to different aspects of the joint focus, using language that would help extend the child's repertoire both cognitively and linguistically. In a simple example, a parent might gently suggest to a young child that their description of the delivery man as 'Daddy' is not correct, by saying 'That's not Daddy, that's Sam, bringing our parcels'. This is the process Bruner called scaffolding – which referred to the collaborative process of creating shared meanings and improving understanding.

Bruner believed that education should be about developing independent learners and thinkers. In contrast to any notion of 'readiness', he thought that children of any age are capable of understanding complex concepts and information if it is presented in an intellectually honest fashion. For instance, very young children are often obsessed with dinosaurs (or trains, diggers etc.) learning the names and shapes of a wide range of different examples, and details of their function, diet or size. This information has usually been gained by sitting with an adult or older sibling, watching a DVD, reading books or researching on the internet. Of course, the child does not have the whole picture, but they can absorb a huge amount of information and will concentrate for long periods on finding out more. The role of the educator is to facilitate learning by helping (scaffolding) the process, so children can discover the relationships between different pieces of information or experiences.

During his studies, Bruner developed a personal view of the way the human brain manages information and proposed that there are distinct ways in which humans encode and store it. In his research on the cognitive development of children, Bruner proposed three modes – different ways in which information or knowledge is stored and encoded in memory. He called them 'representations' and rather than the neat age-related stages of Jean Piaget and others, Bruner saw his representations as having permeable boundaries and only loose relationships with age.

Bruner believed that children represent the world to themselves in three different ways, which he called: **enactive**, **iconic** and **symbolic**.

1. Enactive representation

This mode of representation appears during the first year or so of life, and involves the child in action-based learning. An example of this might be when a young child waves a rattle and associates the sound with a particular movement. When the rattle is dropped, the baby still 'remembers' the movement and expects that when they shake their hand without the rattle, the same sound will result. Such memories are muscular and some of the skills adults acquire can still be more easily demonstrated physically, rather than in pictures or words; often in conversation an adult will almost unconsciously make physical movements as they explain that they were typing, phoning, writing or even driving.

2. Iconic representation

Bruner believed that children under about six years of age start to store information in pictorial form (using images, or 'the mind's eye') with information being stored visually in the brain. When learning to read, children will often use the pictures in a book to help them remember the story, and even adults may still find instructions much easier to follow if they have associated pictures. Bruner saw the infant as an intelligent and active problem solver from birth with intellectual abilities very similar to those of the mature adult, just using pictures instead of words.

3. Symbolic representation

From around seven years of age children begin to use the final style of learning, storing information in language. The symbolic nature of languages means that children can manipulate, order and classify their learning using words, mathematical and other symbols. They can also share their thoughts with others in words. Symbolic representation is used alongside iconic and enactive representation, all three of which remain in use throughout life.

Practitioners would do well to recognise and use all three types of representation in their work so children can learn through physical activity, picture based information and words. Bruner's work clearly outlines an active role for educators in young children's learning, not by telling them things, but by assisting children with their learning. Through scaffolding, the educator provides the child with helpful structured interaction with the aim of helping the child to reach a specific goal.

Legacy and impact

Bruner's observational methods of collecting information about children's learning have influenced practice in many ways. The notion of scaffolding and the key role of language in this process has affected early education by emphasising the importance of making time for talking and encouraging what is now referred to as sustained shared thinking, where adults and children work together, talking about what they are doing and learning as they talk.

Language development is seen as a key factor in the curriculum and although there was a short time during the implementation of the first National Curriculum when speaking and listening disappeared from the documentation in England, there has been a consistent emphasis on language development, of which the National Literacy Strategy and Every Child a Talker are examples. The recognition of the crucial role of communication, language and literacy is evident within the latest documentation for the early years curriculum across all the countries in the UK.

Bruner also proposed that the curriculum should be seen as a spiral, which children revisit at different stages of their learning, rather than a ladder of facts to be learned and skills to be perfected. Within the spiral curriculum there are no topics too difficult or unsuitable for a child – it is the responsibility of the teacher to make the curriculum content accessible by adapting language and simplifying concepts so the child can engage with it at their current level of understanding. This has also encouraged teachers to be less restricted in the information they offer to children and the explorations children undertake.

Bruner's commitment to observational assessment has also been influential. This way of finding out about children's development has been adopted by teachers in early years settings throughout the world, but despite Bruner's work, politicians sometimes still refuse to accept the professional views of practitioners as more reliable than tests, believing that standardised information is more objective than a professional who knows the child and their family well.

Bruner's book, *The Process of Education* (1960) was a landmark text in education, particularly in the United States. It had a direct impact on policy formation in the United States and influenced the thinking and orientation of a wide group of teachers and students of education. Its view of children as active problem solvers who are ready to explore 'difficult' subjects, while being out of step with the dominant view in education at that time, struck a chord with many.

In later years, Bruner added to his advice about teaching:

To instruct someone … is not a matter of getting him to commit results to mind. Rather, it is to teach him to participate in the process that makes possible the establishment of knowledge.
(Toward a Theory of Education, 1966).

One other significant aspect of Bruner's work was his questioning of the principles with which Piaget worked (p 243). Bruner agreed with Piaget that children are predisposed to learning, that they have a natural curiosity, and that their cognitive abilities develop over time, particularly as they begin to understand and use symbols. However, he disagreed with Piaget's stages of development, proposing that cognitive growth is a continuous process. He also argued that language development, instead of being a result of cognitive development, is the cause of it. Humans need language in order to learn about thinking and adults and more developed peers can make a big difference to both language and thinking.

Bruner's thoughts on shared thinking and his emphasis on child observation methods of research have been at the heart of studies by Kathy Sylva. In 1997, she began work with a team of education specialists from the University of London, School of Education to identify the aspects of early education that have the most lasting effects on children's lives later. They have worked consistently with 3,000 children, originally following their progress in pre-school provision – the Effective Pre-school and Primary Education (EPPE) and later in the Effective Pre-school, Primary and Secondary Education (EPPSE). The project has now reported on progress at the end of Key Stage 3 (14 years old). Both the EPPE and EPPSE projects have emphasised the importance of observing children in familiar environments, at home and in schools and settings, talking with parents and carers, and identifying the features of education that are most effective.

The outcomes of this research have influenced practitioners and also the government; there are significant aspects of the government guidance, which would not have been included without the support of this evidence. The enormous expansion of childcare both in the UK and across the world has been supported and funded according to the principles defined by the Sylva research.

Influence on early years practice in the UK

Although not directly named in the latest guidance for the early years across the UK, Kathy Sylva's thinking and influence, together with those of Bruner and Vygotsky are obviously prevalent. From observation, through language development to scaffolding and support for 'sustained shared thinking', there are influences throughout the statutory requirements and the guidance for practitioners. Some examples from the 'Statutory Framework for the EYFS' and 'Development Matters in the EYFS' are included here, but there are many more.

> Communication and language development involves giving children opportunities to experience a rich language environment; to develop their confidence and skills in expressing themselves; and to speak and listen in a range of situations.
>
> (DfE, 2012)

> On-going formative assessment is at the heart of effective early years practice. Practitioners can … observe children as they act and interact in their play, everyday activities and planned activities, and learn from parents about what the child does at home.
>
> (Early Education, 2012)

> Sustained shared thinking helps children to explore ideas and make links. Follow children's lead in conversation, and think about things together. (Early Education, 2012)

> The key person must seek to engage and support parents and/or carers in guiding their child's development at home. They should also help families engage with more specialist support if appropriate.
>
> (DfE, 2012)

England

In the guidance 'The EYFS progress check at age two', newly implemented in England, there are further points for guidance which support the thinking of Bruner and those who followed his views, including Vygotsky:

> Practitioners and parents use their ongoing observations and knowledge of the child to draw up a clear picture of the child's development at a particular point in time.
>
> For any assessment of development to be meaningful and useful, a complete picture of a child should be obtained. This will best be realised when parents, the child, and all practitioners and professionals who know or have involvement with the child, participate fully in the assessment process.
>
> A starting point for all assessment should be an acknowledgement that parents know their children best. They are their child's first and most enduring educators, with in-depth knowledge of their child's, physical, emotional and language development over time. This knowledge should be reflected in both on-going dialogue and in the progress check.
>
> (DfE/National Children's Bureau, 2012)

It is very clear that as early years practitioners we have much to thank Bruner and his followers for.

Things to think about

- How much of Bruner's substantial influence were you aware of? Why do you think this is?

- Sylva and her team have made a significant contribution to the framework for the EYFS in England and in other countries across the world. She says that:

  'For all children, the quality of the home learning environment is more important for intellectual and social development than parental occupation, education or income. What parents do is more important than who parents are.'

  (Sylva et. al., 2004).

- What do you think are the most influential features of the work you do in your setting?

- Sustained shared thinking has been a thread through early education for many years now, and another quote from the EPPE report says:

  'Effective pedagogy includes interaction traditionally associated with the term "teaching", the provision of instructive learning environments and "sustained shared thinking" to extend children's learning.'

  (Sylva et. al., 2004).

- How do you make time for shared thinking with the children in your group?

Jerome Bruner

Cyril Lodovic Burt

Full name: Cyril Lodovic Burt

Born: 1883

Died: 1971

Place of birth: London, England

Countries of residence: England

What he did: Burt is known for his involvement in improving intelligence testing, including working on the 11 Plus test, establishing the first child guidance clinics, and work in educational psychology.

Influences on education today: Although the 11 Plus test is no longer a national test in England, some local authorities still use it to select children for grammar school education, and the notion of standardised testing is now firmly established as one element in assessment in primary and secondary education across the UK.

Theories and areas of work : Developmental psychology, psychometrics

Key influencers and followers: William McDougall, Raymond Cattell, Hans Eysenck

Key works: *Mental and Scholastic Tests* (1921, 1962), Burt also published numerous articles and papers describing and defending his work.

Attainment is a poor measure of capacity, and ignorance no proof of defect.
Cyril Burt, Mental and Scholastic Tests, 1921

Life, love theory and research

Cyril Burt was born in England, the son of a doctor who had very little money. He was educated and worked in England, graduating from the University of Oxford with a degree in psychology, followed by a postgraduate qualification in education. In 1908 he became a lecturer in psychology at the University of Liverpool and in 1913 he went to work for the London County Council to assist in identifying what were then called 'the feeble minded'. He was one of the first to be involved in establishing child guidance clinics, including the London Child Guidance Clinic, and the London Day Training College in Islington, where he carried out much of his research on young children's learning.

In 1909 he embarked on a study comparing the intelligence of boys enrolled in an elite preparatory academy with the intelligence of boys attending a regular school. To control for environmental influences, he chose measures (such as mirror drawing) that were unlikely to have been learned during the students' lifetimes. Since the preparatory school students' scores were higher than the other students', he concluded that they had more innate intelligence. Moreover, he noted that the fathers of the preparatory school boys were more successful in their chosen careers than the fathers of the other boys, which he interpreted to mean that the preparatory school boys had simply benefited from their fathers' superior genetic endowments. These findings reinforced his views that intelligence was a solely heritable aspect, passed down through genes from generation to generation.

Throughout his lifetime, Burt remained committed to proving that intelligence is primarily an inherited characteristic, leading to criticisms by other professionals that he was part of the eugenics movement, believing that the single factor affecting intelligence was in a child's genes, that affluent children are affluent because their parents are more intelligent and that there was little that could change this. The eugenics movement believed that the 'white' races were superior to the less developed or 'savage' races, and that this would not change. Burt's thinking was not that straightforward as he sometimes maintained that environmental factors *could* affect attainment, so he was obviously capable of some complex double-think.

In 1926 Burt began to press for a national testing programme that could identify the brightest children from across all socio-economic groups. He believed that this would give some economically disadvantaged children educational opportunities that they would not otherwise receive. However, because he believed that children from lower socio-economic groups were likely to suffer from genetic disadvantage, he expected that fewer children from this group would benefit from any assistance.

His proposed testing programme was implemented across England in 1944 as a national assessment process referred to as the 11 Plus test (because it was taken by children in their last year of primary school). Results of the exam were used to allocate students to grammar schools (for the small number of high scorers) or secondary modern schools (for the rest). School placements were fixed and there was no second chance. There were obvious advantages for the children who passed the test, but for the majority of children their future had been decided at the age of 11; there was no chance for them gaining a university place, as the universities restricted their intake to applicants from grammar schools. The 11 Plus was discontinued as a universal test in 1976 when the government restructured secondary education by introducing comprehensive schools. However, there are still nearly 200 grammar schools in England today which still use a version of the test to select their students, and it is used in some local authorities that retain grammar schools – the largest of which is the county of Lincolnshire. In Northern Ireland, the 11 Plus is also still used for entry into the few grammar schools there.

During his long working life Burt also investigated gender and emotional differences between boys and girls and found that contrary to beliefs at the time, the differences between boys' and girls' scores were *smaller than common belief and common practice would lead us to expect'* (quoted in *Neuroscience in Education*, Sergio Della Sala 2012). Collation of several threads of his research led him to declare that overall, cognitive differences between boys and girls are negligible, and this has helped to establish educational parity for girls.

In the 1960s, Burt began research on the study of identical twins, particularly those who had been reared apart. He found a very high correlation between the IQs of identical twins reared apart. This research has formed the basis for much recent research, as identical twins provide a firm foundation for statistical comparison and standardisation of tests.

Burt was highly regarded for this research work but his interpretations of the results were controversial, particularly his views that intelligence is heritable, and therefore fixed. He did admit that environmental factors could influence attainment but asserted that any of these could be attributed to genetic influence.

After his death Burt was at the centre of a scandal when it was discovered that all his research papers had been burned. This led to controversy over the reliability of his work and accusations of burning incriminating evidence. There is also evidence that some of his research data for the twin studies was fraudulently obtained to ensure that it supported his views. It may never be proven whether he was fraudulent or merely careless but confidence in his work took a hard knock at the time and tarnished his image permanently.

Legacy and impact

Burt had an enormous effect on education in the UK, particularly during the time when the tripartite system of schooling was being introduced. The government at that time implemented a new policy for secondary education by dividing secondary schools into three types – grammar schools, secondary modern schools and technical schools. Children were allocated at 11 to one of these three types of secondary school, although in many areas, the real choice was between grammar and 'secondary modern' schools, as there were few technical schools at the time, and only a very few more were ever built. All children were tested in their last year of primary school when many of them were still only ten years old, and allocated to one of these schools.

Criticisms about the testing process arose quickly as it soon became evident that children's futures were being decided, and they were 'labelled' for life at the age of 11; either a child had a grammar school education and went to university, or they went to a secondary modern school and were extremely unlikely to go to university. When the 11 Plus test was being used, a focus on practising for the test took over the last year of a child's primary education and children were offered all sorts of incentives by their parents to ensure they were among the few (around 10%) children who passed the test.

Opponents to this system said that children were being labelled at far too young an age, particularly as there was rarely a second chance to take the exam, even for the children who were the youngest in the cohort when they took the test. Since that time there have been many reports on research into the effects of being the youngest in the year group, and the 'summer born effect' is now a well-recognised feature at all stages of education, but particularly at secondary transfer. Test results of summer born children are now weighted to account for the child's birth date, and parents, teachers and government officials are all very aware of the problems associated with standardised tests which do not allow for the age of the child.

It was 32 years before the Labour government of Harold Wilson really took notice of the unfairness and divisive nature of this tripartite school system and declared their intention to introduce comprehensive secondary education for all children. Despite the scandal that followed his death, Burt did valuable work which contributed to ensuring that boys and girls have equity in the education system The findings of his work on twins, although criticised at the time, have been proved to be generally in line with later research; and the child guidance clinics that he worked to establish continued their support for children and their families for two decades.

Influence on early years practice in the UK

Burt had a significant and lasting effect on secondary education. During his lifetime, his work on genetics and intelligence was taken seriously by other psychologists and researchers, teachers and their managers. In the UK we now have a comprehensive education system for all, regardless of background or ability. Of course there are still differences in ability across every cohort and the effect of children's backgrounds on their learning has been recognised. We still don't have all the answers to ensuring equality for all children but we do have equality of access to the early years curriculum for all children and an increasing entitlement to childcare for all.

The principles on which the early years curriculum is built are those of equal respect for all children and their families, and a commitment to do everything possible to support the individual child in achieving the highest standards that they are capable of achieving.

England

The EYFS curriculum in England has a principle that relates directly to Burt's work, as stated in the 'Statutory Framework for the EYFS':

Every child deserves the best possible start in life and the support that enables them to fulfill their potential. Children develop quickly in the early years and a child's experiences between birth and age five have a major impact on their future life chances. A secure, safe and happy childhood is important in its' own right. Good parenting and high quality early learning together provide the foundation children need to make the most of their abilities and talents as they grow up.

(DfE, 2012)

In the guidance document Development Matters:

Every child is a unique child who is constantly learning and can be resilient, capable, confident and self-assured.

Practitioners

- understand and observe each child's development and learning, assess progress, plan for next steps

- support babies and children to develop a positive sense of their own identity and culture

- identify any need for additional support

- keep children safe

- value and respect all children and families equally.

(Early Education, 2012)

Currently the government in England allocates additional funding to support children who are identified as being from disadvantaged families. In the guidance for the use of this funding entitled: 'The pupil premium: Next steps', the government states that:

There is no doubt that the pupil premium *has enabled schools – including many in areas not traditionally seen as facing significant disadvantage – to do more to improve the results of their less advantaged pupils. But equally, the data suggests that we still have much to do to ensure that those from poorer families do as well as their classmates. Some schools have closed that gap, but many still have a long way to go.*

(Sutton Trust and Education Endowment Foundation, 2015)

Schools and settings in England are now expected to collect, collate, evaluate and present statistical evidence about the progress of children qualifying for the pupil premium. It is no longer acceptable to use professional judgement alone to justify continued funding. Practitioners must now use standardised assessments, which give comparative scores.

Since Burt's death, Scotland and Wales have received devolved powers for the management of education and Northern Ireland has some freedom too, particularly in the management of schools. They all include strong statements in their documentation about equality of opportunity for all learners, and today, the 11 Plus test is only used for admission to the few remaining grammar schools in Northern Ireland.

Scotland

The vision statement for the Foundation Stage in Scotland, as detailed in 'The Early Years Framework' includes the following:

> It is clear that no one programme of work or action will be successful in turning around lives affected by complex and ingrained social problems. It will take a concerted and long-term effort across a range of policies and services to deliver the transformational change in early years described in the previous section.
>
> (The Scottish Government, 2008)

Wales

In Wales the curriculum describes in 'Foundation Phase Framework' provision as:

> Educational provision for young children should be holistic with the child at the heart of any planned curriculum. It is about practitioners understanding, inspiring and challenging children's potential for learning. Practitioner involvement in children's learning is of vital importance particularly when interactions involve open questioning, shared and sustained thinking.
>
> (Welsh Assembly Government, 2015)

Northern Ireland

And in Northern Ireland, the documentation 'The Northern Ireland Curriculum Primary' details the commitment to:

> The Northern Ireland Curriculum aims to empower young people to develop their potential and to make informed and responsible choices and decisions throughout their lives.
>
> In the Foundation Stage children should experience much of their learning through well planned and challenging play. Self-initiated play helps children to understand and learn about themselves and their surroundings. Motivation can be increased when children have opportunities to make choices and decisions about their learning, particularly when their own ideas and interests are used, either as starting points for learning activities or for pursuing a topic in more depth.
>
> (CCEA, Northern Ireland, 2007)

However, we still need to acknowledge that there is inequality in education. In 2014, a campaign called 'Read On Get On' was launched in the UK. It aims to have every child 'reading well by 11 across the UK by 2025':

> In Britain primary education for children has been compulsory for at least the last 150 years. Yet to our shame, thousands of children leave primary school each year unable to read well enough to enjoy reading and to do it for pleasure, despite the best efforts of teachers around the country.

New research published here shows starkly that the UK has the strongest link among developed nations between poor literacy and unemployment. This is a ticking time bomb for our long-term competitiveness. We know too that the die is cast early. By the age of 3 we can already see the clearest correlation between family income and the vital language development that leads to reading.

(The Save the Children Fund, 2014)

Key guidance documents for countries in the UK

DfE (2012) 'Statutory Framework for the EYFS'.
Early Education, (2012) 'Development Matters in the EYFS'.
Sutton Trust and Education Endowment Foundation, (2015)The pupil premium: Next steps'.
The Scottish Government, (2008) 'The Early Years Framework'.
Welsh Assembly Government, (2015) 'Foundation Phase Framework'.
CCEA, Northern Ireland, (2007) 'The Northern Ireland Curriculum Primary'.
The Save the Children Fund (2014) 'Read on Get on'.

Things to think about

- Do you think that the children of middle class families do better in your setting than children from less affluent homes?
- How could you reduce the gap between these two groups?
- Do you think that testing very young children produces useful information? How else could you collect this information?
- Currently, schools and settings identify those children who are deemed to be disadvantaged. Additional funding is allocated to these children. How do you think it should be used to ensure that the gap is closed between these children and their more advantaged peers?
- There is a move by the present government to support the building of more grammar schools. Getting a place in one of these schools will probably involve sitting an entrance exam such as the 11 Plus test. Do you think this is a forward looking or backward looking idea?

John Amos Comenius

Full name: John Amos Comenius

Born: 1592

Died: 1670

Place of birth: Nivice, Moravia (now the Czech Republic)

Countries of residence: Moravia, Poland, Transylvania, Holland, Sweden

What he did: Comenius wrote the first picture books for use in education. He supported the concept of school as an entitlement for everyone and that practical subjects and learning about the world should replace the formal, fact based, 'teacher directed' systems in place until his time. He also recognised that parents are their children's first educators and that they should prepare their children for school by teaching them simple skills including nursery rhymes.

Influences on education today: Comenius lived 400 years ago but his work has had a significant effect on many who followed him and on the way education in the primary years has developed.

Theories and areas of work: Educational philosophy

Key influencers and followers: Jean-Jacques Rousseau, Johann Heinrich Pestalozzi, Friedrich Fröebel and many others were followers

Key works: *The Great Didactic* or *Didactica Magna, Orbis Pictus, Janua Linguarum Reserata: Atrium, Vestibulum The School of Infancy: a Primer for Parents. Orbis Pictus* was the first illustrated textbook for young children to be published in Europe and is still available in digtal format from: *www.gutenberg.org.*

Much can be learned in play that will afterwards be of use when the circumstances demand it.

John Comenius ,1649

Life, love, theory and research

Born in Moravia (now part of the Czech Republic), John Comenius grew up to be an influential teacher, thinker and theologian and one of the earliest promoters of universal education. It is a huge shame that his influence on educational theory and practice is not more publicly celebrated, as many of his ideas are as fresh today as they were over 400 years ago.

Comenius became something of a nomad, due to his religious attachment to the Moravian Brotherhood, a protestant sect committed to a simple, natural way of living but persecuted by other religious groups at different times during Comenius's lifetime when there was great religious unrest across Europe, before and during the outbreak of the Thirty Years' War. This meant that once Comenius left Moravia he was never able to return to his homeland. As a result of this disruption he didn't enter school until his teens, where he began to develop an abiding interest in and sympathy for young school children struggling with the myriad of Latin rules; Latin schools were the only means of education at the time.

In the early decades of the 17th century, while he was at university, Comenius came upon the ideas of Wolfgang Ratke and Francis Bacon, who were beginning to question the way children were taught and to promote the ideas which Comenius explored for the rest of his long life. When he finished at university, Comenius was too young to join the church, so he began teaching in what is now Czechoslovakia. He later combined priesthood and school management with teaching in elementary schools and exploring his new ideas about education.

This was a happy time, during which he married and had two children. However, this calm period ended with the outbreak of the Thirty Years' War when the Spanish army invaded the country and looted Comenius's home. His library and all his unpublished writing on education, the work of years, was lost. He moved to Bohemia, but during the next few years Comenius' wife and both children died from disease. Not long after this, the Moravian Brotherhood lost their historical protection by the aristocracy (many of whom also belonged to the brotherhood). The brotherhood was outlawed and Comenius and his friends left for Poland where he settled in the town of Lissa.

During the 13 years of his first stay in Lissa, Comenius began to concentrate on his ideal of a pansophic (encyclopedic) education system, covering all knowledge and organised in an age-graded curriculum from primary to university. He named this system *The Great Didactic* or *Didactica Magna* and completed it in outline form during his stay in Lissa. *The Great Didactic* is a handbook for teachers and although not published until several years later, was one of the first educational 'manuals' to be printed in large numbers. The English translation of this book is still available nearly 400 years later. Alongside *The Great Didactic*, Comenius also produced books for children and for parents as he believed that children should be taught in their own home language and should have books illustrated with pictures that interested as well as instructed them.

From 1642–1648 Comenius travelled widely, visiting different countries where he spoke about his ideas and helped schools to put them into practice. He was invited to England in 1641 but the government of the day was so caught up in the Civil War that they decided not to fund the implementation of Comenius' ideas in English schools, so he moved to Sweden. By this time, he had already written a book on the teaching of language as well as a series of graded readers, and he implemented their use in schools in Sweden. These books all form part of the wider practice of *The Great Didactic*, which was both a philosophy and a series of practical handbooks providing guidance for its implementation.

Later, Comenius returned to Poland, where he was involved more in religion than education but other countries continued to invite him to come and review their education systems. Transylvania (in present day Hungary) made a good offer, so he moved to the north of the country where he drew up a plan for a seven-year school. The programme was successfully implemented, particularly in schools and classes that were taught by teachers trained by Comenius himself.

Due to the increasingly dangerous political times in Europe, Comenius continued to move around the continent until the end of his life, finally settling in Holland, where, among other writings, he produced a thousand page collection of his educational works. Comenius's most famous books included his thoughts on education and his experiences of implementing these ideas in schools. As well as *The Great Didactic*, his publications included:

- **Orbis Pictus: The World in Pictures** – published in 1658, in print until the 17th and 18th centuries and available as a pdf even today. This book is thought to be the first illustrated book for children. It is a wonderful encyclopedia of the world, illustrated with woodcuts and covering the whole of the known and spiritual world: animals, birds, fish, fruits, the heavens, fire, weather and many other aspects, explained in both English and Latin. It is certainly worth a few minutes of your time to look at this wonderful book, which would fascinate any practitioner or child, even today. Comenius believed that children who were interested would learn more easily and his book gained huge popularity and was translated into many languages.

- **Janua Linguarum Reserata: The Door of Language Unlocked** – this book was also encyclopedic but intended for children of older primary and secondary ages. In a hundred chapters, it covered everything from the origin of the Earth to the workings of the human mind. Like the Orbis Pictus, the text was presented in two columns, originally German and Latin. Comenius recommended that each chapter should be read ten times to ensure a real engagement with the material. He believed that as the pupils became more familiar with the text, they understood more.

- **Atrium: The Central Court** – a more advanced text for students who had completed the *Janua*. It deals with parts of speech such as verbs, nouns, pronouns and adjectives which were each explained with examples.

- **Vestibulum** – in practice, the *Janua* proved to be more difficult than Comenius intended, so he wrote *Vestibulum* to be used before it. *Vestibulum* had simpler language, shorter sentences and descriptions: Things at home and school, accidents and qualities of things, and the virtues were some of the sections of the book.

Comenius regretted that he could not illustrate this book, however, this book was also popular and was widely translated.

- **The School of Infancy: a Primer for Parents** – Comenius also wrote books for parents, and this one was extremely popular with mothers. Comenius urged mothers to breastfeed, and not use wet nurses, not to give their child highly seasoned foods, to ensure abundant fresh air, sleep and exercise, and above all, not to administer medicines. These were all enlightened views for the time. He also advised that in preparation for formal education, parents should help their children to learn to count to ten, distinguish different quantities and learn some basic shapes. However, he did urge parents not to push their children too hard or too fast For instance he maintained that children could not understand measurement until around the age of six. In language development, he advised that children should learn the names of objects, plants and animals. He also recommended that parents should encourage children to speak clearly and learn to speak in their own mother tongue before learning another language (Latin should not be taught until at least the age of 12). Poetry, jingles and nursery rhymes were all promoted by Comenius; he said that even if children didn't understand the words they would benefit from the rhythm and rhymes.

Considering his nomadic life and the turbulent times he lived in, it was an enormous achievement to make such an impact on educational thinking and practice. The ideas of Comenius were so successful that they were emulated all over the world, and his ideas are so embedded in current practice that it is surprising to think that they were first promoted four centuries ago.

Legacy and impact

Although he lived at the very beginning of the Renaissance, Enlightenment, and Age of Reason, Comenius's ideas are remarkably contemporary. He paid equal attention to the developing child, the method of instruction and the nature of the subject matter being taught.

During his life, he was influential in developing a theory of education in Europe and beyond, moving teaching away from rote learning and providing knowledge in the child's own language. Jean-Jacques Rousseau, Johann Heinrich Pestalozzi and others followed in his footsteps, and it was unfortunate that in the years between Comenius's time and theirs, educational practice stagnated and in some ways moved backwards into formality and an emphasis on subject knowledge, without the hands-on familiar principles and processes that Comenius promoted and we recognise today.

In his book *Giants in the Nursery*, David Elkind explored the principles that Comenius proposed for successful education. These imply that a good education reflects the way nature operates. It is begun early, working from what is easy to what is more complex, and learning is planned to meet the developmental needs of the child. Children are included in the discussion about what should be taught and teachers recognise and use the power of sensory learning. These principles, summarised from David Elkind's book, match well with the principles we apply to early learning today.

Comenius also recognised the influence of good parenting on children's future wellbeing and educational progress. His book for parents, *The School of Infancy: a Primer for Parents*, was well received and found a place in many homes at the time. Middle class women and those with a religious affiliation to Comenius and his brotherhood were the target for the book and it could be seen as providing a template for parenting books ever since.

Comenius was convinced that children must enjoy their time at school, be active in their learning and start with familiar things. The principles included above resonate with modern education theory and practice, underlining the need for children to use their senses and enjoy learning. The teacher too is advised, as now, to engage with children's interests, differentiate their teaching according to the age and stage of development of the child and ensure consistency in the way they work. He also appreciated that children need to play and that play can provide something the teacher never can. Play has its own important place in learning – not play as recreation but as a real extension of children's learning, to be respected and valued by teachers.

In such social plays with their companions, there is neither the assumption of authority nor the dread of fear, but the free intercourse which calls for the all their powers of invention, sharpens their wits, and cultivates their manners and habits.

(Elkind, 2015)

Influence on early years practice in the UK

The influence of Comenius's work can be found throughout the UK in documentation and in practice. In this short selection, you will find what all four countries have to say about picture books, (Comenius was one of the first to write picture books for children) and nursery rhymes (Comenius was certainly among the first educators to recognise the value of play in learning). These staple ingredients of the early years curriculum are now embedded in our curriculum and we often take their presence for granted, perhaps without questioning why they are important.

England

In England, practitioners are advised to use picture books and pictures in every area of learning and development to enhance and facilitate children's learning. Here are just some of the references in 'Development Matters'. Practitioners should:

- *Have resources including picture books and stories that focus on a range of emotions, such as 'I am happy'.*
- *Provide photographs and pictures of emotions for children to look at and talk about.*
- *Use pictures, books, real objects, and signs alongside your words*
- *Introduce, alongside books, story props, such as pictures, puppets and objects, to encourage children to retell stories and to think about how the characters feel.*
- *Let children handle books and draw their attention to pictures.*
- *Encourage and support children's responses to picture books and stories you read with them.*
- *Provide picture books, books with flaps or hidden words, books with accompanying CDs and story sacks*
- *Use pictures and objects to illustrate counting songs, rhymes and number stories.*
- *Use pictures or shapes of objects to indicate where things are kept and encourage children to work out where things belong.*

There are also many references to the use of rhymes and rhythm, particularly in the areas of Communication and Mathematics. Here are just some:

Mathematics:

- *Sing number rhymes as you dress or change babies, e.g. 'One, Two, Buckle My Shoe'.*
- *Move with babies to the rhythm patterns in familiar songs and rhymes.*
- *Use song and rhymes during personal routines, e.g. 'Two Little Eyes to Look Around', pointing to their eyes, one by one.*
- *Collect number and counting rhymes from a range of cultures and in other languages..*
- *Listens to and enjoys rhythmic patterns in rhymes and stories.*

Communication and Language:

- *Share rhymes, books and stories from many cultures, sometimes using languages other than English, particularly where children are learning English as an additional language.*
- *Introduce 'rhyme time' bags containing books to take home and involve parents in rhymes and singing games.*

(Early Education, 2012)

In the three other countries – Scotland, Northern Ireland and Wales, there are also many references to pictures and rhymes as essential components of the curriculum and as a foundation for reading, particularly for very young children.

Wales

In Wales, there is a clear emphasis in 'The Foundation Phase Framework' on the way pictures can enhance children's reading strategies:

- *Make meaning from pictures in books, adding detail to their explanations (in nursery)*
- *Use pictures to aid understanding of text (in Reception)*
- *Make meaning from visual features of the text e.g. illustrations, photographs, diagrams and charts (in Reception)*
- *Understand the meaning of visual features and link to written text, e.g. illustrations, photographs, diagrams and charts (in Year 1)*

(Welsh Assembly Government, 2015)

Scotland

In Scotland, the learning and sharing of nursery rhymes and songs are suggested as ways to forge a link between home and the early years setting in

'Framework pre-birth to three':

Early literacy starts with attunement between parent and baby. Tuning into the baby's needs by understanding, respecting and responding to first sounds, facial expressions and body language helps to support early literacy development. Offering opportunities for stories, conversations, listening, rhymes, singing, mark making, environmental print, and creative and imaginative play are all effective and fun ways of developing literacy.

Supporting the development of literacy and numeracy by involving parents in their child's learning by providing a home lending library and keeping them informed of the stories, rhymes and songs that the child is learning in the nursery.

(Learning and Teaching Scotland, 2010)

Although Comenius lived so long ago, he uncovered many of the key characteristics of high quality early years practice to which we aspire today.

Things to think about

- Had you realised why you naturally use songs and rhymes when you work with young children? Did you realise that this seemingly new idea had been in existence for so long?

- Try downloading *Orbis Pictus* from the Internet. It is available on line at archive.org/details/orbispictusofjoh00comeiala . Look at its amusing and interesting illustrations. Do you think young children today would be interested in them?

- How much notice do you take of the pictures when you read a book to children? Observe yourself and think about what you find. Do we spend enough time looking at this vital component of the reading process?

- How much support has your training given you in valuing and promoting books, stories and rhymes? Is this enough to give you confidence in using them with children?

Mihaly Csikszentmihalyi (1934–)

Full name: Mihaly Csikszentmihalyi

Born: 1934 (still living)

Place of birth: Rijeka Croatia

Countries of residence: Hungary, United States

What he did: The concept of 'flow' is the central theme of Csikszentmihalyi's life and work.

Influences on education today: The concept of 'flow' and the whole culture of mindfulness and concentration is now recognised as essential, not just for artists and sports people, but for everyone. 'Slow Schooling' is one of the outcomes of these developments.

Theories and areas of work: Humanism

Key influencers and followers: Martin Seligman, Howard Gardner

Key works: *Creativity: Flow and the Psychology of Discovery and Invention* (1996), *Good Work: When Excellence and Ethics Meet,* (2001).

The best moments usually occur when a person's body or mind is stretched to its limits in a voluntary effort to accomplish something difficult and worthwhile. For each person there are thousands of opportunities, challenges to expand ourselves.

Mihaly Csikszentmihalyi, Flow: The Psychology of Optimal Experience, 2008

Life, love, theory and research

Mihaly Csikszentmihalyi is a psychologist who was born in Hungary and now works in the United States. In the Second World War he was imprisoned as a child in Italy and during this time of suffering he found that when he played chess he entered a state in which he could forget his imprisonment, hunger, loneliness and the loss of his family. This experience would eventually lead him to coin a name for this state: the theory of flow.

After a chance experience of hearing Carl Jung speak, Csikszentmihalyi went to America and began to explore further his growing interest in a human's ability to overcome adversity and enter an internal state, making themselves unaware of the world around them. Csikszentmihalyi has devoted the rest of his working life to the study of happiness – what makes people truly satisfied and fulfilled – and this has become the theory of flow. He describes flow as a concentrated state of being where an individual is so involved in an activity that he or she becomes unaware of others or of the passage of time. They will also emerge from this state energised and happy.

Sports and games can also result in flow and many sports people have commented that they also enter a different state during these activities. Here is an example of flow in sport:

Max is a man who loves to run. Not just running, but running marathons, double marathons and competing in Iron Man events. He isn't competitive, except against himself. He just loves the state he gets in when he is running for a long time, pushing himself to the limit. His life, his diet, his sleep patterns, his social contacts are all shaped by his running. Material things are sacrificed to pay for kit and travel. He is prepared to forgo promotion in his work, because a managerial job would mean less flexibility for his training, less opportunity to take a few days off to travel to the places where the marathons are held, in his own country and abroad. When he runs, practising regularly in the gym and on country roads and tracks, he is often uncomfortable and cold, his muscles ache, his lungs hurt, his hands are cold and stiff. So why does he do it?

When Max is running, once his muscles have warmed up, and he is 'in his stride', he enters what Csikszentmihalyi calls the state of 'flow'. He feels free, relaxed, without worries, unaware of other runners or of his own place in the race – almost outside himself – and above all, Max is happy. Experiencing flow makes Max, like others with the same experience, raise the challenge of the activity – next time he may attempt a longer or more challenging run in order to achieve the same feeling.

Over the years of his research, Csikszentmihalyi has found that when a person enters the state of flow, they are happy, positive and energised. Flow floods the body with endorphins that make us happy, and research over many years has found that true happiness can be present in the human body and brain when they enter this state.

It isn't only extreme physical exercise such as skiing, running, surfing etc. that can result in flow; Csikszentmihalyi found that other activities can bring flow too. Creative activities such as, painting, drawing, singing, writing, sculpture and playing music have also been found by Csikszentmihalyi to be ways into flow. People who become very deeply involved in something they enjoy and feel part of are, like Max, prepared to forgo other things even personal relationships or income in order to do the activity that gives them flow.

Young children also enter the flow state and practitioners often see a child who is completely absorbed in what they are doing, so absorbed that they are unaware of what else is going on around them. Time has no relevance, and they don't even respond to an adult voice when they say it's time to tidy up.

When he was working in the United States, Csikszentmihalyi attempted to identify the features of flow and thus of happiness or fulfillment. He began his studies by working with teenagers, trying to establish what made them happy. He provided them with beepers that beeped at random times during the day and the teenagers were asked to record their thoughts and feelings each time their beeper went off. Most of the teenagers indicated that most of the time they were unhappy. However, when they were engaged in a challenging task, they tended to be more positive about their feelings. Csikszentmihalyi found that a balanced combination of challenge and ability – not so much challenge that one feels threatened but sufficient challenge to avoid boredom – made theses teenagers happier than in any other activity. Too simple a task produced the typical response of 'boring', too difficult and they would switch off.

The research moved on to questioning artists and other creative people about flow, as there was clear evidence that creative activities such as music and painting could trigger flow and that creative people often do enter a different state when they work.

The best moments in our lives are not the passive, receptive, relaxing times … The best moments usually occur if a person's body or mind is stretched to its limits in a voluntary effort to accomplish something difficult and worthwhile.

(Csikszentmihalyi, 2008)

Csikszentmihalyi has found that flow is a concentrated form of happiness and the people who took part in his research told him that it was true – flow brought happiness to them. The happiness resulting from flow is not just random chance but a situation that we construct consciously for ourselves, prepared for, cultivated and defended by individuals. In order to facilitate flow, we (like Max) are prepared to sacrifice almost anything.

Csikszentmihalyi's theory was influenced not just by his own experiences and by hearing Jung, but by Abraham Maslow's thinking, illustrated in his hierarchy of need (p 200). Flow is the same as the state of 'self-actualisation' when individuals reach their full potential. In this state they can be aware simultaneously of both their own potential and also their limitations and can meet challenge at an appropriate level.

It is hardly surprising that Csikszentmihalyi found that true happiness comes from within the individual, not from outside. When we focus our energy and time on a goal we have chosen ourselves, Csikszentmihalyi maintains that our psychic energy flows in the direction of that goal, resulting in harmony and contentment. In this state, we are '…so involved in an activity that nothing else seems to matter; the experience is so enjoyable that people will continue to do it even at great cost, for the sheer sake of doing it.' (Csikszentmihalyi, 2008)

Some of the features of flow are:

- there are clear goals every step of the way
- there is immediate feedback to one's actions
- there is a balance between challenges and skills
- action and awareness are merged
- distractions are excluded from consciousness

- there is no worry of failure
- self-consciousness disappears
- the sense of time becomes distorted
- the activity becomes an end in itself.

The key to successful flow is the management of external factors, both positive and negative. To achieve a state of flow we may have to ignore other people and sometimes, this determination to get into flow can undermine relationships, particularly with others who are not particularly interested in achieving it. We forget the restrictions of both time and space and are prepared to abandon other things we should be doing because these will affect flow. This has been described as a merging of the person and the activity.

Legacy and impact

Csikszentmihalyi's work has had significant effects on the professions of psychology and therapy where flow and the concept of mindfulness have to some extent merged. Mindfulness activities and yoga are both activities that can lead to flow. Because the brain is allocating so much power to the activity during flow, the body may well be in discomfort or even in pain but the individual is often unaware of this.

The understanding and appreciation of the power of flow has enabled sports scientists and psychologists to help professional and amateur sports people to focus their minds on developing the relevant skills to encourage flow, both to increase their performance and to accept that in order to be 'in the zone' they may have to make difficult decisions about the priorities in their personal and professional lives. In his book *The Chimp Paradox* Steve Peters, a sports scientist, describes a state with some of the characteristics of flow. He maintains that when we take charge of the different elements of our minds we can enter a state of flow where anxiety and stress can be reduced and we can take control of our lives.

In education, learning more about the theory and features of flow behaviour can help practitioners to understand the place of this state in children's lives. One of the most highly regarded skills of learning is the ability to concentrate and focus on the task in hand. If we are constantly interrupting children to stop the activities that fascinate them, to come and join activities that may not, we do them a disservice and fracture their concentration.

As practitioners and teachers come under more and more pressure to improve their own performance and the attainment of the children they work with, activities such as mindfulness have become one of the ways they can reduce anxiety for both teachers and children. In some schools, yoga, mindfulness and other meditation techniques have been used to help children relax and concentrate and some of these initiatives seem to be having a positive result, particularly with older children.

The principles of mindfulness are not new, although its popularity has increased in the last few years. This ancient Buddhist practice has been revived to help with the management of the stress of modern living. Mindfulness means paying more attention to the present moment, being aware of the world around us, noting the little things and pausing for thought which increases awareness, clarity and acceptance of the present reality. Mindfulness is seen as a way to make space for other activities and this may also lead to Csikszentmihalyi's state of flow.

Influence on early years practice in the UK

As mentioned above, many of the features of flow are reflected in the learning skills promoted in the literature to support early years practice.

England

In the EYFS framework, within the Characteristics of Effective Learning, practitioners will find the following references to some of the key characteristics of flow behaviour:

The Unique Child will show evidence of being involved and concentrating:

- *Maintaining focus on their activity for a period of time*
- *Showing high levels of energy, fascination*
- *Not easily distracted*
- *Paying attention to details*
- *Enjoying meeting challenges for their own sake rather than external rewards or praise*

Enabling Environments – what adults could provide:

- *Help children concentrate by limiting noise, and making spaces visually calm and orderly.*
- *Ensure children have uninterrupted time to play and explore.*
- *Children will become more deeply involved when you provide something that is new and unusual for them to explore, especially when it is linked to their interests.*
- *Notice what arouses children's curiosity, looking for signs of deep involvement to identify learning that is intrinsically motivated.*
- *Ensure children have time and freedom to become deeply involved in activities.*

- *Children can maintain focus on things that interest them over a period of time. Help them to keep ideas in mind by talking over photographs of their previous activities.*

(DfE, 2012)

Flow appears to be a useful tool in learning and we should be encouraging children to understand that control of their own learning is just as important as sitting and listening to an adult. Balancing the pressure on adults to follow a planned curriculum, and the child's need for time and space to develop a 'flow mentality', may prove difficult, but is a constant need.

Northern Ireland

In the section dealing with Personal Development and Mutual Understanding, The Northern Ireland Curriculum Primary includes the following statement, which echoes Csikszentmihalyi's theory that all humans can and should learn to manage their own learning and begin to understand the activities and interests that, for them, can offer the experience of flow:

By the time children enter school their dispositions will have been influenced by their pre school experiences. Teachers should foster children's dispositions to learn by providing a varied and enjoyable curriculum which takes account of their interests. They should help children to progress and achieve by nurturing their motivation, perseverance, curiosity and creativity, by encouraging them to problem solve, and by giving them time for reflection.

(CCEA, Northern Ireland, 2007)

Wales

In Wales, there is an understanding that some of the most powerful learning comes about in and through play, which is often the location of flow 'Play and early years: birth to seven years' states:

Pure play – the play in which the child and their own selected participants can be involved is 'pure' in the sense of being unadulterated with any interference or direction on anyone's part but the children's. When adults are seeking involvement in children's play, they need to do so playfully if they wish to make inroads into children's thinking and actions in play.

(PlayWales, 2013)

Things to think about

- Have you ever seen a child in a flow state? What were they doing? What did you do?

- Do you experience flow in your work, during your studies or in your private life? Which activities do you get so involved in that you experience flow? What are the pressures in your life that prevent you from experiencing flow?

- When you are working, look for children who are so involved in what they are doing that they may be experiencing flow. Watch what happens. How long does their concentration last? Which activities seem to be best for children to move into the flow state?

- Do you think it's possible for more than one child to get into flow together? Could a child get into flow while they are working with an adult?

- Have you practised mindfulness or known anyone who has? What are its real benefits?

Mihaly Csikszentmihalyi (1934–)

John Dewey

> **Full name:** John Dewey
> **Born:** 1859
> **Died:** 1952
> **Place of birth:** Burlington, Vermont, United States
> **Countries of residence:** Burlington, Vermont, United States
> **What he did:** Dewey championed education based on first hand experience, the topic approach and following children's interests, but with a rigorous approach to progression and continuity in the curriculum.
> **Influences on education today:** First hand experience lies at the heart of good practice in the UK, not only in the early years, but throughout the whole education system.
> **Theories and areas of work:** Pragmatism, Educational psychology
> **Key influencers and followers:** Plato, Jean-Jacques Rousseau, Jane Addams and Hull House
> *The School and Society* (1892), *The Child and Society* (1902), *The Relation of Theory to Practice in Education* (1904).

"No one can be really successful in performing the duties and meeting these demands [of teaching] who does not retain [her] intellectual curiosity intact throughout [her] entire career.

John Dewey; To those who aspire to the profession of teaching; 2010; In Simpson, D.J., & Stack, S.F. (Eds), Teachers, leaders and schools: Essays by John Dewey 2010

Life, love, theory and research

John Dewey was born in Vermont, and strangely, was named John after his older brother who had died in an accident. He went to school and university in Vermont and after graduating he worked for two years in a high school and one year in an elementary school before deciding that he was not suited to teaching.

Many educators think that Dewey was the most significant educational thinker of his era and even of the 20th century. As a philosopher, social reformer and educator he challenged and then fundamentally changed the existing approaches to teaching and learning, spending large parts of his life studying the history of current education practice and working as a professor of psychology at a teacher's college and at Columbia University.

Dewey's ideas about education sprang from a philosophy of pragmatism and were central to the Progressive Movement in schooling. His first major publication was *The School and Society* which explored his progressive views on education. At a time when 'progressive education' was fashionable and many progressive schools were established, Dewey thought that children should learn from first hand experience. His reports of the children in his laboratory school in Chicago sound very similar to later topic or thematic approaches which are still popular today. Children did not just sew, they explored the whole process – investigating how cotton was grown and making cloth before embarking on the sewing itself.

In his writing Dewey asked that theory and practice in education should come together. He criticised the schoolroom with its cramped desks suited only for reading or listening and the lack of space for creating, exploring and making. He said children should be 'the centre of gravity' for teaching.

He also criticised the American school system, where transition from kindergarten to elementary school, where changes from a play-based situation to a formal reading and writing curriculum put a brake on children's progress. He equally opposed the transitions later in children's lives when they moved from elementary to intermediate school and then to high school. He thought the way to unify education was by linking it to the outside world, to shops, factories, museums, and offices so that children were in direct contact with the world, making formal classrooms less necessary.

In Dewey's ideal world, teachers would be in control of the curriculum, starting from questions and following children's interests. There would be a curriculum which started from question marks rather than strict rules and the teachers themselves would be available to help answer the questions that would arise from children's explorations.

Dewey maintained that education was a social activity, that schools could be agents of social change and that children should be able to interact with the curriculum, taking part in defining their own learning. School should be a place to learn how to learn, not just a place where abstract content was acquired. He was one of the most famous proponents of hands-on learning and experiential education, believing schools should be places for independent thought and enquiry.

Dewy's involvement in teacher education was a result of his interest in schools. He believed that teachers should love children and be interested in them, not just in disseminating knowledge. Teachers should be lifelong learners, always interested in imparting what they knew, ensuring that the children in their care became intelligent, thoughtful members of society. In this way, education had a chance of changing the society of the future. The best teachers are those who watch the children, understand what they see and are able to respond appropriately. Dewey recognised the stress and hard work involved in being a good teacher and knew it was in a sense never ending; a teacher was always watching, responding, learning and developing themselves, never satisfied, always striving in the interests of the children.

Dewey was constantly opposed to the current model of schools where teachers only taught the knowledge and skills the pupils would need for their working lives, which would mostly be as low paid working class employees. Dewey believed that the knowledge and skills learned at school should be more than just rote-learned information about subjects that are irrelevant to future working life. Dewey also thought that teachers should be more than just the 'funnel' through which facts should be poured into the pupils: 'It is the business of teachers to help in producing the many kinds of skill needed in contemporary life.' (Bodson, 1987).

At the time, there were two conflicting views of education. The first was centred on the curriculum and focused almost solely on the 'subject matter to be taught'. Dewey argued that the major flaw in this methodology was the inactivity of the student, described by him as the 'shallow student who was to be deepened.' In the second view, the curriculum was 'child-centred' with the child as the starting point and continual check on direction for the curriculum. In Dewey's eyes, neither of these was absolutely right. The curriculum should be responsive to the child, but child-centred learning threatened the content of the curriculum, and endangered the role of the teacher. The curriculum should balance these two views, while avoiding dominance by either the curriculum or the child.

His view was that teaching should take the best of both methods, providing children with the tools they would need to survive in society in the future, which meant that teaching should aim to produce citizens who could contribute to a democratic and intelligent community. In other words, the teacher should focus on knowledge and skills that would enable children to respond to a variety of situations and possibilities, rather than filling children's minds with facts or useless knowledge.

The methods Dewey supported were both child-centred and multi-subject, taught through active learning and joined-up subjects. He put a premium on meaningful activity in learning and participation in classroom democracy. Unlike earlier models of teaching, which were teacher dominated, relying on authoritarianism and rote learning, progressive education asserted that students must be really involved in what they were learning. Dewey argued that curriculum should be relevant to students' lives and should rely on learning by doing, with the development of practical life skills at the heart of children's education.

Dewey believed that teachers should be lifelong learners themselves, and that they could not survive long if they were not interested in their own development and that of others in the profession. However this interest in their own development was of no use unless the teacher is also passionate about imparting their knowledge to the children. The combination of being a permanently interested learner and committed teacher is a complex and tiring occupation, a fact which Dewey recognised and understood.

Teachers today will be able to empathise with Dewey's view of teaching, that:

'One of the most depressing phases of the vocation is the number of care worn teachers one sees. While contact with the young is a privilege for some temperaments, it is a tax on others which they do not bear up under very well.'

Teachers, Leaders and Schools: Essays by John Dewey, 2010

However, he maintained that schools would not be successful unless the quality of teaching was improved and then maintained into the future. The most important characteristic of a good teacher was the ability to watch the children and respond to how they related to the subject or lesson presented. This criterion is still among the most powerful indicators of high quality teaching.

Dewey also maintained these indicators of a good teacher:

- a love for working with, and a continuing study of the development of young children

- a natural disposition to inquire about the subjects, methods and other social issues related to the profession and how to match these to the needs and interests of children

- a permanent interest in what makes good classroom practice and a desire to share this knowledge with others.

These were not a set of observable skills, they were best described as attitudes and mindsets. Even now, they are sometimes missed in lists of teacher aptitudes, and because they are not easily measured, they may get missed when a teacher is observed. However they are still some of the most important features of the work of an outstanding teacher and can often be seen reflected in the achievements of children and other adults with whom the outstanding teacher works.

There have always been critics and cynics prepared to undermine the work of innovators in education particularly when there is any move towards giving more power to the learner. In Dewey's time, some critics assumed that, under his more child-focused system, students would fail to acquire basic academic skills and knowledge. Others believed that classroom order and the teacher's authority would disappear. This attitude has never been proven and teachers who share ownership of learning with children usually find that behaviour and attitudes improve.

Teachers in modern schools would recognise the methods Dewey promoted, and the arguments against child-centred learning and student involvement still play out against education practice today, with political and social influences pulling methodology in different directions as government priorities change and new leaders implement ever changing policies.

Legacy and impact

Dewey was such an important influence in his own time that it is difficult to understand why his contribution has not left more of a mark on modern methods. The continual change in of focus in schools, and the repeated swing between formal methods and those with less control held by the teacher, has left the teaching profession confused and lacking in confidence. Many teachers are searching for the most effective balance between child-focused and adult-directed learning. Schools are constantly told they are able to follow their own futures, yet education has never been more centrally controlled, so the insecurity remains.

A good example of recent mixed messages from government was the implementation of the Literacy Strategy in England where a formal hour of literacy teaching was imposed on all primary schools. The extent of the central direction was such that, within the original documentation, a clock indicated the number of minutes to be spent during the Literacy Hour in teaching each of the elements of literacy – spelling, grammar, writing, reading.

In the most recent version of the National Curriculum for England, there is more room for flexibility in adapting the curriculum and teaching methods to the needs of the children. However, despite this supposed reduction of the requirements for lessons, the framework used for inspecting lessons in schools often appears to be founded on a rigid model of teaching, objective setting and progress made by children in individual lessons, leaving teachers confused and lacking the courage to innovate or experiment with alternative methods.

Influence on early years practice in the UK

UK governments have all recognised the importance of education in improving conditions for individuals, not just during their school years, but for the rest of their lives. The two-fold roles of schooling are agreed across the UK – providing children with the skills they need for their working lives, and enriching the lives of individuals by giving them life skills and a lifelong interest in finding out about the world – are well established. An educated workforce is the lifeblood of a successful economy and in the current situation where many people may not stay in the same job for their whole working life, skills such as problem solving will be essential.

England

The latest EYFS Framework and guidance for England, both outline sets of skills that Dewey would recognise, as detailed in the 'Statutory Framework for the EYFS':

> *In planning and guiding children's activities, practitioners must reflect on the different ways that children learn and reflect these in their practice. Three Characteristics of Effective Teaching and Learning are:*
>
> * *playing and exploring – children investigate and experience things, and 'have a go';*

- *active learning – children concentrate and keep on trying if they encounter difficulties, and enjoy achievements; and*
- *creating and thinking critically – children have and develop their own ideas, make links between ideas, and develop strategies for doing things.*

(DfE, 2012)

The guidance for practitioners in supporting these essential skills includes a wide range of practical suggestions, and it is very evident that the role of the adult is crucial in ensuring that the child feels confident to take some of the control of their own learning.

In Playing and Exploring (engagement) adults are encouraged to play with the children, without taking over, or dominating the play. Practitioners need to become strong models of effective learners, encouraging risk taking and using sensitive techniques to enable children to talk about their own learning.

In Active Learning, described as supporting motivation or mastery techniques, adults are again encouraged to stimulate and support children in following their own interests, and introducing the notion of metacognition (thinking and talking about thinking) which involves adults and children in considering the process of learning, not just the product.

In Creating and Thinking Critically (thinking) adults are also encouraged to introduce thinking skills and the language of thinking such as *think, know, remember, forget, idea, makes sense, plan, learn, find out, confused, figure out.* Asking and answering questions, valuing children's ideas giving time for thinking – using the techniques of sustained shared thinking, where adults and children work together as equals to solve problems and work together. Terms such as 'plan', do and review' and 'scaffolding' are often used to describe these processes.

Practitioners are anxious to get the balance right between adult-directed activities and child-initiated learning, and there has been much discussion in an effort to come to an agreement, so practitioners and teachers as well as their managers and those who evaluate their performance can be sure that they agree on what is ideal. The guidance in the Statutory Framework is helpful but does not give any idea of proportions, leaving this to professional discussion. This suggestion is unhelpful to those practitioners who are not confident or experienced enough to make the decision themselves, as detailed in 'Development Matters in the EYFS':

Each area of learning and development must be implemented through planned, purposeful play, and through a mix of adult-led and child-initiated activity. Play is essential for children's development, building their confidence as they learn by leading their own play and by taking part in play which is guided by adults. There is an ongoing judgement to be made by practitioners about the balance between activities led by children, and activities led or guided by adults.

(Early Education, 2012).

There is also an expectation in the English framework that, by the time children reach the age of five, they should be ready for more adult intervention but many teachers in primary schools realise that self-initiated learning should continue for the whole of a child's education and beyond. For instance, in Slow Schools (sloweducation.co.uk), the education programme is planned in long blocks, to ensure that children have time to follow their own interests and work at their own pace on self-motivated projects. In this way creativity, innovation and motivation are being retained, and despite criticisms and opposition, standards are rising in these schools.

There is no doubt that Dewey would recognise the guidance for early education in all four countries of the UK as it reflects the principles for the sort of child-centred education he proposed – an education where the adult and child move forward together, preparing the child for the next steps in learning and eventually for life.

Key guidance documents for countries in the UK

DfE, (2012) 'Statutory Framework for the EYFS'.
Early Education, (2012) 'Development Matters in the EYFS'.

Things to think about

- How do you establish the balance between child-initiated and adult-led activity in your setting?

- Does this balance change as children get older?

- Why are the Characteristics of Effective Teaching and Learning important?

- It is well understood that the 'Characteristics of Effective Learning' are about how a child is learning, not what a child is learning. How do you record and report to parents and carers on children's progress in these areas?

- How would you prepare yourself for working in schools with very different philosophies and ways of working?

Margaret Donaldson

Full name: Margaret Donaldson
Born: 1926 (still living)
Place of birth: Paisley, Scotland
Countries of residence: Scotland
What she did: Donaldson explored children's thinking, and the unique child. She also explores 'embedded thinking' (concepts firmly fixed in a child's thinking) and 'disembedded thinking' which often makes no sense to them. We often expect children to absorb disembedded information just because it is contained in the curriculum.
Influences on education today: Donaldson's work on understanding how children think, and in collecting such a wide range of information about how they turn those thoughts into language has had a significant effect on practice and subsequent research. Her investigations into the validity of Piaget's staged model of development reflected a more general concern about such an influential theory.
Theories and areas of work: Social constructivism; Developmental psychology
Key influencers and followers: Jean Piaget, Jerome Bruner, Lev Vygotsky
Key works: *Children's Minds* (1978), *Human Minds* (1922).

The better you know something the more risk there is of behaving egocentrically in relation to your knowledge. Thus, the greater the gap between teacher and learner, the harder teaching becomes.

Margaret Donaldson, Children's Minds, 1978

Life, love, theory and research

Born and educated in Scotland, and working there for much of her life, Margaret Donaldson is a well-respected theorist with a specialism in studying the minds of children. She believes that learning is an active, constructive process affected by both genetic makeup (nature) and the environment (nurture). Each individual learner constructs their own unique reality with new information linked to existing knowledge, so the way each person sees the world, and therefore the way they respond to it, is unique.

Donaldson, who visited and worked with Jean Piaget, later disagreed with some of his thinking, particularly after she met and worked with Bruner and Vygotsky in the 1960s. She thought that the rigid stages of development proposed by Piaget had resulted from research methods that were suspect in that the instructions to children were difficult for them to understand.

Donaldson examined some of Piaget's tasks to demonstrate that when simple modifications were made, children were able to operate at levels above those predicted by Piaget. In her new tasks she focused on using language and situations that had real meaning for the children, making sense in the child's world. Using these modified tasks and more familiar language, Donaldson showed that children could successfully complete tasks that demonstrated a capacity for deductive reasoning, problem solving, 'conserving' and 'de-centering', which were at the centre of Piaget's experiments.

For instance, Donaldson adapted Piaget's conservation of number task using lines of shapes. (The concept of conservation is the recognition by a young child that quantity does not change with physical rearrangement). In this test, Piaget placed two even rows of different objects in front of a six year old. He asked the child whether there are more circles, more squares, or the same number of each kind. The expected answer is 'the same'.

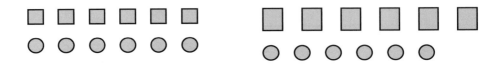

Piaget then rearranged the row of squares as shown and asked the same question again. This time around a child would usually say 'there are more squares'.

In re-structuring this test, Donaldson introduced the concept of a 'Naughty teddy' who had theoretically disturbed one of the rows of shapes, and in this way, the child was able to relate to the concept and understand that the random row of counters still had the same number, even though the appearance of the line of shapes was different. Piaget's stages of development have become (and still are) the foundation for early years planning and practice.

During her experiments, Donaldson developed her theories of 'embedded' and 'disembedded' thinking. Embedded thinking is thinking that has been securely placed in familiar contexts and linked with existing knowledge. At this point, the child can use the new learning confidently and in the right context which Donaldson called making 'human sense' of what they are asked to do. When children are asked to do or learn something outside their limits of experience, their thinking is 'disembedded', making no sense to them and affecting the amount of information they retain. Obviously practitioners should try to focus on embedded thinking, although it is not always possible when they are expected to present information to children which is disembedded.

Donaldson also advised practitioners working with young children to learn to 'decentre' themselves, so they can understand the world from the viewpoint of the child. In this way, they will be able to make the activities they plan and the questions they ask more relevant to the children's experience.

Donaldson has written books and many papers about her thinking and the most well known of these is *Children's Minds* published in 1986. This book, widely read in education circles was described by Jerome Bruner as, 'One of the most powerful, most wisely balanced and best informed books on the development of the child's mind to have appeared in 20 years. Its implications for education are enormous.' (Bruner, 1978).

Her main interest has been in applying her theories to human thought and language – particularly the difference between what is said and what is meant, and *Children's Minds* explores the place of language, particularly at the point when children begin to attend school. Her focus is the difference between the way that adults and children perceive and use language. Children live in the moment and often we talk to them about things that are not in the moment, leaving them confused.

The shortcomings of the recent theories about the growth of the mind can be seen as related to a failure to pay enough attention to the difference between language as it is spontaneously used and interpreted by a child and language as it has come to be conceived of by those who develop the theories.

(Donaldson, 1978).

Donaldson proposes that when we talk to children, they are influenced by three things:

- Their own knowledge and experience of language
- Their own assessment of what they think we intend (and of course this may be very different from our own intention)
- The way he or she would represent the situation to himself or herself if we were not there at all.

This proposal throws a spotlight onto our conversations with children and how they sometimes misunderstand what we say, and how we should always give them time to ask us to clarify. Young children have less knowledge of how language works so they are less confident about using language themselves and interpreting the language they hear. Consequently, children are more likely to rely on non-linguistic cues, such as visual cues from their immediate surroundings, where they are more confident.

As early years practitioners, we devote much of our time to creating a stimulating environment in our settings. However, Donaldson proposes that many young children find it extremely difficult to focus on the details of language when they are in a situation where there are many other stimuli to distract them.

Even when children appear to have a good grasp of language and are able to listen to us and concentrate on what we are saying, they may not always understand everything we say. Knowing what a word means is a developing skill which is enhanced by using and hearing it in many different situations and by the development of the brain in handling language: '... it is a common but naïve assumption that the understanding of a word is an all-or-none affair. But it is not so. Knowledge of word meaning grows – it undergoes developmental change.' (Donaldson, 1978)

This results in the surprisingly complex language used by some children. When children go to nursery or school, some of this language is 'learned' and some is copied from others and repeated without an understanding of its complexity. For example, a child comes home from nursery and at a family meal repeats a new phrase he has heard. He announces in a loud voice, 'This place is rubbish!' His outburst is not a condemnation of his caring home, simply the attempt of a young language learner to try out a phrase that his friend used at nursery which got a response from practitioners that impressed him.

We also need to understand that most children and adults know what they mean when they speak and it is easier to produce language than it is to understand the language spoken by others. This mismatch continues into adult life, so even when we think we understand what everyone says to us, it is very easy to misunderstand, particularly when we lack context and facial expression. When we are on the phone or using social media and we can't see the speaker, we are at a considerable disadvantage. Knowledge of language and its meaning is never complete; it continues to develop for our whole lives.

Donaldson wrote that initially, children's early language is embedded in the situations a child experiences, meaning that the young child considers the language they hear in context and as a whole, rarely considering words out of context. Children come to school as accomplished thinkers, but their thinking is focused outwards. Until a child can internalise what they see and hear, and start to generate a range of possible options for action and response, they will not become effective communicators or thinkers. Such responsive thinking and interpretation comes from being able to generate responses and plan them for themselves.

Children who are constantly trying to figure out what other people mean must be capable of realising that other people have intentions that may be different from their own, and this is a complex concept: 'A child who is trying to figure out what other people mean must be capable of recognizing intentions in others.' (Donaldson, 1978)

Language is an essential tool for humans and Donaldson's work has been the basis for our commitment to language development as a crucial skill for success in education. Our society places great emphasis on thinking and thinking needs language, both to express ourselves and to understand what others are saying. This is a difficult enterprise for young minds and some children find it so difficult that they shut down completely, refusing to talk in public situations or even becoming an elective mute – a child who can speak but refuses to do so.

Donaldson maintained that there has been and still is, a division between:

- those who **think** (implying that these people have a monopoly of the language skills), and
- those who **do** (people who work with their hands and bodies, and are presumed not to need complex language).

Becoming aware of language itself, free from the immediate context is a key stage in language development. The realisation that language is a distinct system is a significant point in development and learning to read is central to this process, because the written word is permanent and free from non-linguistic content. It is the word on its own that determines meaning. So learning to read is a very important part of learning about language as a whole. The first step is to make the child more aware of spoken language and that speech can be written down as words. Children should have time to reflect on what they are reading and should be presented with texts that are neither too easy nor too difficult. It is vital that children can use the reading process as early as possible to develop their reflective awareness and increase the complexity of both their spoken language and their language for thinking.

When teaching reading Donaldson believes it is a mistake to insist on a 'one to one' correspondence between letters and the sounds they make which she believes can undermine the natural urge to master speaking, reading and spelling. This could pose a problem for practitioners when they have directives telling them exactly the opposite; that they have to teach disembedded information to children, when the best readers have embedded skills.

Maintaining a positive self-image is vital. Very early in their school careers, children form an impression of the type of learner they are and those who see themselves as 'stupid' or 'slow' are very likely to withdraw from difficult tasks rather than see them as challenges to be tackled and overcome. Failure becomes a self-fulfilling prophecy, which is a concept that has been explored and developed by Carol Dweck. Donaldson asks us to reconsider the traditional way of encouraging pupils by offering rewards – gold stars, treats or privileges. Sadly, children who don't receive such rewards will instantly view themselves as failures and external rewards can actually decrease the enthusiasm of those who received them for an activity.

The link with Donaldson's work and that of Howard Gardner is worth making here (p147). Gardner encourages us to value every sort of intelligence, whether this is mathematical, linguistic and literary intelligence, which we have traditionally valued OR musical, kinaesthetic or naturalist intelligence.

Legacy and impact

Donaldson's greatest influence has been in the education of young children and particularly in the development of early language. She maintained that early years practitioners should concentrate on closing the gap between less advantaged, language delayed children and more fluent, advantaged children. This issue is now central to the thinking and policy of governments across the developed world and has resulted in many initiatives to address the issue, prompted by several reports concerning children's language development and the need to 'close the gap'. A report entitled 'Promoting speech and language: a themed study in fifteen local Sure Start Programmes' states:

> Children growing up in impoverished circumstances are generally exposed to language that differs both qualitatively and quantitatively from the experience of more fortunate children. A social class gradient in language skills is already emerging by the time a child is two years old and the gap widens substantially by the time children reach statutory school age.
>
> (Melhuish et. al., 2007)

Every Child a Talker (ECaT) was a five-year project in the UK (2008–2013), which aimed to:

- raise children's achievement in early language
- improve practitioners' skills and knowledge
- increase parental understanding and involvement in children's language development.

The project was rolled out throughout England, with subsequent associated initiatives in Scotland, Northern Ireland and Wales, and has resulted in improvements in practitioner understanding of communication development, in working with parents on communication skills at home, and in identification of children at risk of language delay. However, the intended expansion of the strategy to all settings in the country has been a real problem. Due to the sheer number of early years settings and practitioners, some were never included in the phased roll-out of the project, and financial restraints and reduced funding for early years initiatives have curtailed these, and other language development programmes.

The Read On Get On Project document, led by Save the Children Fund, aims to get every child reading well at the age of 11 across the whole of the UK by 2025. The launch report of the current position in Scotland includes the following information about early language development:

> Evidence suggests that by age three, 50% of our language is in place and by age five, 85% of is in place. In addition, evidence from England shows that a two-year-old's language development can strongly predict their reading skills on entry into school, as well as later attainment. Yet a child's background has a significant impact on acquiring these all important early language skills.
>
> (Save the Children Fund, 2014)

The report goes on to identify the difference in comprehension and language development between children from lower socio-economic backgrounds who enter school having heard a million fewer words than their middle class peers.

The crucial place of language development is now accepted in every country, but the gap between less and more advantaged children remains as stubbornly present as it ever was and in some countries even appears to be increasing, despite the efforts of governments, practitioners and managers in settings and schools.

Donaldson was one of the researchers who first identified the power of high quality early years education in improving language development, particularly for children in deprived areas. Her work, with that of other researchers, has influenced governments to make significant investments in early years provision, and making this an entitlement for four year olds, then three year olds, and increasingly for two year olds, particularly those from poor families. 'Early years pupil premium and funding for two-year-olds' states: 'Research has found that high quality pre-school education is especially beneficial for the most disadvantaged pupils and for those with low qualified parents, in promoting better outcomes at age 11.' (DfE, 2014). However, The Sutton Trust has identified a probable gap of 19 months between the least advantaged and the most advantaged children, and that this gap widens as children go through their school years: 'Eradicating this inequality is fundamental to ensuring all children get the best start in life'. (DfE, 2014).

Donaldson gave a tremendous push to the communication debate and *Children's Minds* continues to be a core book for study in universities and colleges.

Influence on early years practice in the UK

Helped by the work of such thinkers and researchers as Donaldson, communication and language has become a core area of learning in government guidance across all the countries in the UK. In Scotland, the Literacy Commission emphasises that even before birth, language development can be delayed by the negative effects of disadvantage and poor ante-natal care. 'A vision for Scotland: The report and final recommendations of the literacy commission' states: 'Some children arrive at nursery at the age of three or even four with barely any language and poorly developed social and motor skills.' (Scottish Parent Teacher Council, 2009)

The guidance in 'Pre-birth to three' in Scotland advises practitioners to work with mothers and young children, ensuring that language development is supported both at home and in the setting:

Early literacy starts with attunement between parent and baby. Offering opportunities for stories, conversations, listening, rhymes, singing, mark making, environmental print, and creative and imaginative play are all effective and fun ways of developing literacy.

(Learning and Teaching Scotland, 2010)

The EYFS Statutory Framework for England includes the following information on the importance of language development, identifying it as one of the three Prime Areas of development, which should be at the centre of provision, particularly before the age of three:

Three areas are particularly crucial for igniting children's curiosity and enthusiasm for learning, and for building their capacity to learn, form relationships and thrive. These three areas, the Prime Areas, are:

- *communication and language; (communication and language development involves giving children opportunities to experience a rich language environment; to develop their confidence and skills in expressing themselves; and to speak and listen in a range of situations.)*
- *physical development; and*
- *personal, social and emotional development.*

(DfE, 2012)

The work of Donaldson, along with that of Vygotsky, Bruner and other recent thinkers has resulted in a new look at the way children learn, moving away from Piaget's rigid stages of development to a more flexible approach, and a view that children are much more capable than we think, do not develop in strict stages, and need to link new learning with their existing knowledge. The central place of talk in early years practice indicates an acknowledgement of the work of Donaldson alongside that of other constructivist theorists.

Key guidance documents for countries in the UK

Save the Children Fund, (2014) 'Read On Get On, Scotland'.
Literacy Commission, Scottish Parent Teacher Council, (2009) 'A Vision for Scotland: The Report and Final Recommendations of the Literacy Commission.'
Learning and Teaching Scotland, (2010) Pre-birth to Three.
Melhuish et. al., (2007) 'Promoting speech and language: a themed study in fifteen local Sure Start Programmes'. DCSF Publications.

Things to think about

- Language is a crucial tool. How much help have you had during your training that enables you to feel confident in supporting language development?

- How much of your time do you spend in conversations with children?

- How do you make time for talk in your setting?

- How do we as practitioners find out what children are thinking and how they reason so we can really get inside their thinking?

- Embedded thinking is thinking that has been securely placed in familiar contexts and linked with existing knowledge. At this point, the child can use the new learning confidently, making 'human sense' of what we are saying. How do we find out children's levels of existing thinking?

- Donaldson advises practitioners working with young children to learn to 'decentre' themselves, so they can understand the world from the viewpoint of the child. How easy is this to do in the real world? How could you make more time for this?

Carol Dweck (1946–)

Full name: Carol Dweck

Born: 1946 (still living)

Place of birth: New York City

Countries of residence: United States

What she did: Dweck explores the relationship between motivation, effort, intelligence, and mastery-oriented learning.

Influences on education today: Mastery-oriented learning has become a centre of interest for practitioners, their managers, and is now included in inspection schedules.

Theories and areas of work : Social and developmental psychology

Key influencers and followers: Claudia Mueller

Key works: *Mindset: The New Psychology of Success* (2006), *Mindset: How You Can Fulfill Your Potential* (2012)

After seven experiments with hundreds of children, we had some of the clearest findings I've ever seen: Praising children's intelligence harms their motivation, and it harms their performance.

Carol Dweck, Mindset: The New Psychology of Success, 2006

Life, love, theory and research

Carol Dweck is a psychologist, currently working at Stanford University in the United States. She is particularly interested in intelligence but not in defining or measuring it. She has spent her working life studying the effect of motivation on learning, particularly in children. She feels that there has been too much emphasis on intelligence (an external measure of cleverness or ability) and too little on the way that motivation can affect the quality of learning, even for children who have been deemed to have low levels of measurable intelligence.

Her work has focused on the reasons why some people succeed more easily than others and how to foster success in those who find it hard to succeed. She believes that 'there is no relation between students' abilities or intelligence and the development of mastery-oriented qualities' (Dweck, 2012) – in other words, there are some bright children who avoid activities that they perceive as too challenging, give up easily and seem to 'wilt' in the face of difficulty. At the same time, there are some apparently less-able children who have a strong 'can-do' attitude, persisting in activities even when they get very difficult. These children seem to thrive when challenged and often accomplish far more than their teachers or their parents expect. They are not interested in proving how clever they are and they tend not to worry about whether they can do the task or whether others think they can. Instead, they just put all their effort into the task itself. Dweck has named this attitude as having 'a Growth Mindset'.

Dweck and Claudia Mueller (Professor of Surgery, Stanford University) conducted six studies, and all had significant results. In these studies, older primary-aged pupils with similar levels of attainment were given a set of problems, which they were able to complete successfully:

- Some of these children were given praise for their intelligence, including such things as telling them how clever they were. It turned out that praising students' intelligence did make them feel good, but only in the short term. These children were hesitant to attempt the next level of problems in the research, because they felt they might be proven to be 'dumb'. They were so keen to look smart that they were afraid of the next level of challenge.

- In contrast, the other group, who were praised for their effort had many positive outcomes. When these children were offered the chance to go on with the research tests, 90 percent of them wanted to proceed to the more challenging learning opportunity. They accepted that a harder task needed more effort and, when offered, they even accepted the chance to take the new tasks home to practice.

In the next part of the study, the children who were praised for their intelligence did significantly worse than before, while the children who had been praised for their effort did significantly better than before. The groups of children who had similar levels of performance at the start of the study were now far apart.

Dweck went on to collect information from older students, and found that learners of all ages can be taught that their intellectual skills can be expanded and improved by their own hard work and confrontation of challenges. When they are taught this, they seem to become more eager to take on challenge, work harder and are more able to cope with obstacles in their learning.

Practitioners and teachers should continue to give praise, but praise the process (the effort, the strategies, the ideas, what went into the work), not the person. Dweck became convinced that labelling children as 'gifted' or 'of high IQ' could have problematic effects, putting pressure on these children to perform to their label and resulting in these children losing confidence and under-performing. IQ tests can pinpoint current levels of attainment, but some children who have been thought to have a low or average IQ have gone on to become some of our most inspiring adults in the world of creative, scientific, literary and sporting achievement.

Another interesting result of Dweck's research is that girls receive much more praise for their work in the primary years, with boys being criticised for lack of attention and effort. She thinks this may give boys useful lessons in the importance of effort, which may serve them well later. Girls, on the other hand, do not receive so much criticism, so they learn less about the power of effort, and may think that the criticism of others implies low ability. This may not be a problem in primary school but when learning becomes more difficult, seeing criticism as a message about their ability may result in girls avoiding subjects such as maths and sciences, where it is easier to identify mistakes and errors.

Carol Dweck's work has involved helping teachers to be aware of the benefits of mastery-oriented learning which also focuses on children's efforts, not just on their abilities. When working with Carol Dweck, teachers are encouraged to help children become aware of their own learning, focusing on their own efforts rather than just their ability, and they are encouraged to adopt a 'can-do' attitude, identifying their own mistakes and deciding what they could do next to put them right. This is referred to as a 'mastery-oriented' attitude.

A key ingredient in creating mastery-oriented learners is having teachers who value effort and particularly the sustained effort needed to complete challenging tasks:

> Rather than praising students for doing well on easy tasks, they should convey that doing easy tasks is a waste of time. They should transmit the joy of confronting a challenge and of struggling to find strategies that work.

(Dweck, 2012)

Successful teachers hand over responsibility for learning to the children, helping them to focus on their own efforts and those of others, not just the grades or test levels they achieve, but the quality of the learning itself and the enjoyment and satisfaction they experience when they achieve their goals. The aim should be to recognise and value intrinsic rewards – the reward of achieving the goal, rather than extrinsic rewards – prizes, stickers or competitive grades. For Dweck, the best mix is a combination of valuing learning and challenge and valuing grades or test scores but seeing these as merely an index of current performance, not a sign of intelligence or worth.

During Dweck's own childhood, classes were arranged in IQ order, with extrinsic rewards for the successful pupils. The result was that the higher-ability pupils lived in fear that their next test would result in demotion and the lower-ability pupils felt under-valued and unable to achieve the higher status, as their intelligence was a fixed characteristic and could never be changed, stifling the desire to learn and resulting in high stress for everyone.

Thoughtful teachers opposed this style of classroom management which was obviously unhelpful to everyone. It was followed by a swing towards a style where copious amounts of empty praise were used, in the belief that this would boost children's self-esteem and thus their progress in learning. It was not surprising that this method did not work either, as it simply resulted in children who were uninterested and unmotivated; success was too easy to achieve and praise was almost irrelevant.

The current emphasis on testing conveys to children and their families that the only important thing is to do well on these tests, such as phonic screenings, maths tables, SATs, standardised tests, with no indication that such tests just assess the individual's performance on a particular day, rather than a helpful spot check of their current development and what needs to be focused on in future.

Dweck recommends that children should be clear that any measure of their skills reflects their current performance, not their intelligence or worth. If your results are not what you expected: 'Work harder, avail yourself of more learning opportunities, learn how to study better, ask the teacher for more help, and so on.' (Dweck, 2012)

Her recommended methods are similar to the training methods used by many top athletes who are very performance-oriented. They do not see a negative outcome such as losing a game or a race as reflecting their underlying skills or potential to do better. Between games they are very learning-oriented. They watch tapes of their past game or race, trying to learn from their mistakes, talking to their coaches about how to improve and working tirelessly on new skills.

Dweck feels that teachers should behave like trainers, teaching children to value hard work and challenge in learning. They should also be teaching children how to cope with disappointment by planning new approaches and giving the more power and influence over their own learning.

One of the key times when children fail to succeed is at times of transition, when they move from class to class or school to school, resulting in significant loss of momentum in learning. At these points, children facing more difficult work or different teaching styles sometimes believe that they are just not clever enough to succeed and they give up. Previously able learners can lose their confidence and become anxious. Instead of concentrating on giving effort to their learning they begin to withdraw and stop trying.

Other children who have a mastery-oriented approach take the challenge of a new class or school in their stride, often surprising their teachers and parents. They see the harder work as a challenge to be mastered. The central message is that it's not the level of your skills that matters, it's the mindset you bring to your learning.

Legacy and impact

Dweck has had a significant influence through the books she has written and in her training for teachers on raising motivation and 'mastery-oriented' behaviours. These have been adopted in upper primary and secondary schools, and many schools across the world have adopted her methods reducing the emphasis on grades, test results and IQ scores, and moving into methods where the children have much more ownership of their own learning and are praised for genuine effort, rather than for test scores. However, this is a long-term investment for schools and it is often difficult to manage in a culture where test scores and summative assessments provide the information for judging individual or school performance and are particularly important to parents.

One of the recent tensions for practitioners and teachers is that they are advised in curriculum documentation to develop a problem-solving, learning focused approach, where the learner has involvement in the direction of their learning through regular evaluation and 'next steps'. However, the link between simple summative assessments and test scores and the pay of individual practitioners and teachers can result in an over-emphasis on observable outcomes rather than the effort a child makes in getting there.

Dweck's Growth Mindset methods have been implemented in many primary schools across the UK. On its website, Mereworth school in Kent, where Growth Mindset has been implemented, have published how they've tailored the main aspects to their school, encapsulating the principles of Growth Mindset such as learning from making mistakes, learning from each other, challenge, risk taking and involvement. They end their statement by saying: 'We remember that the brain is making new connections all the time – the only thing you need to know is that you can learn anything!' You can find the full statement on their website at mereworth.kent.sch.uk/growth-mindset

Influence on early years practice in the UK

England

In the most recent guidance for practitioners in England, 'Statutory Framework for the Early Years Foundation Stage', there is an emphasis on the Characteristics of Effective Learning, and the section on creative and critical thinking has much in common with the views of Carol Dweck:

> *Characteristics of Effective Learning are:*
> - *playing and exploring – children investigate and experience things, and 'have a go';*
> - *active learning – children concentrate and keep on trying if they encounter difficulties, and enjoy achievements; and*
> - *creating and thinking critically – children have and develop their own ideas, make links between ideas, and develop strategies for doing things.*
>
> (DfE, 2014)
>
> *These characteristics include many of the essentials that Dweck identified for successful learning. The clear link between the EYFS curriculum and motivation is in the section entitled Active Learning, where practitioners are advised to offer opportunities for children develop their*

motivation through: 'Being involved and concentrating, keeping trying, and enjoying achieving what they set out to do.'

(DfE, 2014)

Children's progress in demonstrating these characteristics, which focus on effort rather than attainment, is included in annual reports to parents, and should help to counteract the current emphasis on simple levels of attainment. Other Characteristics of Learning, such as engagement; thinking, having a go, choosing ways to do things also underpin the essential skills of the effective learner, with a Growth Mindset. This advice, reflecting the central principles of early education, encourages adults to offer young children ownership of their learning, freedom to choose ways that they learn best and the chance to follow their own interests as they build their abilities to concentrate and thus increase their motivation.

Guidance for early years practitioners working in the other countries of the UK each carry their own messages about the central importance of motivation, high self-esteem and confidence.

Wales

In the 'Curriculum for Wales; Foundation Phase Framework', the guidance to practitioners is that they should plan a programme where:

Motivation and commitment to learning is encouraged, as children begin to understand their own potential and capabilities. Children are supported in becoming confident, competent and independent thinkers and learners…They experience challenges that extend their learning.

(Welsh Government, 2015)

One of the desired outcomes for learning by the time children are around seven years of age also echoes the Dweck ethos:

They (children) are competent in identifying problems and coming up with solutions to solve them. They are able to demonstrate skills of perseverance, concentration and motivation. They demonstrate appropriate self-control. They understand how they can improve their learning and can be reflective.

(Welsh Government, 2015)

Northern Ireland

In Northern Ireland, the Primary School Curriculum Framework detailed in 'Thinking skills and personal capabilities for Key Stages 1 and 2' has the following commitment to developing Personal Capabilities of Self-Management and Working with Others that underpin the whole curriculum:

The Personal Capabilities of Self-Management and Working with Others underpin success in all aspects of life. Developing Personal Capabilities means creating opportunities for pupils to:

- *experiment with ideas;*
- *take initiative;*
- *learn from mistakes;*
- *work collaboratively; and*
- *become more self-directed in their learning.*

(CCEA, 2007)

It is evident from these short examples from curriculum statements across the UK, that developing motivation and other personal skills that enable children to become independent, is very close to '*mastery-oriented*' learning. One can only hope that the pressure to perform in tests and the use of other limited measures of intelligence does not overtake these worthy and scientifically proven aims.

Key guidance documents for countries in the UK

DfE, (2014) 'Statutory Framework for the Early Years Foundation Stage'.
Welsh Government, (2015) 'Curriculum for Wales: Foundation Phase Framework.'
CCEA, (2007) 'Thinking skills and personal capabilities for Key Stages 1 and 2'.

Things to think about

- Dweck is very much opposed to testing, ranking and other simplistic measures of intelligence which do not take into account the notion of effort. Do you think she is right?
- Some settings and schools use the Characteristics of Effective Learning to inform their planning and practice and report on these rather than the areas of learning when talking to parents. How evident are the Characteristics of Effective Learning in your setting?
- How hard is it to ensure that children have inspiring and motivating experiences in the early years? Can we make learning exciting and child-centred in these days of constant measuring by test and summative assessment?
- How might you incorporate some of Dweck's principles into your work, particularly if you are new to the setting or school?

Hermann Ebbinghaus

Full name: Hermann Ebbinghaus

Born: 1850

Died: 1909

Place of birth: Barmen, Prussia

Countries of residence: Germany, England, Poland

What he did: Ebbinghaus explored memory and described the learning curve (and the forgetting curve). He developed the use of psychometric tests for reading and intelligence using 'nonsense' words of three letters to assess memory and reading ability. He also invented 'cloze procedure' (sentences and passages with blanks in for the child to complete).

Influences on education today: Ebbinghaus's work lives on in national tests, particularly those using nonsense words. His learning and forgetting curves are still used and his structure for scientific reports is now standard practice across the world.

Theories and areas of work: Educational psychology, psychometrics

Key influencers and followers: Gustav Fechner

Key works: *Memory, A Contribution to Experimental Psychology* (1885), *Psychology: An Elementary Textbook* (1908)

A poem is learned by heart and then not again repeated. We will suppose that after a half year it has been forgotten: no effort of recollection is able to call it back again into consciousness.

Herman Ebbinghaus Memory: A Contribution to Experimental Psychology, 1885

Life, love, theory and research

Hermann Ebbinghaus was a philosopher, born and educated in Prussia whose work would probably be seen as nearer to that of a psychologist's. Little is known of his early life and even in his young adulthood, he moved about regularly within Europe.

Ebbinghaus pioneered the systematic study of memory and he was the first person to describe the details of the learning curve. He was convinced that memory should be studied using systematic research methods more often associated with the physical sciences, something that was not thought possible at the time.

He began his studies of memory in 1897, becoming interested in how we remember words and letters. In attempting to develop memory tests he began to abandon the use of 'real' words, as he thought that using existing memories of real words and numbers in his tests, would undermine his results. He began to develop a system of using 'nonsense syllables', three letter CVC collections consisting of a consonant, followed by a vowel and ending in a consonant. These syllables were deliberately screened to avoid existing words (such as DOT), or those that sound like existing words (such as BOL, which sounds like BALL). Among the CVC words which could be used were DAX, BOK, and YAT.

Ebbinghaus collected over 2,000 of these CVC words and wrote each one on a separate card. At first he tested his own memory by pulling a random group of cards from a box and writing them in a list in his notebook. He then read the words to the rhythm of a metronome and attempted to memorise the list, saying them back again at the end of the investigation. In one investigation he undertook 15,000 recitations of groups of these syllables.

This work, although thorough, was limited by the fact that Ebbinghaus only used himself in the study so the results could not be used to make judgements across the population. His role as both researcher and subject also caused some criticism, as this makes any research less reliable. However, the use of 'nonsense' words continues today in some intelligence tests and phonics screenings (see below).

Ebbinghaus's work is also included in this collection because he was the first psychologist to describe the learning curve, which examines the way we all learn and remember things. When we try to remember a new piece of information, the biggest increase in our memory happens as we first try to recall the information. After this, less and less information is retained with each subsequent attempt to remember. Reviewing the information within 24 hours appears to help to embed it.

The so-called 'forgetting curve' has the same pattern, with a human tendency to halve their memory of newly learned knowledge in a matter of days or weeks unless they consciously review the learned material. Ebbinghaus's work on remembering, the technique of reviewing recent information, has been adopted by teachers working across the age range from early years settings to university tutorials, where regular plenary and review sessions are recommended.

Ebbinghaus also did some research into a factor that many practitioners and teachers recognise well – the way that children's mental ability, concentration and stamina decline as the school day progresses. Unfortunately the details of these studies and the way they were conducted have now been lost.

Ebbinghaus did leave one other lasting influence on the whole of the scientific community, not just psychology. His method for presenting research papers in four sections has been adopted throughout the world, with the majority of scientific papers now being presented in this way:

- the introduction
- the methods
- the results
- a section for discussion.

Ebbinghaus only lived until he was 59 and had few followers or close contacts during his working life. Even though he was criticised for his methods, his papers on memory, the learning and forgetting curves and particularly his pioneering work on researching areas unexplored at the time had a notable effect on his contemporaries.

Legacy and impact

Several of Ebbinghaus's research findings have been influential in educational and social fields:

- The use of 'nonsense syllables' in intelligence and reading testing has become common.
- Ebbinghaus pioneered the use of completion of sentences or inserting missing words into a piece of text. These are now widely used in tests and in curriculum work, particularly to reinforce learning – this method is now called cloze procedure.
- Mnemonics: Ebbinghaus believed that memory could be improved by the use of mnemonics – remembering information through rhymes, sequences and other easily remembered tricks – such as singing the alphabet, remembering the colours of the rainbow by saying 'Richard Of York Gave Battle In Vain' (red/orange/yellow/green/blue/indigo /violet), or using 'My Very Easy Method Just Speeds Up Naming Planets' to remember the names and order of the planets in our solar system (Mercury, Venus, Earth, Mars, Jupiter, Saturn, Uranus, Neptune, Pluto).

Reviewing recent learning to ensure it remains in the memory has a secure place in the teacher's toolbox and the importance of revision of knowledge before exams has become universally recognised.

The use of flashcards in the teaching of reading, the recognition of specialised vocabulary, and in learning foreign languages, is a development from Ebbinghaus's nonsense syllable cards.

Influence on early years practice in the UK

The single most important link between Ebbinghaus and the current policy in England for the teaching of reading is the Synthetic Phonics method for teaching reading. Synthetic Phonics is a method where children are taught to read letters or groups of letters by saying the sound(s) they represent, before progressing to sounding out words letter by letter. 'Development Matters in the EYFS' states:

> When children are ready (usually, but not always, by the age of five) provide regular systematic synthetic phonics sessions. These should be multisensory in order to capture their interests, sustain motivation and reinforce learning.
>
> Demonstrate using phonics as the prime approach to decode words while children can see the text, e.g. using big books.

(Early Education, 2012)

When children are six years old, the Statutory Phonics Screening is used to establish the child's progress in learning to read through phonics. The screening uses 'nonsense syllables' such as 'pon', 'hab' and 'ulb', which can have a range of pronunciations, particularly if the child speaks a dialect form of English. The 'Phonics Screening Check and National Curriculum Assessments at Key Stage 1' documentation says:

> Phonics Screening check
>
> This is a statutory assessment for all pupils in year 1 (typically aged 6) to check whether they have reached the expected standard in phonic decoding. All state-funded schools with a year 1 cohort must administer the check. Those pupils who did not meet the standard in year 1 or who were not tested, must be re-checked at the end of year 2 (typically aged 7).

(DfE, 2015)

Flash cards have been used for many years to teach reading, and before the current emphasis on Synthetic Phonics, a majority of teachers taught reading through a range of methods including 'Look and Say' and 'Whole Word Recognition', both of which rely on the use of flashcards to help children to recognise and remember words by sight, rather than by breaking them down into component sounds. This method has generally been replaced by a government directed phonic approach to the teaching of reading. However, the use of flashcards to help children who respond to visual rather than auditory stimuli is still included in Letters and Sounds, support materials for the teaching of reading through a wide variety of methods including real flashcards, and 'virtual' versions of these on an interactive whiteboard. The DfE documentation 'Letters and Sounds' says:

> Flashcards
>
> Purpose

To say as quickly as possible the correct sound when a letter is displayed

Resources

*Set of A4 size cards with a letter on one side and its **mnemonic** (a pictorial clue) on the other (e.g. the letter s on one side and a picture of a snake shaped like an s on the other)*

Procedure

- *Hold up the letter cards the children have learned, one at a time.*
- *Ask the children, in chorus, to say the letter-sound (with the action if used).*
- *If the children do not respond, turn the card over to show the mnemonic.*
- *Sometimes you could ask the children to say the letter-sounds in a particular way (e.g. happy, sad, bossy or timid – mood sounds).*
- *As the children become familiar with the letters, increase the speed of presentation so that the children learn to respond quickly.*

(DfE, 2007)

There has also been a recent emphasis on helping children to remember what they have learned, by using a variety of techniques, many of which were invented or at least recommended by Ebbinghaus:

- Plenary sessions at the end of lessons or sessions where children are offered opportunities to talk about what they have done and what they have learned
- Small group times when children can recall what they have learned
- The use of photos so practitioners can talk with children about what they have been doing
- Feedback either during or after an activity which helps children to review their own progress and learning
- Sustained shared thinking where adults and children work alongside each other, discussing, repeating and evaluating what is going on and what they are learning.

In the three other countries of the UK, there is more emphasis on using a variety of techniques for teaching reading so children can use a wide range of cues, including reading words on sight and phonics.

Scotland

In Scotland, more caution is advised and retaining a wide variety of reading strategies is recommended, as stated in 'Building the curriculum 2 (3–18): Active learning in the early years':

Children will develop a range of skills including literacy and numeracy which are built on in preschool education from their experiences at home. However, a more formal approach, for example to reading and writing, should be introduced only when staff feel that children are developmentally ready to benefit from this. Each child, each group of children and indeed each day might demand fresh thinking.

(Scottish Executive, 2007)

Wales

In the Foundation Phase in Wales, there is also guidance for practitioners that a wide range of strategies will support all children to reach these goals by the end of the Reception year. The 'Foundation Phase Framework' emphasises using phonic methods only when these are known:

- *recognise that words are constructed from phonemes (sounds) and that phonemes are represented by graphemes (written letters):*
- *orally blend combinations of known letters*
- *orally segment combinations of known letters*

apply the following reading strategies with support:

- *phonic strategies to decode simple words*
- *recognition of high-frequency words*
- *context cues, e.g. pictures, initial sound*
- *repetition in text.*

(Welsh Assembly Government, 2015)

Northern Ireland

In Northern Ireland, Communication across the Curriculum is a significant area of learning and has the following aims for reading in primary schools:

READING (CEA NI Curriculum)

Pupils should be enabled to:
- *read a range of texts for information, ideas and enjoyment;*
- *use a range of strategies to read with increasing independence;*
- *find, select and use information from a range of sources;*
- *understand and explore ideas, event and features in texts*;*
- *use evidence from texts to explain opinions.*

The preservation of different strategies for teaching and learning in three of four countries is an unusual situation and the outcomes of adherence to Synthetic Phonics by the DfE in England will be an interesting policy to follow in coming years.

Key guidance documents for countries in the UK

Early Education (2012) 'Development Matters in the EYFS'.

DfE (2015) 'Phonics Screening Check and National Curriculum Assessments at Key Stage 1 in England'.

DfE (2007) 'Letters and Sounds'.

Welsh Assembly Government (2015) 'Foundation Phase Framework'.

Scottish Executive; (2007) 'Curriculum 2 (3–18); Active learning in the early years'.

Things to think about

- Do all children respond to the same way of teaching reading? Why do you think this is?

- Do you use synthetic phonics in your setting? Do you think it is the best way to teach reading or do you think that a more mixed and broader range of teaching is better?

- Sustained shared thinking in small groups is suggested as one of the best ways to help children to revisit and evaluate their own learning. Some practitioners find this very difficult to fit into a busy schedule. Do you have any tips or ways to find the time, now you know how essential it is for children to revisit what they have learned?

- Do you have any tricks for remembering information? What do you find helpful in remembering things?

- How much research have you done into reading methods? Will this be enough to help you when you begin work in a setting or school?

Hermann Ebbinghaus

Hans Eysenck

Full name: Hans Eysenck

Born: 1916

Died: 1997

Place of birth: Berlin Germany

Countries of residence: England

What he did: Eysenck studied personality and personality disorder, and took forward the nature/nurture debate.

Influences on education today: The nature/nurture debate is still very much discussed today, particularly since the work of the Human Genome Project has produced so much information about our heredity.

Theories and areas of work: Psychology

Key influencers and followers: Cyril Burt, Richard J. Herrnstein

Key works: *Intelligence: A New Look* (1998), *Sense and Nonsense in Psychology* (1956), *Race, Intelligence and Education* (1971), *The Inequality of Man* (1973)

Modern education does no favour to the children it is supposed to teach when it de-emphasizes facts; although facts are not the only important things in life, in science, and in the arts, they nevertheless constitute the absolutely essential substructure without which nothing worthwhile can be built.

Hans Eysenck, The Inequality of Man, 1975

Life, love, theory and research

Hans Eysenck was a psychologist who was born in Germany but spent his adult working life in Great Britain. His work spanned many areas of psychology and his wide-ranging written output has been cited more frequently than any other psychologist of his time.

Eysenck's work was most influential in the areas of personality and individual differences. However, despite his extensive work and widely read books – he published 75 books and some 700 articles during his lifetime – some of his research was later questioned by the public and his peers for the validity of its research basis. His main emphasis was on the genetic nature of much human behaviour and because of this some of his views were considered to be racist. Although these interpretations can all be made from reading his scientific writings, in his autobiography he admits to the important additional influence of environment and upbringing on intelligence.

Eysenck's work on genetics involved him in exploring IQ differences between people from different racial groups, taking him into the realms of comparing IQ scores from people with African and Eastern heritage with those of white people. This research added to concerns about whether this work was racist in focus.

> *All the evidence to date suggests the... overwhelming importance of genetic factors in producing the great variety of intellectual differences which we observe in our culture, and much of the difference observed between certain racial groups.*
>
> (Eysenck, 1971)

He also made some statements about the heritability of intelligence which resulted in accusations of supporting the eugenics movement. This was reinforced when he agreed to contribute to magazines published by Nazi supporters.

> *... the whole course of development of a child's intellectual capabilities is largely laid down genetically, and even extreme environmental changes... have little power to alter this development.*
>
> (Eysenck, 1973)

One of Eysenck's major contributions to our thinking about early years education, to psychology and post-Freudian psychotherapy was his theory of personality which was based on research into what he described as the two dimensions of personality. The model described the interaction between extraversion and neuroticism, and the balance between these dimensions in each individual:

- extraversion – being predominantly concerned with influences from outside the self, evidenced by individuals being enthusiastic, gregarious and enjoying contact with others
- neuroticism – which is characterised by anxiety, fear, moodiness, worry, envy, frustration, jealousy and loneliness.

Eysenck proposed that extraversion was triggered by levels of arousal in the cortex (the cerebral cortex is the outer layer of the brain) and that neuroticism was caused by imbalances and individual differences in the limbic system (a complex system of nerves in the brain which influences emotions). He maintained that these dimensions were caused by physical aspects of brain processes which influenced extraverts to engage in interactions and situations which provide more stimulation, while introverts seek lower levels of arousal. He believed that the balance of each individual personality was the result of the individual's genes and physiology.

This work resulted in the development of psychometric tests to establish personality types and thus support the treatment of people with personality disorders. The tests usually involved people in rating themselves, usually from 1 to 5, against a range of descriptive adjectives such as shy, outgoing, wild, introverted etc. For example, a shy person might rate themselves as 5 on 'shy' but only 1 on 'outgoing' – a more extrovert person would probably score the reverse. Eysenck's research found two major dimensions from the information – neuroticism and introversion-extroversion. He could then place each person on the scale between normality and neuroticism.

Further research followed, as Eysenck and his team looked at why individuals could be so different. They explored the sympathetic nervous system which is responsible for automatic, unconscious actions within our bodies. This system is triggered in response to messages from the brain, particularly in situations of stress, danger and in emergency response situations. For instance, the limbic system can instruct the liver to release more sugar for energy, enlarge the pupils in the eyes, give you 'goosebumps' by raising the hairs on your arms, or release more adrenaline from the adrenal glands. In this way, you can run away from danger, see a wider view and respond in 'flight or fight' mode. One of the most severe responses is a 'panic attack', which Eysenck described as similar to the feedback sound you get when you put a microphone next to a speaker, sending the sound round and round from mike to speaker and back again, amplified every time until it comes out as a loud scream. Panic attacks stem from a frightening experience which triggers your sympathetic nervous system. This makes you even more nervous and anxious, more susceptible to nervous stimulation and so on, until you are in fact responding to your own panic, not the original stimulus.

Eysenck thought that some people have much more responsive sympathetic nervous systems than others and some of us manage stressful situations such as having an accident more easily than others. This group of people may be terrified by relatively minor incidents and are much more likely to suffer from neurotic disorders.

His descriptions of introversion and extraversion were very similar to those of Carl Jung – the nervous/outgoing, quiet/loud dimension being present to a different extent in us all. However, how we each handle the balance between these two extremes is also different between individuals. At the extreme introversion end are people with many phobias or obsessive disorders who tend to be more introverted than people further along the dimension. When Eysenck extended his research to mental institutions of the time, he decided to add a third factor to his theory which he labelled as psychoticism, a personality pattern typified by aggressiveness and interpersonal hostility.

Eysenck was a behaviourist, obsessed with the collection and interpretation of masses of data on human behaviour and physiology. His belief in the dominance of genetic factors, controversial at the time, is perhaps more understandable as we explore the genome mapping available to scientists today.

Legacy and impact

Throughout his long life, Eysenck was dedicated to scientific principles of research based on collection of data and analysis of this. Although there was some criticism of his methods, in particular the size and constitution of his samples, his ideas have influenced the world of psychology and psychotherapy. Synthesising and expanding thinking that goes as far back as the philosophers of Ancient Greece has presented us with a structure for understanding those aspects of human behaviour that are visible, yet have invisible causes. His analysis of personality and its possible disorders is presented in a form that allows professionals and the general public to understand the features of our behaviour, using a shared vocabulary and terms that are easily understood.

The concept that we all rest somewhere on a spectrum between extreme introversion and extreme extraversion is helpful, if rather simplistic. Eysenck's later work on expanding that concept to explore the notion of psychoticism which goes beyond the usual range into psychological illness makes the spectrum more relevant.

The continuing influence of Eysenck on educational thinking is that his work adds to the 'nature/nurture' debate; the discussion about whether children's genetic makeup or their upbringing has the most influence on how they behave and learn. There is still no clear answer to the balance of influence – do families have more influence or does genetic make-up? And does the culture in which children are raised have any impact on personality?

Children's personalities affect their development in many ways. A fearful child will take more time to adjust to new situations and people than a more extravert one. Small events, such as collecting mini-beasts or using masks or balloons for role-play may trigger panic or enjoyment in different children, so knowing as much as possible about individual children is very important. Home visits, introductory sessions and staggered starts to settings are all helpful to both children, parents and practitioners in the 'getting to know you' process. Home/setting diaries where significant events and information are exchanged, and the central contribution of the 'key person' approach are all aimed at helping a child to adjust, wherever they might be in Eysenck's dimensions of personality, without triggering their sympathetic nervous systems.

Influence on early years practice in the UK

Eysenck's work has influenced the way in which we respond to children with emotional and behavioural difficulties. We now understand much more about the way children's personalities affect the way they learn and we are now much more able to identify problems at an early stage and work with their parents to share the responsibility of support. Children's emotional stability is just as important as their physical growth or intellectual development. 'Pre-birth to three' states:

> *The key person meets the needs of every child in their care and responds sensitively to their feelings, ideas and behaviour. They offer security, reassurance and continuity, and are usually responsible for feeding, changing and comforting the child.*
>
> (Learning and Teaching Scotland, 2010)

This selection of guidance notes from Development Matters, the EYFS guidance for England identifies some of the places where we can see Eyenck's influence and gives practitioners some idea of the important role they play in helping children to manage their own behaviour and emotions:

- *Make sure the key person stays close by and provides **a secure presence** and a refuge at times a child may be feeling anxious.*
- *Provide areas to mirror different **moods and feelings** - quiet restful areas as well as areas for active exploration.*
- ***Name and talk about a wide range of feelings** and make it clear that all feelings are understandable and acceptable, including feeling angry, but that not all behaviours are.*
- ***Use Persona Dolls** to help children consider feelings, ways to help others feel better about themselves, and dealing with conflicting opinions.*

> (Early Education, 2012)

Throughout the Foundation Stage, practitioners are expected to support children's personal development, with the expectation that by the end of the reception year, at around the age of five, they can demonstrate the following characteristics.

> *Children talk about how they and others show feelings, talk about their own and others' behaviour, and its consequences, and know that some behaviour is unacceptable. They work as part of a group or class, and understand and follow the rules. They adjust their behaviour to different situations, and take changes of routine in their stride.*
>
> (The Statutory Framework for the EYFS, DfE, 2014)

Children who do not achieve this goal may be identified as having additional needs in behavioural and social development. Of course, this may be that they are young for their age group or that they may really have an emerging need for support. Practitioners who have concerns about a child's behaviour can refer to documentation specifically provided for the purpose of identifying the problem and contacting support services. This is usually located within the support for children with special needs, as stated in the 'SEN and disability code of practice 0–25 years':

A delay in learning and development in the early years may or may not indicate that a child has SEN, that is, that they have a learning difficulty or disability that calls for special educational provision. Equally, difficult or withdrawn behaviour does not necessarily mean that a child has SEN. However, where there are concerns, there should be an assessment to determine whether there are any causal factors such as an underlying learning or communication difficulty.

Children and young people may experience a wide range of social and emotional difficulties which manifest themselves in many ways. These may include becoming withdrawn or isolated, as well as displaying challenging, disruptive or disturbing behaviour. These behaviours may reflect underlying mental health difficulties such as anxiety or depression, self-harming, substance misuse, eating disorders or physical symptoms that are medically unexplained.

(DfE and DH, 2015)

It is evident from the documentation produced throughout the UK that support for children with emotional needs is available, although ensuring support from professionals trained in psychotherapy requires persistence and very detailed information gathering.

Scotland

In Scotland, schools and settings are advised to evolve systems for managing crises in children's behaviour by supporting adults during, and after they happen. The documentation 'Focusing on inclusion' states:

Do the school's systems for exchanging information, providing advice and dealing with behavioural crises give staff enough support to enable them to understand and relate to children and young people with emotional and behavioural difficulties?

(Scottish Executive, 2006)

Wales

In the SEN documentation available to practitioners working in Wales 'Practical approaches to behaviour management in the classroom', the following reference is made to the power of environmental pressures on children's behaviour. It makes reference to the research carried out by Eysenck and others that studied twins who were reared apart compared to twins reared together:

Research evidence has come from studies around twins separated at birth and early infancy. This goes to show that both nature and nurture are involved in our development, although when dealing with behaviour attention needs to be paid to creating a positive environment and experiences to promote good behaviour.

(Welsh Assembly Government, 2012)

Some children have difficulties that require short-term specialist support, or are outside the range of mainstream schooling. Helpful advice, such as that contained in the documentation for practitioners in Wales is invaluable in ensuring that children's behaviour is managed without the practitioner or the child feeling guilty or lacking in professional competence.

Key guidance documents for countries in the UK

Learning and Teaching Scotland, (2010) 'Pre-birth to three'.
Early Education, (2012) 'Development Matters in the EYFS'.
DfE, (2014) 'Statutory Framework for the Early Years Foundation Stage'.
DfE and DH, (2015) 'SEN and disability code of practice: 0–25 years'.
Scottish Executive, (2006) 'Focusing on inclusion'.
Welsh Assembly Government, (2012) 'Practical approaches to behaviour management in the classroom: a handbook for classroom teachers in primary schools'.

Things to think about

- In the past, it was considered unhelpful to identify children's additional learning needs until they were seven years old. Currently, practitioners are encouraged to identify such needs as early as possible. Do you think this is too young?

- The Key Person system gives real support to some children and their families but there are some children who are in danger of slipping through this safety net. Why does this happen? Can you think of ways to ensure that these children have the support they need?

- What do you think has most influence over the development of our personalities:
  - Friends, family and the people we meet?
  - Genes that you inherit from your parents?
  - Education from nursery to further education?
  - The environment we live in, including the influences of social media, TV, films and celebrities?

Hans Eysenck

John Flavell

Full name: John Flavell
Born: 1928 (still living)
Place of birth: Rockland, Massachusetts, United States
Countries of residence: United States
What he did: Flavell invented the term 'metacognition' and did some of the early research into thinking about thinking. He continues to collect and synthesise research in this field.
Influences on education today: Metacognition has become a familiar term in education associated with thinking skills and problem solving. Children from their early years are encouraged to 'think about thinking.'
Theories and areas of work: Cognitive development, Psychology
Key influencers and followers: Jean Piaget
Key works: *The Developmental Psychology of Jean Piaget* (1963)

Metacognition is especially useful for a particular kind of organism, one that has the following properties. First the organism should tend to think a lot. By definition, an abundance of metacognition presupposes an abundance of cognition.

John Flavell, Speculations about the Nature and Development of Metacognition,1987

Life, love, theory and research

John Flavell is an American psychologist who specialises in children's cognitive development and learning and has been influenced by the work of Jean Piaget. He is regarded as one of the first researchers into metacognition in young children and its link with intentionality and the ability of the mind to form mental representations of behaviour, which should not be confused with concrete intentions.

The prefix meta- is used in psychology and learning theory to indicate about – for instance, metadata refers to data about data. Flavell used two terms which have now become familiar in education and psychology:

- Metacognition – a higher order thinking skill which involves humans in active control over the thinking process (thinking about thinking).
- Metamemory – a type of metacognition, the knowledge of what can help us to remember things, and the self-monitoring and management of memories.

Flavell's theme of metacognitive research has continued for more than 30 years and he has often encouraged others to contribute to the study of metacognition.

Flavell and many other scientists think that the skill of metacognition is a skill unique to human beings although some higher order animals such as apes can demonstrate intentionality. In 1987, Flavell attempted to describe the sort of organism that has developed the use of metacognition. He said that the organism needs to think a lot, should be capable of monitoring its own thinking (in other words it should be conscious of the thinking process), and the organism should want to communicate with others, explaining its thinking to other organisms. Planning ahead and evaluating future plans are crucial features of the metacognitive process. Flavell felt that human beings are organisms with these properties.

Intentionality is another thinking characteristic Flavell used, although it was first used in medieval times. Intentionality is the state of being directed towards a specific goal or thing – in other words, being intentional in an action. Piaget, whose work Flavell has always admired, proposed that until children reach the age of 8–12 months they are not able to show intentionality in their actions. An example of this is the fact that until a child can use a stick to get to something that is beyond their own reach, they have not achieved intentionality – intentional activity depends on a child's ability to form a plan and carry it out.

Flavell maintains that the ability to consciously direct your thinking towards a plan or an evaluation of your success is a sign of both intentionality and metacognition. This implies that the brain is not only active during thinking but that the thinker is an active participant in the activity and has a definite goal in mind as he or she is thinking. The thinker is able to adapt the plan as the activity proceeds, ensuring that progress towards the goal is maintained so they reach their intended goal.

Flavell explored the process of thinking as deliberate, purposeful and aimed 'towards a specific goal', not just abstract thought but a conscious process. In exploring this concept, he used the term metamemory to describe an individual's ability to manage the input of new information into memory and organise the storage, search and retrieval of this information. This was originally thought by Flavell to be an entirely conscious process, although later research appears to have found that some metacognitive activity happens in the subconscious.

Metacognitive activity usually precedes and follows cognitive activity – the child needs to use knowledge and skills already learned as they plan, solve problems and identify their own goals. Cognitive and metacognitive activity are closely interrelated and mutually dependent ⇀ metacognitive knowledge can lead the individual to engage in or abandon a particular cognitive enterprise based on its relationship to his or her interests, abilities and goals. This may involve the child in 'switching off' from externally imposed learning activities when they do not interest them or fail to give opportunities for metacognition, which in turn gives them ownership of the learning.

Flavell described three groups of variables that affect learning:

1 **Personal knowledge** – All the things I know about myself as a learner – Can I do the task? Am I interested in doing the task? Do I learn best by listening or reading? Will I need to work on my own or with other people? Is the task presented in a way that appeals to me? This is sometimes referred to as declarative knowledge.
2 **Task knowledge** – All the things I know about the task – How much information have I already got? How well is it organised? Is it interesting? How difficult is that task? Am I likely to be successful in completing this task? This is sometimes referred to as procedural knowledge.
3 **Strategy knowledge** – Planning and organising my approach – When and why will I need to use the person and task knowledge? What strategies and skills will I need? What are the goals and sub goals for the task? This is sometimes referred to as conditional knowledge.

These questions can be addressed in any order and either consciously or even unconsciously as we deliberate on whether to attempt a task. Responses such as the likelihood of success or failure are also important during the period before deciding whether to get involved in any task.

Likelihood of success is also a factor in metacognition – Will I be able to do it? Do I have the right skills and abilities? Can I do the maths? Am I good enough at descriptive writing? Do I need to produce a final outcome such as a written report, calculations or a presentation?

However, three skills appear to be particularly important for metacognition:

• **Planning**: What are the strategies and resources that could affect the progress and success of my performance of the task? What do I need and how could I begin the task?
• **Monitoring**: How do we know how the task is going? Are we still on the right track or do we need to change our approach?
• **Evaluating**: How well did we do the task? Is the final product what we expected? How well did we do it? How well did we work together?

Although metacognition is closely aligned to cognition and there are some overlaps between the two, there is a significant difference in thinking processes between the simple adding of numbers and the process of building a model with complex stages, which involves planning, organisation and concentration. Unfamiliar or new experiences, or those

John Flavell

with important consequences, will be more likely to involve the learner in metacognition but are also more stressful and may result in panic or refusal. Of course, tasks that interest a child are more likely to engage them immediately and involve metacognition, and very young children can often begin the process if they are able to work closely with an adult or other child to solve a shared problem or complex task.

As early as 1987, Flavell was encouraging teachers and practitioners in the early years to teach the skills that children need for the metacognitive process and to offer opportunities to practise and explore these skills in a range of interesting projects. Metacognition has a critical role to play in successful learning for life, and this means that teachers themselves should also be able to demonstrate the skills for successful thinking. Practitioners must also have the skill and the courage to ask questions, to plan flexibly, to change course if needed, and to evaluate their own and the children's work in conversation with the children.

Additional skills that children and teachers need to support metacognition include:

- **Understanding the roles of others** – particularly in shared tasks
- **Communication skills** – talking and listening
- **Memory** and 'remembering' skills
- **The ability to research** effectively during the task.

In his extensive work with young children, Flavell found that those children whose parents talked to them frequently developed these skills at an earlier age. Children who demonstrate these skills do better in learning tasks and in exams, and even better if they are taught by teachers who also understand the principles of metacognition. They are self-regulated learners who are able to select thinking tools and strategies for the tasks they attempt, and are able to switch strategies during a task to make sure they always use the most effective way to solve the problem or complete the task.

Much of Flavell's later research has been done with preschoolers attending the Bing Nursery on the Stanford University campus and in this research, he and his team observed very young children and found that they understand a lot about thinking. They know that it is different from other activities such as talking, seeing or knowing. They know that thinking can involve things that have already happened or that have not yet happened.

'However preschoolers greatly underestimate the amount that they and others think, and they have difficulty perceiving that other people think. In other words…although preschoolers know that rocks do not think, they also don't believe that their parents think all that much.

(Alic, 2001, Gale Encyclopedia of Psychology 2nd edition)

Flavell has taught us that we may be underestimating and also misunderstanding the way children think and perceive the world. Talking about, demonstrating and teaching the skills of thinking about thinking will help children and the adults who work with them, to become more proficient learners, problem solvers and independent explorers.

Legacy and impact

Flavell and his team have influenced practice in schools across the world. Training for teachers in using thinking skills and courses for schools that involve the children are now widespread. Major research has been undertaken in universities and there are initiatives among groups of schools to adopt the methodology as they learn of the improved outcomes for children who have learned to use metacognition, often referred to as Thinking Skills.

Carol McGuinness, Professor of Psychology at Queen's College, University of Belfast has been involved in developing a curriculum with thinking skills at its heart, and her work is particularly evident in the latest National Curriculum for schools in Northern Ireland where thinking skills …*are embedded and infused…at each key stage and pupils should have opportunities to acquire, develop and demonstrate these skills in all areas of the curriculum.* 'Thinking Skills and Personal Capabilities' (CCEA, 2007) The guidance for Key Stages 1 and 2 contains the following diagram:

When planning	When adapting	When evaluating
How am I going to do it? Is it similar to anything I've done before? Is it one of those?	Do I understand it so far? Do I need to ask a question? Am I on the right track? Am I still on task? Is there a better way?	How did I do it? What method/strategy worked? What did I learn? Did my plan work out? Can I learn from my mistakes? Can I do better next time?

There is also an overt commitment to involving children in talking about and learning the skills of metacognition.

A useful 'Literature Review of Thinking Skills' was produced in 2005 by NFER Nelson. It is available as a free download from https://www.nfer.ac.uk/publications/TSK01/TSK01.pdf .

Thinking aloud is a key cognitive skill for younger children, and practitioners should recognise and encourage this as a thinking skill. If, as part of sustained shared thinking, practitioners model thinking aloud, describing what they are doing, what they think they might do next, how and why, commenting on any problems and difficulties encountered, they will help children to understand and accept that it is quite acceptable to do this too.

Influence on early years practice in the UK

The profile of thinking skills has been raised within the latest guidance for the early learning across the UK. It is now recognised as a powerful way to encourage independent learning and problem solving approaches where children are intensely involved in their own learning, whether they work alone, with other children, or with adults.

England

In England, thinking is a significant element in the Characteristics of Effective Learning as detailed in the 'Statutory framework for the EYFS', and practitioners are now expected to report regularly to parents on children's progress in these areas, which concentrate on how children learn rather than what they learn:

> In planning and guiding children's activities, practitioners must reflect on the different ways that children learn and reflect these in their practice. Three Characteristics of Effective Teaching and Learning are:
>
> - playing and exploring – children investigate and experience things, and 'have a go';
> - active learning – children concentrate and keep on trying if they encounter difficulties, and enjoy achievements; and
> - creating and thinking critically – children have and develop their own ideas, make links between ideas, and develop strategies for doing things.
>
> (DfE, 2014)

The guidance on thinking critically is expanded in the 'Development Matters in the EYFS' document, which supports the Framework. It runs through every area of learning, and has its own set of indicators for children's learning, which consist of:

Having their own ideas

- Thinking of ideas
- Finding ways to solve problems
- Finding new ways to do things

Making links

- Making links and noticing patterns in their experience
- Making predictions
- Testing their ideas
- Developing ideas of grouping, sequences, cause and effect

Choosing ways to do things

- Planning, making decisions about how to approach a task, solve a problem and reach a goal
- Checking how well their activities are going
- Changing strategy as needed
- Reviewing how well the approach worked.

(Early Education, 2012)

These indicators have much in common with Flavell's work, as well as reflecting the best principles of early learning.

Northern Ireland

However, it is in the curriculum guidance for Northern Ireland that the work of McGuinness and her team at Queen's College, Belfast has had the most significant effect. 'Northern Ireland Curriculum Primary' has thinking skills and personal capabilities at its heart, as the following short references will demonstrate:

At the heart of the Revised Curriculum lies an explicit emphasis on the development of pupils' skills and capabilities for lifelong learning and for operating effectively in society. By engaging pupils in active learning contexts across all areas of the curriculum, your teachers can develop pupils' personal and interpersonal skills, capabilities and dispositions, and their ability to think both creatively and critically.

(CCEA, Northern Ireland, 2007)

In the Revised Northern Ireland curriculum, thinking skills and personal capabilities are broken down into five strands:

- Managing information
- Thinking, problem-solving and decision-making
- Being creative
- Working with others
- Self-management.

Each of these strands is described in detail and practitioners and teachers are given advice that the strands should thread through the curriculum, not become a separate and additional subject of the curriculum. They are encouraged to plan 'infusion lessons' where subject knowledge and specific thinking skills are combined. There is also a clear definition of metacognition as *'the ability of the learner to plan, monitor, redirect and evaluate how they think and learn.'* (CCEA, Northern Ireland, 2007)

The guidance continues with useful strategies for thinking skills in the classroom. In the document for the Foundation Stage in Northern Ireland the references to thinking skills are more general, but the definition of thinking skills and personal capabilities as an essential component of the curriculum is at the centre of provision from the earliest age.

I find it hard to believe that children who do more cognitive monitoring would not learn better…I also think that increasing the quantity and quality of children's metacognitive knowledge and monitoring skills through systematic training may be feasible as well as desirable.

(Flavell, 1979)

Key guidance documents for countries in the UK

DfE, (2014) 'Statutory Framework for the Early Years Foundation Stage'.
Early Education, (2012) 'Development Matters in the EYFS'.
CCEA, Northern Ireland, (2007 'The Northern Ireland Curriculum Primary'.
CCEA, Northern Ireland, (2007) 'Thinking skills and personal capabilities for Key Stages 1 and 2'.

Things to think about

- Thinking skills and metacognition are time consuming activities even in the best run settings where they are integrated into other activities. How do you manage to fulfill the requirements of the EYFS in a busy setting with a large number of young children?
- How do you demonstrate your own skills as a thinker to the children in your setting?
- Children who have mastered 'thinking about thinking' can be very demanding and ask some very difficult questions, such as, 'What is milk made from?', 'Who is God?' or 'I've been thinking about where babies come from'. How do you cope with these?
- Are thinking skills more important than physical skills, areas of learning or subject content? Why?
- How would you begin to introduce 'thinking about thinking' to a class of very young children?

Paulo Freire

Full name: Paulo Freire
Born: 1921
Died: 1997
Place of birth: Recife, Pernambuco, Brazil
Countries of residence: Brazil, United States, Switzerland
What he did: Freire studied the transformative role that education can play in the lives of people, particularly those who are poor or disadvantaged.
Influences on education today: Friere's influence has expanded throughout the world to influence government policy and educational practice in enabling children from disadvantaged families to access education.
Theories and areas of work: Critical theory, Pedagogy of the oppressed
Key influencers and followers: Plato, Karl Marx
Key works: *Pedagogy of the Oppressed* (1970), *Education as the Practice of Freedom* (1967)

No pedagogy which is truly liberating can remain distant from the oppressed by treating them as unfortunates and by presenting for their emulation models from among the oppressors. The oppressed must be their own example in the struggle for their redemption.

Freire, Pedagogy of the Oppressed, 1970

Life, love, theory and research

Paolo Friere was a Brazilian, born to a middle class family that suffered poverty as a result of the death of his father and the subsequent Great Depression of the 1930s. He is best known for his work in critical pedagogy and his internationally studied book *The Pedagogy of the Oppressed* published in 1968. In school, he fell four grades behind his year group and he maintained that he was not unintelligent or disinterested but that it was the combination of poverty and hunger that were the cause of his inability to learn. The experience led him to dedicate the rest of his life to improving the lives of the poor by providing a better education. His experience had also affected his view of the way education should be organised and implemented.

Although he studied law he never practised, instead choosing to work in secondary education teaching Portuguese. As he continued to work among the illiterate poor of the State of Pernambuco in Brazil, he began to develop his educational theory which was rooted in liberation theory – a moral and theological reaction to the poverty and social injustice of the government at the time, where the ability to read was a requirement for voting in presidential elections.

His first major opportunity to practise his theories was in Refife University where he taught 300 sugar cane workers to read in 45 days. This achievement affected reforms to education policy throughout Brazil, which were brought to a halt by a military coup in 1964 when Friere was imprisoned and had to leave the country.

In 1967 Friere published his first book *Education as the Practice of Freedom*, followed in 1968 by his most influential book *The Pedagogy of the Oppressed*. Although they were not published in his native country until the 1970s these books, published in the United States, resulted in an offer to work as a visiting professor at Harvard University. Friere's theories were influenced by his reading of Plato and by Marxist writers, particularly those who championed the plight of the poor across the world.

As he became better known outside his own country, Friere worked as special education adviser for the World Council of Churches in former Portuguese colonies in Africa. At this stage he was focused on the position of poor people in ex-colonial countries in Africa, identifying the continuing tension between the oppressor (the colonist) and the oppressed (the indigenous inhabitants of the country). He felt strongly that people who had previously been oppressed must be allowed to regain their place in their own countries and that education was the means to achieve this. However, the 'old-style' colonial education was not the right way to achieve these ends. Rather than treating them as 'unfortunates' (Friere's word), the previously oppressed people must be able to participate in developing a new model of education, abandoning what Friere described as the Banking Model, where the student was viewed as an empty account to be filled by the teacher.

This concept was not new. Jean-Jacques Rousseau's view of the child as an active learner had already moved thinking away from the 'blank slate' model. Contemporaries of Friere were also critical of the model of learning as simply transmitting facts, instead, it should be an agent of political and social change. Friere's critical pedagogy model updated the idea by placing it firmly in political and religious contexts, where aspiring learners were silenced and suppressed. He appeared to be able to weave together aspects of many other philosophies into a new whole.

Friere believed that oppressed learners, particularly in less-affluent countries, should learn to develop critical consciousness where they can question the education they are presented with by a dominant culture or a previous colonial power. He maintained that education cannot be totally free from politics; the way children are taught and the content of the curriculum always have a political agenda. Even individual teachers bring their own political views into the classroom.

Some have pronounced Friere as the most significant educational thinker of the 20th century and his contributions, which will particularly appeal to those in education who promote a more informal approach, have included the following:

- Effective education must be a transformative process. The learner must be transformed in a way that enables them to be successful in the future. The sugar cane worker example described above is one of these transformative experiences, where learning to read enabled them to qualify for a vote.

- There should be an emphasis on dialogue between the teacher and the learner, built on respect from both sides. One should not be 'the banker' making deposits in the account of the other.

- The curriculum should be built on praxis – activity and method informed by thoughtful reflection on practice, with an emphasis on practice rather than written theory.

- Friere's invented the concept of a pedagogy of literacy which involves the learner and the teacher in not only reading words, but in reading the world. The learner must make sense of their own world with the intention of creating a new society for themselves and others. The teacher must be out in the community, learning the language of the local people, gathering local vocabulary and learning about issues important to them. In this way the learner and the teacher can communicate and learn together, knowing what is important to the community, and changing it together.

- The central idea of building a pedagogy of the oppressed is a conscious model of education informed by the situation in which the learner lives. This curriculum would be entirely informed by the lives, situations and vocabularies and interests of the learner, not the teacher. This would transform the 'pedagogy of the oppressed' into a 'pedagogy of hope'.

- Friere used many metaphors drawn from Christianity, and his intention was that the teacher should suppress their intentions in the interests of the learner, something he called the 'class suicide', or 'Easter experience' of the teacher, during which the teacher is transformed from a 'banker' into a educator, while the learner is transformed into an educatee resulting in a teacher/learner situation. In this way the teacher and the learner work together in partnership as they have much to learn from each other during the educational process.

Some educators found the religious or mystical nature of some of Friere's work difficult to accept, although he later modified his written style to a more accessible approach. Other educationists say that Friere's model of education is in some ways very like existing models and should be read with some reservations.

Legacy and impact

Freire's work was about transforming people's lives, and practitioners who use his ideas seek to change existing practices, rules, traditions and understandings as a way of achieving this transformation. They support children by wanting them to be able to critically analyse their daily experiences and learning, and help them to reflect on taken-for-granted practices in their experiences within and outside their setting. Practitioners and children talk, explore ideas and learn together about different ways of constructing their world, thereby improving and transforming the conditions in which their learning takes place.

Current approaches to early education resume a more collaborative approach where children and adults work together to transform learning. Practitioners are expected to adapt learning experiences to take into account the cultures, communities and interests in children's lives. The transformative approach is epitomised by programmes which involve whole families, take place at least partly within the community and focus on activities and experiences that have relevance for individual children and their families.

Education across the world is inevitably affected by politics, whether those are the effects of change of political leadership in a single country, the massive political shifts associated with the current mass migration of populations, the responses to terrorism and repercussions of war or the continuation of oppression by dictatorships in more countries than we would hope. Friere believed that politics and education were inextricably bound together and his commitment to 'a pedagogy of hope' is an admirable intention, however fraught with difficulty.

Influence on early years practice in the UK

The commitment to collaborative learning, where adult and child work together, is epitomised in the work of the EPPE project (Effective Provision of Pre-school Education) carried out by the University of London, Institute of Education.

One of the most influential findings of this long-term research project is the powerful effect on children of 'sustained shared thinking' – which occurs when two or more individuals 'work together' in an intellectual way to solve a problem, clarify a concept, evaluate an activity or extend a narrative etc.

England

Sustained shared thinking, a collaborative approach where adults and children learn together, has been incorporated in the statute and the guidance for the EYFS in England and appears in several places, including the Development Matters guidance:

- Sustained shared thinking helps children to explore ideas and make links. Follow children's lead in conversation, and think about things together.

- Prompt children's thinking and discussion through involvement in their play.

- Give children 'thinking time'. Wait for them to think about what they want to say and put their thoughts into words, without jumping in too soon to say something yourself.

- Help children to become aware of their own goals, make plans, and to review their own progress and successes. Describe what you see them trying to do and encourage children to talk about their own processes and successes.

- Ask children to think in advance about how they will accomplish a task. Talk through and sequence the stages together.

(Early Education, 2012)

During the most recent stages of this important long-term research project, later re-named the Effective Pre-school, Primary and Secondary Education 3–14 Project (EPPSE 3–14), researchers have investigated the attainment and development of approximately 3,000 children, following them from preschool to the end of Key Stage 3. Among other intentions, the project evaluated the impact of high quality preschool, primary and secondary school experiences (singly and combined) on students' later outcomes, and how these change over time. The findings of this research chime well with the thoughts of Friere on the purposes and priorities of education, particularly for children from less affluent families:

Student's who succeed 'against the odds' had:

- Higher levels of individual agency, determination and active participation from themselves as well as from the people around them;

- Parents who valued learning and had high aspirations and standards of behaviour for their children. Their children had social networks that provided emotional and practical support which enhanced their self-efficacy, enabling them to become 'active agents' in their learning. These parents' resilience in the face of hardship provided a role model for their children's effort in learning.

(DfE, 2012)

Wales

In Wales, the 'Foundation Phase Framework' commits itself to partnership with the children's parents, involvement in the community and wholistic education:

The Foundation Phase encompasses the developmental needs of children. At the centre of the statutory curriculum framework likes the holistic development of children and their skills, building on their previous learning experiences and knowledge. The Foundation Phase curriculum promotes equality of opportunity and values, and celebrates diversity. Positive partnerships with the home are fostered and an appreciation of parents/carers being the children's first educators is recognized.

(Welsh Assembly Government, 2015)

Paulo Freire

The work of Friere has influenced the whole movement towards a shared model of education where children, their parents and their teachers work closely to personalise a programme which suits the individual. However, the constant pressures of national politics will continue to influence the pace of its progress.

Key guidance documents for countries in the UK

Early Education, (2012) 'Development Matters in the EYFS'.
DfE, (2012) 'Effective Pre-school, Primary and Secondary Education 3–14 Project (EPPSE 3–14) Final Report from the Key Stage 3 Phase: Influences on Students' Development From age 11 – 14.'
Welsh Assembly Government, (2015) 'Foundation Phase Framework'.

Things to think about

- Is it possible, or desirable, in the 21st Century to follow Friere's philosophy and become the ideal teacher/learner?
- Do you think the current early years curriculum is a 'banking' model where children are seen as empty vessels to be filled?
- How well do you feel you and your colleagues know the local community of your school? How could you get that 'pedagogy of literacy' about the local area that Friere says will help you to understand the needs of the children you teach?
- When does sharing ownership of he curriculum become total abdication by the teacher of their role?
- Do you think you will have a lasting effect on the lives of children you work with in the future?

Friedrich Willhelm August Fröebel

Full name: Friedrich Willhelm August Fröebel

Born: 1782

Died: 1852

Place of birth: Oberweisbach, Germany

Countries of residence: Germany, Switzerland

What he did: Fröebel explored the benefits of early education, and invented the concept and description 'kindergarten'. This was focused on following children's curiosity and exploration, outdoor learning, work with the Fröebel 'Gifts' and play as the child's right.

Influences on education today: The kindergarten movement has had a deep and lasting effect on early years education throughout the world. Many features of current practice can be traced back to the influences of Fröebel, including the importance of outdoor learning, play, and hands-on experiences.

Theories and areas of work: Pedagogy

Key influencers and followers: Heinrich Pestalozzi, Jerome Bruner

Key works: *The Student's Fröebel* (1990). Other works in German, not translated.

Children are like tiny flowers; they are varied and need care, but each is beautiful alone and glorious when seen in the community of peers.

Play is the highest expression of human development in childhood for it alone is the free expression of what is in a child's soul.

Friedrich Fröebel, The Education of Man, 1826

Life, love, theory and research

Friedrich Fröebel was born and lived in Germany, where he completed most of his work. His early life in the woods and hills of Thuringia moulded his philosophy and instilled his commitment to active outdoor learning. The methods he developed during his life time are fundamental to present day early education, particularly his commitment to play being at the heart of learning and the importance of the outdoor environment where children can be physically active, grow things, climb, sing and dance.

In his own early years, Fröebel was not successful in school, particularly in writing and reading, so he turned his attention to those subjects which he enjoyed and did well in – geometry and geography, particularly map making, which led him to take architecture as his major subject at university. However, shortly after he left university, perhaps following a conversation with a friend or tutor, he decided that education rather than architecture would be a suitable career, and he went to work at one of the first schools to become inspired by his pedagogical approach. After a period away at war, and some time working in a mainstream school, Fröebel got a job in a museum classifying gemstones and crystals, and it was here that he began to formulate a theory that the geometric structures of minerals, and particularly of crystals, mirrored the growth of animals and human beings.

Two years later Fröebel moved to work at a school at Yverdon. As he worked with Pestalozzi he began to refine his own ideas about the education of young children and the central themes of this emerging approach were:

- Play is the major vehicle for learning, as children explore their environments
- Teachers must plan education for the whole child
- Teachers should encourage children to use their curiosity and sense of exploration (one of Fröebel's major principles)
- Active learning should replace the hours of lecturing and rote learning of the past.

These were revolutionary thoughts at a time when children were expected to behave as miniature adults, only of use when they were old enough and well trained enough to work. Education was a time for sitting at uncomfortable desks listening to teachers, learning facts by rote, and copying from the blackboard.

In 1816, Fröebel turned down the offer of a scientific job in Sweden and in 1817 he opened his own school in Switzerland where he could put his educational ideas into practice. The first school was Universal German Educational Institute in Gieshelm where he was the principal. He was able to start implementing his ideas, but his most famous initiative, the kindergarten (or garden for children) had to wait another 24 years until he could open the first kindergarten in Blankenberg, Germany in 1840 – Fröebel's Play and Activity Institute which was renamed Kindergarten. Before this initiative, even rich children did not go to school until they were seven years old and most did not attend school at all.

A kindergarten was a place where they could play freely and observe and interact with nature but also a place where they themselves could grow and develop free from the imperatives of adults. Major components of the kindergarten day were:

- observing and nurturing plants in a garden to stimulate awareness of the natural world

- singing, dancing and gardening for healthy activity
- creative play with specially developed resources called gifts and occupations.

From the time of opening the first kindergarten, Fröebel was also demonstrating a commitment to the training of teachers to work with the kindergarten children. Training schools in Europe and later in the UK, offered courses for women who wished to work with young children.

Fröebel's experience of geology generated a belief that guided handling and manipulation of three-dimensional geometrical objects could help children's learning and brain development. At the time most children didn't go to school at all, many worked in mines and factories and by the time they were seven they were treated as adults. Rich children's toys were very ornate and unsuitable for the sort of play that Fröebel believed supported early education; examples of these were rocking horses, china dolls and tin soldiers, all intended for use in the quiet, controlled environment of the homes of the day.

As Fröebel began to shape his own views on learning he looked at existing toys and their suitability for the play-based, nature dependent learning central to his educational theories and practice. It was obvious that existing toys would not be suitable, so Fröebel set about designing and making his own. These were made from natural materials (such as unpainted wood, simple metal, coloured fabric and card and wool), and were natural geometric shapes (spheres, cubes, sticks etc). These toys reflected his work in geology and crystallography, resembling 'the 'building blocks' of the physical world. The objects became the 'gifts and occupations' that were used by Fröebel and his followers in the first kindergartens, and are still a feature of teaching and learning in Fröebel schools today.

The gifts and occupations are a staged series of objects, mostly wooden and mostly 3D, each with their own attributes and instructions for how they should be used and each in their own wooden box. The gifts were used by children alone or with one or two companions. Despite their appearance, these gifts are not resources for maths or science but had a wide variety of applications. Fröebel maintained that with the right support from teachers, this series of resources and the activities that accompany each one would take children into the realms of Forms of Knowledge (math/science), Forms of Life (relating to objects found in a child's life/world) and Forms of Beauty (abstract patterns and designs).

As well as the simple blocks and divided blocks, the gifts included other resources such as sticks and woollen balls. Each gift was given to the child in a particular order, at a suggested age. Fröebel divided these objects into two groups: boxes one to six are the 'six gifts', and boxes seven to ten are the 'four occupations'. The difference between the groups was that the gifts could and should be returned to their original form at the end of play, by returning them to the box which they neatly fitted into while the constructions made with the occupations had to be deconstructed at the end of play.

By using the gifts and occupations, Fröebel believed that children could progress in their understanding from material experiences to those that are more abstract and creative. The series of gifts and occupations was:

- **Gift 1** – a wooden box containing six small balls made of crocheted cotton, of six different colours.

- **Gift 2** – a wooden box containing six 3D wooden shapes – two cubes, two spheres, two cylinders, one of each shape has holes drilled in it.

- **Gift 3** – the 'divided cube', a wooden cube, the same size as the cubes in gift 2, divided into eight one-inch cubes which fit neatly in the box.

- **Gift 4** – the two-inch cube has now been divided into eight oblong blocks two-inch by one-inch by half an inch which fit neatly in the box as in gift 3.

- **Gift 5** – a three-inch cube divided twice in each direction, with some cubes divided diagonally into triangular prisms – 21x1" cubes, 6 half-cubes, and 12 quarter-cubes.

- **Gift 6** – the classic building blocks. More varieties of rectangular prisms, including 18 oblong blocks, 12 flat square blocks, and six narrow columns to be used for building.

- **Occupation 7** – a set of parquetry tablets containing a variety of geometric shapes, made from wood, plastic or paper and consisting of seven different shapes.

- **Occupation 8** – sticks and rings, some rings halved, for making pictures and patterns.

- **Occupation 9** – small circular objects, often in a variety of colours representing the point, big enough for the child to pick up but small enough to make complex patterns, shapes and pictures.

- **Occupation 10** – a box of spheres and sticks, often referred to as 'peas work' because the original spheres were soaked dried peas, to be connected with thin sticks like modern cocktail sticks. This gift influenced many modern construction sets such as Tinkertoy.

Fröebel's ideas about childhood development and education interested people in academic and royal circles, mostly as a result of promotion by Baroness Bertha Marie von Marenholtz-Bülow who introduced Fröebel to royalty and high society in Europe. One of these prominent personalities offered the use of one of his hunting lodges where Fröebel trained the first group of Fröebel teachers.

Sadly, shortly before Fröebel's death, the kindergarten movement received a real blow. The Prussian court of the day, possibly feeling threatened by the freedom and innovation central to the movement, banned all kindergartens, leaving some of Fröebel's closest followers to try and keep the original school at Keilhau open until the beginning of the 19th century, when the kindergarten movement would return and really become established. The school still thrives today as an accurate example of the work of Fröebel. It is now a residential school for children with special needs.

There are still Fröebel schools in the UK and United States, following his methods and ensuring that the children have the outdoor holistic education that Fröebel 'invented'. Fröebel training for teachers continues to this day.

Legacy and impact

Fröebel training for teachers was first established in England at the Fröebel Institute in West Kensington, London, in 1895. Teacher education in Fröebelian methods continues to flourish in several university colleges now, most famously at Roehampton University, London. Teachers with Fröebel training often go on to work in Fröebel schools or schools where a Fröebelian method is promoted. This includes providing early years education for children up to the age of eight.

Fröebel was originally intending to become an architect. It is interesting that the American architect Frank Lloyd Wright said that the Fröebel blocks were an inspiration for some of his most famous buildings and he bought boxes of Fröebel blocks for himself and for his own children – they can be seen in his home and studio today. He used the blocks to inspire his plans and designs, and it is possible to see the influence of Fröebel in his houses, particularly those in Chicago.

Many of the resources and games used in early years settings have changed little from Fröebel's original gifts and occupations. Practitioners across the world will know the appeal of building with wooden blocks and using construction sets where temporary buildings and objects can be made and remade. Other familiar construction sets, such as Lego® and Stickle Bricks, pegboards and shape boards echo the lines and points in the gifts, and Trio, Meccano and Polydron add to the variety, many producing abstract shapes as well as the possibility of building recognisable objects. Schools in Reggio Emilia, as well as the Fröebel schools, promote the use of natural materials and muted, natural colours which seem to have calming properties that are conducive to learning.

The Fröebel message has travelled across the world. For instance, in 1948, when Germans were fleeing from the revolution, the kindergarten initiative moved to the United States. Martha Schurtz, a trained kindergarten teacher, opened the first kindergarten in her home, teaching her children and their cousins in German. The first school was followed by others, gradually expanding across the country, but sometimes with a diluted Fröebelian message.

In the later part of the 19th century the kindergarten movement continued to expand, sometimes struggling to preserve the purity of Fröebel's methods, and to defend the ways in which the teachers worked with parents and with children. By the early 20th century, every major city in the United States had a public kindergarten and they became more and more pressured to include the teaching of 'subjects', although 'nature study', home and community life, literature, music and the arts were still at the core of kindergarten provision. There was also friction with some psychologists who were against 'motherly love' in the kindergarten, insisting on a focus on subject matter and learning objectives, and helping children to adjust to the social environment of school. Kindergartens were increasingly incorporated into publicly funded schools, and the kindergarten curriculum has been incorporated into the K-12 curriculum. Children from three to four are able to attend pre-school settings, before entering compulsory education at the age of five.

Fröebel still lives on in the kindergarten movement in the United States as exemplified in an article in the New York Times in the summer of 2015:

> Concerned that kindergarten has become overly academic in recent years, this suburban school district south of Baltimore is introducing a new curriculum in the fall for 5-year-olds. Chief among its features is a most old-fashioned concept: play.
>
> New York Times; June 2015 Kindergartens Ringing the Bell for Play Inside the Classroom

There are many Fröebel kindergartens across the world, including those in the United States, Europe, Australasia, India and Pakistan. Most of these are fee-paying and some adhere more strictly to Fröebel's principles than others.

However, as Fröebel said before his death:

> The last word of my theory I shall carry to my grave, the time is not yet ripe for it. If three hundred years after my system of education is completely, and according to its real principle, carried through Europe, I shall rejoice in heaven.
>
> (Fröebel, 1782–1852)

Influence on early years practice in the UK

Fröebel has had a significant effect on early education in the UK. The following aspects of his beliefs are included in the current versions of curriculum documentation:

- the importance of outdoor play
- active learning at the heart of the curriculum
- music, rhythm and rhyme as a support for early communication and language development
- creative play and construction.

Across the countries of the UK, guidance for these aspects appears to ensure that Fröebel's principles are carried forward into the future of early years education:

The 'Statutory Framework for the EYFS' says:

Providers must provide access to an outdoor play area or, if that is not possible, ensure that outdoor activities are planned and taken on a daily basis.

(DfE, 2014)

The 'Curriculum for Wales: Foundation Phase Framework' says:

Indoor and outdoor environments that are fun, exciting, stimulating and safe promote children's development and natural curiosity to explore and learn through first-hand experiences. The Foundation Phase environment should promote discovery and independence and a greater emphasis on using the outdoor environment as a resource for children's learning.

(Welsh Government, 2015)

'Pre-birth to three' says:

Being outdoors has a positive impact on mental, emotional, physical and social wellbeing. The outdoors, which refers to the immediate environment attached to the setting, the local community and beyond, can provide opportunities for participating in new, challenging and healthy experiences. Most staff in early years settings understand that they have an important responsibility to ensure that regular and frequent outdoor experiences are integral to everyday practice for all children.

(Learning and Teaching Scotland, 2010)

For many children, opportunities to be, or play, outdoors are few and far between. Staff in early years settings therefore have an important responsibility to maximise outdoor play experiences for children as it may be the only time they have to play freely and safely outside. . . . outdoor play does not necessarily mean purchasing expensive equipment, as the natural environment itself contains a whole range of materials which can be adapted, explored and enhanced in a variety of ways. High quality provision ensures that outdoor play extends beyond the outdoor area belonging to the early years setting and into the local and wider community.

(Learning and Teaching Scotland, 2010)

Outdoor play in particular can also be a major contributor to outcomes around physical activity and healthy weight. Developing play spaces, and play opportunities for children and removing barriers to play is therefore a priority.'

('Play' from the Foundation Stage guidance, Scottish Government, 2008)

Active learning is another Fröebelian essential. The 'Statutory Framework for the EYFS' says:

In planning and guiding children's activities, practitioners must reflect on the different ways that children learn and reflect these in their practice. One of the three characteristics of effective teaching and learning is:

- *active learning – children concentrate and keep on trying if they encounter difficulties, and enjoy achievements.*

(DfE, 2012)

'Pre-birth to three' says:

From the earliest days, children can experience the joy of physical activity through play both indoors and outdoors and in all weathers. Play and movement are essential for brain development as it is often through play that babies and young children learn about themselves, others and the world around them. These experiences also offer important opportunities for the development of fine movements, gross motor skills and social skills.

(Learning and Teaching Scotland, 2010)

'Understanding the foundation stage' says:

Children learn best when they:

- *have opportunities to be actively involved in practical, open-ended and challenging learning experiences that encourage creativity;*
- *have opportunities to initiate experiences that capitalise on their individual interests and curiosities; are actively involved in planning, reviewing and reflecting what they have done.*

(Northern Ireland Curriculum, 2006)

Making music is another central theme of Fröebel's philosophy, and this is also reflected in curriculum guidance, in such statements as the following from 'Pre-birth to three':

When making provision for outdoor experiences, staff can:

- *enhance the outdoor area by ensuring the provision of a range of resources, such as natural materials, musical instruments, dressing up clothes and tents.*

(Learning and Teaching Scotland, 2010)

Creative activities also have a key part to play in Fröebelian education, and across the UK guidance, practitioners are expected to offer a wide range of creative activities. The 'Statutory Framework for the EYFS' says:

Expressive arts and design involves enabling children to explore and play with a wide range of media and materials, as well as providing opportunities and encouragement for sharing their thoughts, ideas and feelings through a variety of activities in art, music, movement, dance, role-play, and design and technology.

(DfE, 2014)

Being imaginative: children use what they have learnt about media and materials in original ways, thinking about uses and purposes. They represent their own ideas, thoughts and feelings through design and technology, art, music, dance, role-play and stories.

(DfE, 2014)

'Pre-birth to three' says:

Resources should also be selected according to a wide range of factors, including the changing needs and interests of individuals and groups of children, the time of year, weather conditions and so forth. Children derive most benefit from resources when they are presented and organised in imaginative and creative ways.

(Learning and Teaching Scotland, 2010)

Play is at the heart of Fröebel's methodology, and learning through play is now a cornerstone of early years education across the UK.

The 'Statutory Framework for the EYFS' says:

Each area of learning and development must be implemented through planned, purposeful play and through a mix of adult-led and and child-initiated activity. Play is essential for children's development, building their confidence as they learn to explore, to think about problems and relate to others. Children learn by leading their own pay and by taking part in play which is guided by adults. There is an ongoing judgement to be made by practitioners about the balance between activities led by children and activities led or guided by adults.

(DfE, 2014)

'Pre-birth to three' says:

There are many different types of play and children learn and play in diverse ways, as they have individual preferences, interests and needs.

Play enables children to:

- *make important connections so that they can make sense of their world*
- *consolidate and celebrate what they know and can do*
- *act out and process day-to-day experiences*
- *thrive, develop self-confidence and social skills*
- *experiment with and manage feelings.*

(Learning and Teaching Scotland, 2010)

As the reader can see from the selection of quotes above, play, active learning, access to the outdoors and a creative curriculum remain not just priorities, but entitlements for children right across the UK.

Key guidance documents for countries in the UK

DfE, (2014) 'Statutory Framework for the Early Years Foundation Stage'.
Welsh Assembly Government, (2015) 'Foundation Phase Framework'.
Learning and Teaching Scotland, (2010) 'Pre-birth to three'.
CCEA, (2006) 'Northern Ireland Curriculum: Understanding the Foundation Stage'.

Things to think about

- If you could, would you add any other entitlements to the ones identified by Fröebel?
- Have you ever seen the Fröebel gifts? Why not look them up online? They are very interesting.
- Fröebel said that practitioners should use natural objects and natural colours in their settings. Many early years catalogues and toyshops are full of bright colours and plastics. What do you think is better?
- Do the children in your setting take advantage of the outdoor activities you plan or do they prefer to follow their own activities and interests? How could you make your outdoor area more appealing?
- During your training, have you learned about Fröebel? How much do you agree with his methods?

Howard Gardner

Full name: Howard Gardner

Born: 1943 (still living)

Place of birth: Scranton, Pennsylvania, United States

Countries of residence: United States

What he did: Gardner has defined the concept of multiple intelligences, a new way of looking at intelligence.

Influences on education today: Initially, practitioners enthusiastically adopted Gardner's theory, and went to great lengths to find out children's dominant intelligences and teach to these. More recently, practitioners have recognised that the important thing to remember is that each child is different and may need to use different intelligences as they learn and develop. This does not need detailed planning for each child.

Theories and areas of work: Developmental psychology/ Humanism

Key influencers and followers: Jean Piaget, Jerome Bruner, Claude Levi-Strauss

Key works: *Frames of Mind* (2011), *The Unschooled Mind* (2011), *Multiple Intelligences: The Theory in Practice* (2006)

Anything that is worth teaching can be presented in many different ways. These multiple ways can make use of our multiple intelligences.

Howard Gardner, Interview for Huffington Post 'Living Legends', 2013

Life, love, theory and research

Born and brought up in the United States, the son of German immigrants, Howard Gardner was a studious child who enjoyed playing the piano. At Harvard University he studied under Erik Erikson, graduated in Developmental Psychology, and worked for some years after graduating at the Boston Veterans Administration Hospital. Since 1986, he has worked at Harvard University School of Education, where he has had a significant impact on how we think about intelligence.

Gardner's interest in defining and exploring intelligence was really sparked during his time at Harvard when he become fascinated by Erikson's work. Jerome Bruner was another inspiration and these people changed Gardner from a budding lawyer to a eminent psychologist. As he developed his ideas on intelligence, he disagreed, and publicly countered Jean Piaget's theories of a staged approach to development, declaring that it was quite common for a child to be at several stages of development at once.

While Gardner was working on a project called the Project of Human Potential, he constructed a theory that there was not just one intelligence but many, and the theory of Multiple Intelligences was born. This work was published in 1983, in the book *Frames of Mind: The Theory of Multiple Intelligences* where Gardner gave detailed information about his work.

He was very interested in the way that in western society (although not in some others) we value some attributes such as mathematical or linguistic ability more highly than musical or athletic abilities, raising the first to the level of 'intelligence' while dismissing the latter as just 'skill'. In this way, the efforts and achievements of talented athletes, pop singers or artists are often less highly rated than being able to speak Cantonese or do quadratic equations.

We have this myth that the only way to learn something is to read it in a textbook or hear a lecture on it. And the only way to show that we've understood something is to take a short-answer test or maybe occasionally with an essay question thrown in. But that's nonsense. Everything can be taught in more than one way.

(Gardner, Interview for Edutopia, 1997)

Gardner's original list of intelligences contained seven different types but he has since added another, 'naturalist intelligence', and freely admits that his list may not be complete. The seven original intelligences proposed by Gardner were:

- **Linguistic intelligence** – the ability to learn and use language effectively. Children with linguistict intelligence are often expressive and outgoing talkers. They have a natural instinct for using language and as they grow more confident, they will ask questions about what words mean and will often develop an ability to play with words, using nonsense words and even made-up languages. They love talking and contribute with enjoyment to discussions, stories and rhymes.

- **Logical/mathematical intelligence** – the ability to manipulate and understand numbers, problems and mathematical calculations. Children with logical/mathematical intelligence will often become fascinated with patterns and pattern making. They notice patterns in nature and the world around them, spotting similarities, matching objects, and organising toys such as cars or books with care. These children are often good at problem solving and making links in learning.

- **Musical intelligence** – ability both in playing instruments and singing, these people often have skills in rhythm and pitch, enjoy singing and making sounds. They learn songs and rhythms easily, sometimes singing before they learn to talk fluently and enjoy any activity where rhythm, rhyme and sound are used.

- **Kinesthetic intelligence** – these children know the position of their own body in space, are good movers, well coordinated, and often good at sports and games. They usually develop both gross and fine motor skills at a faster pace than others of their age, and they enjoy learning on the move, outdoor activities often being favourites. They also enjoy using tools and other small implements.

- **Spatial intelligence** – the ability to recognise patterns and use these to solve problems. Young children with spatial intelligence can often recreate objects, either copying real objects using construction toys such as Lego® or found materials, recreating scenes or structures they have made previously.

- **Interpersonal intelligence** – the capacity to understand the intentions, motivations and wishes of other people. Young children with this intelligence are good friends, playing cooperatively, taking turns and being aware of others. They often choose to play with others rather than alone. They are often the first to notice that another child is distressed and sometimes react strongly to stories with emotional content.

- **Intrapersonal intelligence** – the capacity to understand ourselves and appreciate our own feelings and motivations. These children are very aware of their own feelings and emotions and can talk about how they feel. They respond thoughtfully to stories including emotional or moral problems and have a strong sense of what is right.

- **Naturalistic intelligence** – the ability to be highly in tune with nature and interested in the patterns and relationships of nature. Many children have a real interest in animals and the living world but children with a strong naturalist intelligence are absolutely fascinated with anything that is or has been alive, from ants to dinosaurs, from a dead butterfly to the features of their friends' faces. They love being out of doors and would stay there all day whatever the weather.

Gardner's book was very popular and was widely read in Europe and the USA although it now seems that many people only read the section on multiple intelligences, choosing to ignore Gardner's detailed warnings about simplistic interpretation of his work. He was always keen to emphasise that every person has all the intelligences, just in different proportions, and that the idea of multiple intelligences should be used to 'empower learners, not restrict them.' One child might be linguistically and interpersonally intelligent and grow up to be an international translator, another might have musical and kinesthetic intelligence and be destined to be a dancer.

Gardner was also concerned about the confusion between Multiple Intelligences (MI) and learning styles, and there were some proposals that he found offensive where MI was used to make statements about race and intelligence. Gardner has also been much more involved in how MI might be used in education, not as a labelling device, but as an enabler, helping teachers and pupils to access their special intelligences as they explore topics and projects.

20 years after the publication of *Frames of Mind*, Gardner published a paper about what had happened in the meantime, to him and to the theory of MI – the full paper is available

at http://howardgardner.com/multiple-intelligences/. In this short paper, he followed the progress of MI and how he had worked on its clarification and promotion,

He was conscious at this point that unleashing an idea (he called it a 'meme') into the community was as risky as unleashing one's child onto the world. There must be a point at which the idea must, like a child, be able to stand on its own feet but it is always difficult for the parent. He admits that there is much work still to do to explore the theory – more intelligences are and will be proposed, and more ways will be found to unlock the potential of the ideas. Meanwhile, Gardner intends to continue his work in ensuring that MI continues to be explored, influencing such things as the types of courses available in universities, the use of MI in education and the ways in which new information about the brain and body might affect thinking about MI.

A second paper, published in 2011, 30 years after the original publication of *Frames of Mind*, began with a repetition of much of the previous information, and went on to update Gardner's latest work. This paper includes information on Gardner's involvement in education, links with individual schools, and teacher training about MI, for which he has travelled all over the world. He began to feel that education before university should cover all the disciplines (science, mathematics, history, and the arts) but recognises the difficulty of covering such a wide-ranging curriculum.

His solution may be included in this paper, 'Multiple Intelligences: the first thirty years' Harvard Graduate School of Education; 2011. In this paper he suggests that two key factors in successful teaching are:

- individualising – knowing as much as possible about the intelligences of each learner in the group and
- pluralising – teaching in multiple ways to meet differing intelligences, so the teachers 'strikes' as many intelligences as possible.

Gardner's work on MI has had its critics, including from some of the most well-known experts on learning, intelligence and brain development. In the 2011 paper, Gardner recounts the ways in which he has answered these criticisms. Here is a taste of his replies:

I'm much more interested in measures of interpersonal intelligence which examine directly how a person works with a group of peers than in paper-and-pencil measures that involve selecting the correct answer out of a multiple choice array.

(Gardner, 2011)

Other criticisms of Gardner's work include:

- The absence of any methods for testing MI to collect statistical data, which Gardner countered by saying he was not interested in becoming a psychometrician.
- The list of intelligences constructed by Gardner. Critics have suggested that this should be extended to include spiritual, sexual, digital and even pedagogical intelligence (the

ability to teach others) – an additional intelligence that Gardner himself proposed, and particularly interests him.

Gardner agrees that MI needs to be updated, in part to take into account the complexity of modern society and the new findings in genetics, engineering, and information technology. However, he retains his view that seeing each other through the lens of multiple intelligences enables us to understand and appreciate the unique nature of each of us. We all behave and learn in unique ways, with some having a single major intelligence and others with a much flatter profile across them all. Gardner suggests that these differences might be imagined as a spectrum, with individuals with 'focused laser intelligence' at one extreme and broader 'searchlight intelligence' at the other. The rest of us would be somewhere on the spectrum between these two extremes:

> I think it would be worthwhile to study in detail the differences between those who deploy a focused laser intelligence and those who display an ever-vigilant and shifting searchlight intelligence.

> (Gardner, 2011)

Thinking in this way may make it much easier for us to understand each other and realise that 'better' or 'worse' cannot be used in this concept, we are all just different.

Legacy and impact

Unfortunately, one of the results of Gardner's defining of multiple intelligences was that some people, and particularly some teachers, misunderstood the detail of the theory. Perhaps they didn't read the whole book but they thought that children were either linguistically intelligent or mathematically intelligent, either interpersonally intelligent or intrapersonally intelligent, and if a child had one sort of intelligence, they couldn't have another. The concept of a profile for each child, with the intelligences appearing proportionally escaped these teachers, and children were labelled, trapped in a persona which did not really describe them. Assessments and questionnaires were invented (not by Gardner), which appeared to be able to identify levels of each of the intelligences, and some teachers even began to group the children according to their major intelligence, failing to understand that the full picture was needed in order to really understand the whole child.

At about the same time as MI was becoming well-known, the education profession also became interested in learning styles (sometimes referred to as VAK). The idea came from several sources and there were several definitions of what learning styles were, but the most popular and easily understood was that we can learn in several different ways and each of us has a preferred learning style:

- **Visual learners** learn best when they use their eyes and have information presented to them in a visual way.
- **Auditory learners** learn best when they hear information and can absorb it through listening.
- **Kinesthetic learners** learn best when they can touch and handle the resources and feel happier learning on the move.

Because VAK was easily understood and explained, even to younger children, it became fashionable to teach children according to their learning style and VAK became so popular that the phrase 'learning styles' is now in common usage, and even the early years curriculum documentation for England specifically refers to it.

Unfortunately, a lot of teachers took the relatively simple VAK solution to explain the differences between individual learning preferences, and applied it indiscriminately it to MI. Self generated and self administered MI 'tests' were published and used to identify predominant intelligences (the ones that scored most highly in the home made tests) and these were used to limit children's learning abilities rather than unlocking them. This simplistic interpretation resulted in criticism of Gardner's original work which was unfairly blamed for the simplistic interpretation by enthusiasts.

The general opinion now is that learning styles do exist, and we can learn to recognise our own preferred learning styles and intelligences as we do have many and they are complex, depending on many influences, not least the time of day, the subject matter and or even whether or not we are hungry.

More recently, Gardner's theory has lost its initial influence. Although the theory is still an interesting one and can throw useful light on our own and our children's behaviours and interests, it should not be used as a way to corral children into scientists, linguists or athletes. Gardner has said that his interest and work on intelligences was 'just a hunch', and is not based on statistical evidence – and he never claimed that it was. We all have talents, skills and interests (not necessarily intelligences), some of which are genetically inherited, some developed during our lives, and all of these may affect how we learn. However, it is possible for children who are physically talented to be thought less of than those who are linguistically, mathematically or sociologically talented, and we should try to eliminate a traditional way of thinking, with an ideal result that all intelligences are valued equally.

Gardner's work was useful in bringing to our attention that all intelligences are important, all to be valued and used by teachers and learners alike. Educators, parents and children should never assume that some skills, talents or attributes are more important than others. However, in a world where linguistic and mathematical abilities are still more highly valued, and music, arts and sport are sometimes seen as 'frills', not even assessed in some countries, and in others only offered as 'extra-curricular' activities, we still have a long way to go before we can even pretend that all intelligences are equal.

Gardner also joined Mihaly Csikszentmihalyi in establishing the Good Works Project (now known as the Good Project), which aims to identify and celebrate 'good works' – described on the Good Works website as 'work that is excellent in quality, socially responsible and meaningful to its practitioners'. Since 1996, Gardner has concentrated much of his effort in this project. On the Good Works website, Gardner is quoted as saying:

> *Doing things in a new way is easy; we call this novelty. What's challenging is to do things in a new way that eventually gets accepted by others; we call this creativity. What's even more challenging is to do something in a new way that is ethical and advances the human condition; we call this 'good work.'*

> (Gardner, www.thegoodproject.org)

Influence on early years practice in the UK

Early years practitioners always try to focus on the special aptitudes and abilities of the individuals in their care, building on these and using them as starting points for learning. They have shown great interest in Gardner's work, and they have welcomed the opportunity to look at children's individual intelligences. Outstanding practice in the early years focuses on individuals, their interests and existing skills, which practitioners use to build the confidence needed for the next steps in learning. In the guidance on the Characteristics of Effective Learning, the EYFS Development Matters has the following relevant advice:

- *In planning activities, ask yourself: Is this an opportunity for children to find their own ways to represent and develop their own ideas? Avoid children just reproducing someone else's ideas.*
- *Support children's interests over time, reminding them of previous approaches and encouraging them to make connections between their experiences.*

> Statutory framework for the early years foundation stage; DfE; 2014

Although there is no direct reference to Gardner's work, except in recommended reading, the supporting documentation for practitioners across all four countries of the UK demonstrates a commitment to the individual nature of children's learning. In each country there are statements that encourage practitioners to locate and build on children's existing and emerging interests:

In Wales, the 'Foundation Phase Framework' says:

> *Settings/schools should teach all programmes of study and frameworks in ways appropriate to children's developing maturities and abilities and ensure that children are able to fully use their*

preferred means of communication to access the curriculum. In order to extend their learning, children should experience a variety of learning and teaching styles.

(Welsh Government, 2015)

In Northern Ireland, 'Understanding the Foundation Stage' says:

This flexibility allows teachers to follow the interests of the children, encouraging them to see links in their learning and to appreciate that the skills they learn in one area can be applied elsewhere.

(CCEA, Northern Ireland, 2006)

In England, the 'Statutory Framework for the Early Years Foundation Stage' says:

The EYFS seeks to provide: a secure foundation through learning and development opportunities, which are planned around the needs and interests of each individual child and are assessed and reviewed regularly.

(DfE, 2014)

Ongoing assessment (also known as formative assessment) is an integral part of the learning and development process. It involves practitioners observing children to understand their level of achievement, interests and learning styles, and to then shape learning experiences for each child reflecting those observations.

(DfE, 2014)

These statements, from the documentation across all four countries, support a provision for children which is adapted according to individual needs, learning styles and interests. However, there remains a risk that in future, the curriculum might be narrowed, by making some areas of learning more important than others. For instance, in the curriculum guidance for England 'Statutory Framework for the Early Years Foundation Stage', there is a possibility that creativity, so important to young children, could be relegated to a 'second class' area of learning:

All areas of learning and development are important and inter-connected. Three areas are particularly crucial for igniting children's curiosity and enthusiasm for learning, and for building their capacity to learn, form relationships and thrive. These three areas, the prime areas, are:

- *communication and language;*
- *physical development; and*
- *personal, social and emotional development.*

(DfE, 2014)

In identifying three areas of learning as 'prime areas', or areas needing particular focus, thus becoming more important than the others, there is a danger that practitioners will relegate the other four areas, including those with a creative or technological focus to 'second class areas', rather than incorporating these by teaching them through the medium of Literacy, Physical or Personal development.

In this way, a child who had an intense interest in technology could still access literacy through computers, tablets, cameras and other technology, and a child with an intense love of nature could do more learning out of doors, where her physical development and fine motor skills can be linked to an active search for mini-beasts. In this way, the early years curriculum could be a vehicle for projects and topics where the intelligences and enthusiasms of all children would be engaged, not a place where children are trapped on a carpet in endless activities labelled 'literacy', as stated in the 'Foundation Phase Framework' for Wales:

> *While we acknowledge that skills development for younger learners, in particular, may be more erratic, effective cross-curriculum planning for skills and a framework for continued development is important for all learners.*

> (Welsh Government, 2015)

And in 'Understanding the foundation stage':

> *In the Foundation Stage teachers have flexibility to interpret the programmes to suit the needs, interests and abilities of the children. Throughout the Foundation Stage children need to be observed closely so that:*
>
> - *teaching builds from the children's current stage of development;*
> - *children's needs and interests lead the learning;*
> - *appropriate support can be given to those children who require it;*
> - *children are motivated and their learning challenged;*
> - *children have high expectations of themselves.*

> (CCEA; Northern Ireland; 2006)

Key guidance documents for countries in the UK

DfE, (2014) 'Statutory Framework for the Early Years Foundation Stage'.
Welsh Assembly Government, (2015) 'Foundation Phase Framework'.
CCEA, (2006) 'Northern Ireland Curriculum: Understanding the Foundation Stage'.
Learning and Teaching Scotland, (2010) 'Pre-birth to three'.

Things to think about

- Have you ever thought about your own intelligences? Is your collection of intelligences likely to give you a 'focused laser intelligence' or a broader 'searchlight intelligence'? Just search for Multiple Intelligences questionnaire and you will find lots of examples. Just remember, it's just a questionnaire, not a scientific exercise!

- Have you looked systematically at the children in your group to try to find out what their unique collection of intelligences might be?

- Does a child's collection of intelligences sometimes frustrate them, or you?

- Some people have been influenced by pressure from parents or teachers to follow their dominant intelligence and ended up in a job they didn't enjoy. This might result in a young person becoming an accountant when they would really like to be an opera singer. Do you know anyone like this?

- In your future career, how well do you think you will cope with the continuing changes in research and advice on teaching and learning?

Arnold Gesell

Full name: Arnold Gesell

Born: 1880

Died: 1961

Place of birth: Alma, Wisconsin, United States

Countries of residence: United States

What he did: Gesell's pioneering work was in observing the developing child, both those of normal abilities and those with disabilities and learning difficulties. The Gessel Development Schedule which was published in 1925 was very helpful in setting out child development in stages, and proved a breakthrough in infant ability testing, even though it was based on observation.

Influences on education today: Gessell's work was influential in reinforcing the notion of tracking children's development through stages related to age. This has underpinned the early years curriculum which now contains overlapping stages of development, which practitioners use to assess and report on progress and attainment.

Theories and areas of work : Developmental psychology

Key influencers and followers: Frances Ilg, Jean Piaget

Key works: *Infant and Child in the Culture of Today* (1943), *The Child from Five to Ten* (1946)

The child's personality is a product of slow gradual growth. His nervous system matures by stages and natural sequences. All of his abilities, including his morals, are subject to laws of growth. The task of childcare is not to force him into a predetermined pattern but to guide his growth.

> Arnold Gesell Infant and Child in the Culture of Today – The Guidance of
> Development in Home and Nursery School, 1975

Life, love, theory and research

Arnold Gesell was born in a village in Wisconsin, America, the eldest of five children and son of a photographer and a teacher. His earliest experiences of observation were when he observed his siblings during their early days in the small town where they lived. He studied history and psychology at the University of Wisconsin, graduating with a degree in philosophy in 1903.

He started his working life as a teacher, and became a principal of a high school before re-entering university to study psychology and child development. His experience in teaching and in visiting schools for children with learning difficulties and disabilities qualified him well for his later work in child psychology.

In 1911, he was appointed an Assistant Professor of Education at Yale, where he established the Yale Psycho-Clinic (later the Clinic of Child Development), and served as the director of the clinic from 1911 until 1948. This clinic became the main centre in the United States for the study of child behaviour, and there Gesell conducted numerous studies and developed the theories for which he became famous.

He was initially interested in the development of children with disabilities, particularly with Down's syndrome and cerebral palsy. However, he realised that he could not continue his work without research into the development of 'normal' children but prior to the early 20th century, scientific observations of children were not common so he set about collecting the information himself. In this research, keen to be as unobtrusive as possible, Gesell used the most up-to-date methods of photography and video to observe young children without interrupting their play. These included using one-way mirrors and a specially developed one-way mirrored dome.

Gesell's detailed observations, particularly of children under five, provided a wealth of new information. Working at the beginning of the 20th century, he observed a large number of children and documented patterns in the way these children developed. He collected enough information to be convinced that all children go through the same developmental stages, although individuals may go through these stages at different rates.

Gesell is best known for his work on child development. From 1923 to his death, he wrote and published many books, some of which were turned into films, and most focused on the development of early childhood. In 1925, he published his work on developmental stages – *The Gesell Developmental Schedule* – which set out a series of stages through which every child would pass. It was based on a longitudinal study, exploring the various stages of development and how they unfolded over time. Two child rearing guides, *Infant and Child in the Culture of Today* published in 1943, and *The Child from Five to Ten* published in 1946, were popular with parents and practitioners alike.

Gesell defined internal and external factors that he believed affect children's intellectual and physical progress. The internal influences included genetics, temperament, personality, learning styles and physical and mental growth. However, there were also some external factors that Gesell thought affected development. These included the environment of childhood, family background, parenting styles, cultural influences, health conditions and early experiences with peers and adults.

This work was influential because in this thorough work of studying stages of develop-ment Gessel had carried out observations in a field of research that had never been explored before. He was also the first researcher to demonstrate that chronological age and developmental age could be different:

> *The Gesell Developmental Observation-Revised (GDO-R) is a comprehensive multi-dimensional assessment system that assists educators, and other professionals in understanding characteristics of child behavior in relation to typical growth patterns between 2½ to 9 years of age.*
>
> (www.gesellinstitute.org)

At the time, the Gesell Developmental Schedule was a breakthrough in infant ability testing and Gesell's scales are still used today. They are one of the oldest and most well-used intelligence measures for young children and form the 'normative approach': establishing 'normal' stages or milestones in development. The results of the test are expressed first as developmental age (DA), which is then converted into developmental quotient (DQ). The assessment shows whether the child is above, below or at the expected level for their chronological age. He established developmental milestones in ten major areas:

- motor characteristics
- personal hygiene
- emotional expression
- fears and dreams
- self and sex
- interpersonal relations
- play and pastimes
- school life
- ethical sense
- philosophic outlook.

Gesell established normative trends for four areas of growth and development, which were covered in the schedule:

1 Motor
2 Adaptive (cognitive)
3 Language
4 Personal-social behaviour.

The scales, based in observation, give a result – called the Gesell Developmental Observation (GDO).

Gesell's theory of development was known as a maturational-developmental theory. It was ground-breaking work and was the first in a long line of such investigations.

Arnold Gesell

Observing and identifying the stages that children went through as they developed became a serious occupation for psychologists and paediatricians, influencing both those who study 'normal' development, and those who work with children with disabilities and learning difficulties.

The six-month stages that Gesell outlined were predictable and could be used to monitor the progress of any child, even from before birth. He used the concept of a spiral to illustrate his thinking, with each cycle of the spiral encompassing the time it takes to move through six stages, (half-year increments of development).

These six-month stages were named by Gesell as:

- Smooth (0–6 months)

- Break-up (6–12 months)

- Sorting out (12–18 months)

- Inwardising (18–24 months)

- Expansion (24–30 months)

- Neurotic 'fitting together' (30–36 months).

He maintained that children passed through these cycles more quickly than adults, with the rate slowing down as the individual aged.

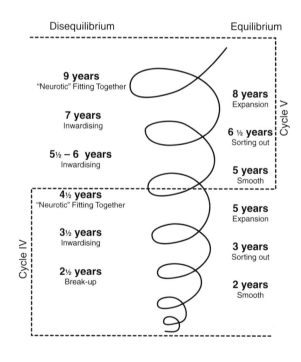

Overall , Gesell made a huge contribution to our knowledge of child development, both in the way he collected information and in the way he enabled the process to be used by professionals other than researchers.

Gesell's scales, although widely used until very recently, were finally considered to have psychometric weaknesses, and the assessments were replaced in 2012 by a new version, called the Gesell Developmental Observation-Revised for ages two and a half to nine years. This assessment is even more comprehensive in its evidence base and construction – the research base for the new schedule involved the observation and assessment of 1,300 children aged from two years nine months to six years three months, and included a sample of public, private, urban and suburban schools; 55 sites in all, spanning 23 US states. The assessment can be used to monitor the progress of children from three and a half to nine years of age, giving a grading of either 'age appropriate', 'emerging', or 'concern' for each area, and a developmental age.

Legacy and impact

During his lifetime, Gesell contributed to the nature/nurture debate by emphasising the influence of both, and said that there was much more complexity to identifying special needs than simple genetics or the influence of the environment. His observations and the Gesell Developmental Schedules have had an enormous effect on the study of child development and how this affects the way children learn, not only those in the 'normal' group but those with disabilities and learning difficulties.

His views of parenting were also influential. He maintained that children who experienced 'reasonable guidance' were more likely to become stable adults. He believed that the balance between control and freedom should be carefully managed by parents and teachers to ensure that there is neither strict control nor excessive freedom. His work and ideas on the best way to raise and educate children were very influential across the fields of research in child psychology, education and child rearing.

However, Gesell's work was criticised on several grounds. One was that he only used white, middle-class parents and children for his subjects, thus decreasing the validity of his studies. He was also accused of ignoring individual and cultural differences in growth patterns, for instance in cultures where the left hand is used exclusively for sanitary purposes.

In time, the following of Gesell's ideas gave way to theories that stressed the importance of environmental rather than internal elements in child development, as the ideas of Jerome S. Bruner and Jean Piaget gained prominence. However, Gessel's suggested stages of development have been influential, especially in England, where the early years curriculum is structured in six-month stages which match Gessel's, although it is emphasised that the borders must be considered to be 'permeable'.

Influences on early years practice across the UK

Gesell's work in defining stages of child development and the wealth of observations which underpinned these have been one of the greatest influences in the structures of early education. He was also one of the first psychologists to argue for universal nursery education in the USA and his assessment schedules were internationally respected.

England

When assessing the developmental progress of children, there is still an emphasis on the use of six-month developmental milestones or stages in development, with a consistent note of caution that expected levels should not be taken as essential steps for individuals. In the 'Development Matters in the EYFS' guidance for England, every page has the following footnote:

> *Children develop at their own rates, and in their own ways. The development statements and their order should not be taken as necessary steps for individual children. They should not be used as checklists. The age/stage bands overlap because these are not fixed age boundaries but suggest a typical range of development.*

> (Early Education; 2012)

Practitioners, teachers and parents have always been keen to know whether children are at the expected stage for their age, and how to identify where problems exist for individuals with Additional Needs. In different countries, this process is tackled in different ways. For instance, in England, practitioners are provided with a set of indicators across all areas of learning, which are structured in broad age ranges for use in assessment and planning, but practitioners are cautioned that they should use these as a 'best fit' model, rather than an observation schedule:

> *Development Matters might be used by early years settings throughout the EYFS as a guide to making best-fit judgements about whether a child is showing typical development for their age, may be at risk of delay or is ahead for their age. Summative assessment supports information sharing with parents, colleagues and other settings.*

> (Early Education, 2012)

Where a child's development raises cause for concern, practitioners are advised to refer to additional documentation such as the 'SEND Code of Practice' either at the two year old check or at the end of the Foundation Stage:

In assessing progress of children in the early years, practitioners can use the non-statutory Early Years Outcomes guidance as a tool to assess the extent to which a young child is developing at expected levels for their age. The guidance sets out what most children do at each stage of their learning and development. These include typical behaviours across the seven areas of learning.

(DfE/DoH, 2015)

Wales

In Wales practitioners are advised that, as in Gesell's work, they should avoid focusing solely on age-related outcomes but should look at developmental stages, as specified in the 'Foundation Phase Framework':

Throughout their formative years, children's learning develops more rapidly than at any other time…Children should move on to the next stages of their learning when they are developmentally ready and at their own pace.

(Welsh Assembly Government, 2015)

However the 'Foundation phase child development assessment profile' for Wales states that practitioners should refer to the 'Descriptions of Behaviour', which are age related in broad bands, very like those used in England. However, the Welsh document provides practitioners with much more detailed examples of observational assessment and advice on how to use the Descriptions on entry and throughout the Foundation Phase:

The Descriptions of Behaviour, which comprise each Developmental Area, are made up of seven steps that span the developmental age equivalents of 18 to 84 months. The upward and downward extension is necessary to cater for children who may be at an early stage of their development and also for those who are more able.

(Welsh Government, 2011)

For children with emerging special needs, practitioners are advised in the 'Foundation phase profile handbook':

However, it is not the intention that the profile will have sufficient detail to fully assess SEN or ALN children. While the lower steps support very early stages in children's development they reflect developmental norms and emergent skills.

(Welsh Government, 2015)

Arnold Gesell

There is still a heavy reliance on age or stage related norms and even where there are warnings to be cautious and include additional information, there is an ever-present pressure to make simplistic judgements. This is particularly the case where adult child ratios result in heavy assessment loads, and these are compounded by government imperatives and inspection pressures resulting in requests for information in simple single numbers, rather than the richer information contained in Learning Stories, or observations.

Key guidance documents for countries in the UK

Early Education, (2012) 'Development Matters in the EYFS'.

DfE/DoH, (2015) 'SEND Code of Practice'.

Welsh Assembly Government, (2015) 'Foundation Phase Framework'.

Welsh Assembly Government, (2015) 'Foundation Phase Child Development Assessment Profile'.

Welsh Assembly Government, (2015) 'Foundation Phase Profile Handbook'.

Things to think about

- How do you use age or stage related statements to track and report on children's progress and achievements in your setting?

- How much time do you spend observing children? Is this long enough?

- If the stage related statements are not suitable for assessing children with additional needs, what would you suggest?

- How could you ensure that the hard work put into collecting observation evidence is incorporated into children's reports and transfer records?

- How much practice have you had in observing and assessing children's developmental stage? Is this easy to do? What would make it easier for you to be accurate?

Daniel Goleman (1946–)

Full name: Daniel Goleman

Born: 1946 (still living)

Place of birth: Stockton, California, United States

Countries of residence: United States

What he did: Goleman introduced the general public to the concept of Emotional Intelligence (EI), and the Emotional Intelligence Quotient (EQ), as things that should be considered in addition to Intellectual Intelligence and Intelligence Quotient (IQ).

Influences on education today: The concept of Emotional Intelligence has really resonated with teachers, and many schools and settings have initiated work with children which helps them to become more emotionally intelligent. This aspect of development is usually incorporated within Personal, Social and Emotional Development.

Theories and areas of work : Humanism, Psychology, Neuroscience

Key influencers and followers: Howard Gardner

Key works: *Emotional Intelligence* (1995), *The Brain and Emotional Intelligence; New Insights* (2011)

Emotional Intelligence begins to develop in the earliest years. All the small exchanges children have with their parents, teachers, and with each other carry emotional messages.
   Daniel Goleman, Emotional Intelligence: Why it Can Matter More Than IQ, 1996

Life, love, theory and research

Daniel Goleman is a psychologist, writer and son of university professors, who was born and has spent the majority of his working life in the United States. He has also lived in India, which gave him the inspiration for his first book about the Indian sub-continent. Following a university career at Amhurst and Berkeley Universities, he won a scholarship to Harvard where he studied psychology.

The concept of Emotional Intelligence was first explored in the 1960s by Michael Beldoch in *Communication of Emotional Meaning* (1976), but the concept of Emotional Quotient appears to have been first used by Keith Beasley in a 1987 article in the Mensa Magazine. However, Goleman was the first to bring the concept to the attention of the general public in his book *Emotional Intelligence – Why it can matter more than intelligence (1955)*.

When Emotional Intelligence began to attract the public attention, there were a few model programmes outside the United States, of which, two were described in Goleman's book. As the benefits of Emotional Intelligence have become more widely recognised and investigated, several new strategies have been designed to assist schools and practitioners to focus on Emotional Intelligence. Schools in many countries have implemented programmes to raise the profile of Emotional Intelligence, and they report good results.

Alongside these programmes and projects, there has been careful collection of data referring to their success. These have included reports of improved educational outcomes for up to 50% of the pupils, lower incidence of unacceptable behaviour, 44% fewer suspensions, rising attendance rates and 60% of pupils showing more positive behaviour. These would be remarkable results for any programme. In these settings and schools, adults and children can function at their best, managing their inner and exterior lives without pressure, leaving them more space for others, not just children, but parents and colleagues.

Goleman is now known worldwide for his subsequent writing and lecturing on Emotional Intelligence, following the publication of this book which remained on the New York Times bestseller list for 18 months. At the heart of his work on Emotional Intelligence (EI), or Emotional Quotient (EQ) is his conviction that non-cognitive skills matter as much, if not more than IQ, both in work and business leadership. He followed the success of *Emotional Intelligence* with another title, *Social Intelligence*, which examines the power of human relations. More recently he has worked on combining information from all his previous books with material from leadership programmes at Yale University.

Goleman's central theme is that, in order to understand and make connections with others, we must be able to empathise not just sympathise with them. Knowing how others are feeling, not just what they are saying or doing, or what their faces tell us, is not enough – we must be able to climb into their skin to really understand their inner feelings.

The elements of Emotional Intelligence identified by Goleman are:

Self-awareness – the ability to know one's own emotions, strengths, weaknesses, drives, values and goals and recognise their impact on others also using gut feelings to guide decisions

Self-regulation – controlling or redirecting one's disruptive emotions and impulses, and adapting to changing circumstances

Social skill – managing relationships to move people in a desired direction

Empathy – considering other people's feelings especially when making decisions

Motivation – being driven to achieve for the sake of achievement.

These are the elements that have been used in most of the Emotional Intelligence programmes now in place throughout the world.

According to Goleman and educators who follow his theories, EI (the most common abbreviation of Emotional Intelligences in the UK) also helps children to be more resilient and to recognise and remember the places and people who enabled them to feel such a sense of safety. However, Goleman emphasises it is not only the support of one teacher that makes the difference, the feeling of security comes when everyone in the school or setting is able to support the development of EI. In such settings children are able to take 'safe risks' with their emotions and relationships. It is also vital that the managers in these settings or schools also care about their staff so they in turn can feel safe, take risks, innovate and empathise with the children.

Empathetic concern, Goleman believes, is the best basis for a caring classroom. In such a classroom, the teacher models kindness and concern for her pupils and they embody this concern for their classmates. Such a classroom, he maintains, is the best place for learning – a warm and supportive atmosphere, with a feeling of security and closeness, somewhere safe and connected. In such a place, children's brains can flourish and they feel safe enough to reach out and understand others. Children suffering abuse, neglect or deprivation outside school will usually thrive in such a setting.

Goleman's more recent involvement in the Life and Mind Institute has enabled him to be involved in many projects with educators and researchers who are trying to identify the essential ingredients of EI and put them in a curriculum, initially for younger children (first and second grades in the United States (six to either year olds) before rolling this out to other age ranges. An example of this work is 'Just like me' where children think about the joys and pains of their lives and then share these with other children, possibly from different backgrounds, helping to reduce negative stereotyping, racism or bullying.

EQ continues to be a growing initiative as results show improvements in cognitive standards and there appears to be more evidence that children's personal development and positive behaviours continue to rise. It is not only the behaviour and academic improvements that have surprised researchers. There is now evidence of a change in brain functioning through EQ programmes. Children in elementary (primary) schools are showing a marked improvement in attention skills and working memory, demonstrating a possible change to the part of the brain that controls these impulses, the pre-frontal cortex. This effect, known as neuroplasticity, means that the children's brains may be changing their physical structure in response to the positive effects of EQ programmes. However, there have been criticisms of the methodology of collecting data on improvements through EQ programmes and more research needs to be undertaken to underpin the claims.

At the heart of Goleman's work on Emotional Intelligence (EI) or emotional quotient (EQ) is his conviction that non-cognitive skills also matter as much, if not more than IQ, both in work and business leadership. He has followed the success of Emotional Intelligence who another title, Social Intelligence, which examines the power of human relations. The concept of EQ testing has not replaced the IQ (intelligence quotient) testing as a measure of intelligence but there is a general feeling that simple IQ testing may not be enough to encompass the whole individual. Goleman's central theme is that in order to understand and make connections with others, we must be able to empathise not just sympathise with them. It is also important to understand that our emotions affect our thinking, possibly more than we currently realise.

The more recent focus of Goleman's work has expanded to include work in business management, following research that appears to show that improving Emotional Intelligence has a good effect on interpersonal relationships in school, at home and at work, and leads to better academic achievements.

He has contributed to the work of the Yale Child Studies Centre, and Chicago University, with a focus on collecting information and research about Emotional Quotient (EQ) from across the world and supporting schools in incorporating EQ/EI work into the curriculum. He has worked most recently at Rutgers University, where he is continuing his investigation into the application of Emotional Intelligence. Goleman is also co-founder of the Collaborative for Academic, Social, and Emotional Learning (www.casel.org) which is involved in identifying evidence based initiatives in emotional literacy to schools across the world.

There has been some continuing criticism of Goleman's work, particularly of his use of 'intelligence' to describe this area of work. In *Intelligence, a New Look*, (2000) Eysenck wrote that attributing the word 'intelligence' to any new behaviour was unfounded in scientific evidence or in fact – and maintained that Goleman's theory was based 'on quicksand'.

Legacy and impact

In 2005, The Association of Teachers and Lecturers in the UK looked into Emotional Intelligence and reported in 'An intelligent look at Emotional Intelligence' that they had less confidence in the published results, particularly the evidence provided for programmes in the United States which was weaker than that provided in the UK, as it was based on 'enthusiastic anecdotes' and lacked a statistical basis.

Among these were the lack of control groups, no evidence that the impact of the programme lasts into the future or into real life, even that statistically significant effects are often disappointingly small in size and subject to the 'Hawthorne effect' – in which improvements are due solely to a novelty effect and teacher enthusiasm.

However, the ATL Report concludes on a more positive note, which reinstates the position of Emotional Intelligence work. They welcome the interest among teachers in Emotional Intelligence which has a chance of countering the problems of the school curriculum, which they say has been '…focused, traditionally, on the desiccated certainties of text-book academia', and recognising that emotionally stupid people can do 'cruel and destructive things'. (ATL, 2005)

Goleman's work has provided a real opportunity for schools and settings (and the business world) to recognise and celebrate the importance of emotional education, and this recognition has extended to the British government where a recent document called 'Promoting children and young people's emotional health and wellbeing' states:

> …head teachers, governors and teachers should demonstrate a commitment to the social and emotional wellbeing of young people…by ensuring social and emotional wellbeing features within improvement plans, policies, systems and activities.
>
> (Public Health England, 2015)

The document gives clear guidance to primary and secondary schools in the specifics of provision which are now included in Ofsted inspection schedules in England.

Goleman is the person whose name is usually associated with Emotional Intelligence, particularly in education, but others preceded his work and there are many who have followed his theories. More recently John Mayer and Peter Salovey, American psychologists, became involved in the way that EI could support teachers and pupils in schools. They believe that Emotional Intelligence is a subset of social intelligence and is about a person's ability to:

- perceive emotion in oneself and others
- integrate emotion into thought
- understand emotion in oneself and others
- manage or regulate emotion in oneself and others.

They redefined Emotional Intelligence as: '…the capacity to reason about emotions, and of emotions, to enhance thinking.' (Salovey, et.al. 2004)

Mayer and Salovey have also been influenced by recent discoveries in neuroscience, where scientists have been able to identify the emotional centres in the brain and how they are different from the parts of the brain (the neocortex) where thinking and learning are processed. Most scientists now believe that Emotional Intelligence has far more influence on our behaviour and our success in life than has ever been thought before.

Salovey and Mayer continue to research and add to their database of international research on the effect of Emotional Intelligence which they maintain has such a huge effect on what makes us human. They are also working on refining measures to test levels of Emotional Intelligence in children and adults and whether it can be improved or altered. The most recent (the Mayer-Salovey-Caruso Emotional Intelligence Test), is based on standard IQ tests, giving an emotional 'score' through specially developed versions of traditional tests. A disadvantage of this test is that it does not give 'right or wrong' answers. Responses are compared with large, international samples from across the world.

These psychologists recognise the huge effect that Goleman's book had in popularising the concept of Emotional Intelligence, but maintain that some of his claims about the nature of Emotional Intelligence and its influence were premature and exaggerated.

In the UK, proponents have tended to use the term 'Emotional Literacy' rather than 'Emotional Intelligence', and their work has been focused on the difference between two very important components of success in learning:

- Self-esteem – the child's perception of their own usefulness and value in school and the outside world

- Emotional Literacy – the child's ability to know and manage their own feelings and to recognise the feelings of others.

In each of the four countries in the UK there have been initiatives which pick up on the work of Goleman, and of Salovey and Mayer. In England, Southampton was the first Local Authority to use Emotional Intelligence as a way to address anger management. The success of this scheme led to an extension of the programme to other areas of EI such as social skills and self-esteem, and to school staff, including lunchtime supervisors. Schools nationwide followed, integrating elements of EI into their curriculum, and in 2003 (for primary schools), and 2005 (for secondary schools) government funded schemes were implemented to support the development of personal and social education using the principles of Goleman's book.

The Primary Behaviour and Attendance Strategy pilot was implemented in 25 Local Authorities as part of a key priority within the Primary National Strategy to promote positive behaviour and full attendance. Six Local Authorities, and 54 secondary schools were selected to take part in the secondary school pilot named Social, Emotional and Behavioural Skills (SEBS). This project took the five key concepts of Goleman's work and provided resources and training for use with eleven and twelve year old pupils. In the evaluation of the pilot for this initiative, one consultant felt that it had helped make a link between emotional wellbeing and learning, 'there is now a more accepted link between academic achievement and emotional wellbeing…it is much clearer and believed'. (Public Health England, 2014)

The project was linked with the Secondary SEAL (Social and Emotional Aspects of Learning) programme, and with the Healthy Schools Initiative, and although elements of these still exist in many secondary schools, changes of government and particularly changes in the management of secondary schools due to the implementation of Academy status in England have combined to make it unlikely that such programmes will be reinstated in the future, unless individual schools or groups of schools decide to do so.

In Scotland, there is information for teachers on the Government research website The Journey to Excellence (www.journeytoexcellence.org.uk), and the Scottish Government encourages schools to consider using the principles of EI when discussing improvements to support for children with emotional and behavioural difficulties. A recent initiative, The Emote Project (gaips.inesc-id.pt/emote) connects schools across the Economic Union in exploring how learning with robots can improve Emotional Intelligence, as children from 11–13 play games in which their companion is a robot who shifts 'between guided and exploratory learning'.

The Charity Family Links UK (familylinks.org.uk) has taken over some of the role of disseminating information on wellbeing and Emotional Intelligence, by linking parents and teachers to the work of Carol Dweck, Goleman and a range of schools and individuals who have been involved in this work.

EI projects are not confined to schools; their effectiveness in exploring emotions has been used in social work, health and community projects. Evaluation of all available information about the effectiveness of EI projects has been done and the results are impressive.

'It (EI) should not be in addition to learning. It's central to learning', says James Park, director of Antidote (www.antidote.org.uk), an organisation set up in 1997 to campaign for wider understanding and practice of Emotional Literacy.

As reported above, EI has not been without its critics – an article in the Times Educational Supplement asked whether the initiative was – 'Touchy-feely mumbo-jumbo or a revolution in our schools? Common sense or neuroscience?' (TES, 11 May 2008). Educators and others who believe in the benefits of Emotional Intelligence will say it can boost health and happiness, tackle challenging behaviour and improve academic performance. Critics suggest it's just a fad.

Influences on early years practice across the UK

The four component countries of the UK put a heavy emphasis on Personal, Social and Emotional Development in the early years, agreeing that it is one of the most important aspects of education for children before and during statutory schooling. This area of learning is the home of development in Emotional Intelligence and it is good to find that it has high status in each of the countries' documentation, and is described in ways that show sensitivity to the development of EI, although there is little direct reference to Goleman's work.

England

Within the 'Statutory Framework for the Early Years Foundation Stage' in England, Personal, Social and Emotional Development is, along with Communication and Language, one of the three prime areas of learning, with three aspects:

Personal, social and emotional development involves helping children to develop a positive sense of themselves, and others; to form positive relationships and develop respect for others; to develop social skills and learn how to manage their feelings; to understand appropriate behaviour in groups; and to have confidence in their own abilities.

The aspects are:

- *Self-confidence and self-awareness:*

- *Managing feelings and behaviour:*

- *Making relationships.*

(DfE, 2014)

Wales

In Wales, the area of learning is called Personal and Social Development and Cultural Diversity, and includes Personal Development, Social Development, Moral and Spiritual Development, and Wellbeing. The area is promoted in a separate booklet, as well as within the whole curriculum document. The booklet called 'Personal and social development, well-being and cultural diversity' contains the following statement, which echoes Goleman's work on Emotional Intelligence:

Personal and Social Development, Well-being and Cultural Diversity is at the heart of the Foundation Phase and children's skills are developed across all Areas of Learning through participation in experiential learning activities indoors and outdoors.

(Welsh Assembly Government, 2008)

The two core components of this area of the curriculum are:

Personal Understanding and Health (understanding themselves)

Mutual Understanding in the Local and Wider Community (relationships with others, including family and friends)

(Welsh Assembly Government, 2008)

Scotland

In Scotland, the 'Curriculum for excellence' describes Emotional Well-being as:

Health and wellbeing includes experiences and outcomes for personal and social development, understanding of health, physical education and physical activity, and elements of home economics.

(Scottish Government, 2006)

Scotland's curriculum documents apply to the whole statutory age range from 3–18, so the curriculum statements are broad but they do also include a description of the teachers' role in PSHE:

Learning through health and wellbeing promotes confidence, independent thinking and positive attitudes and dispositions. Because of this, it is the responsibility of every teacher to contribute to learning and development in this area.

(Scottish Government, 2006)

Northern Ireland

In Northern Ireland, in 'Understanding the foundation stage', Personal Development is described as:

Personal Development and Mutual Understanding, including Personal Understanding and Health and Mutual Understanding in the Local and Wider Community.

(CCEA, Northern Ireland, 2006)

And in the Primary Years, Personal and Mutual Understanding is included in the whole curriculum aims and described as:

Personal Development and Mutual Understanding (focusing on emotional development, social skills, learning to learn, health, relationships and sexuality education and mutual understanding in the local and global community).

(CCEA; Northern Ireland, 2007)

All four countries have responded in different ways to the complex issues around PSHE and EI. Only time will tell whether one is more effective than the others although it would seem sensible to look at those programmes where there is rigorous research into effectiveness.

In the curriculum for Scotland 'Building the Curriculum 2 (3–18)', there is a statement which sums up the whole intention for personal and social development across the UK:

Developing confident individuals

If children and young people are healthy and emotionally secure they will be more able to develop the capacity to live a full life. With a sense of wellbeing they will be better able to deal with the unexpected and cope with adversity. This sense of wellbeing encompasses many aspects including resilience, fitness, confidence, a sense of mastery and control, optimism and hope, and the ability to sustain satisfying personal relationships.

(Scottish Executive, 2006)

Emotional and Social Development are now recognised as key components in the curriculum but in the best early years settings they are woven throughout the day, the week and the year, in a way that makes them the bedrock of education. It is unfortunate that as children grow older, in most schools this cross curricular concept is increasingly seen as a 'subject', often delivered through external programmes in timetabled lessons.

Key guidance documents for countries in the UK

DfE, (2014) 'Statutory Framework for the Early Years Foundation Stage'.
Welsh Assembly Government (2008) 'Personal and Social Development, Well-being and Cultural Diversity'.
Scottish Government, (2006) 'Curriculum for Excellence'.
CCEA, (2006) 'Northern Ireland Curriculum: Understanding the Foundation Stage'.
Scottish Executive (2006) 'Building the Curriculum 2 (3–18): The contribution of the curriculum areas'.

Things to think about

- How much time do you spend on activities which encourage Emotional Intelligence?
- Do you have a programme or a policy for promoting PSED in your school or setting? Do you know what it contains? How do you make sure that new staff know about this advice?
- Have you ever used the SEAL resources for the Foundation Stage? Although these have been available for some time, and the present government is not promoting them, they are still available on the Internet, and the box of resources was sent to every school.
- Do you think children today are emotionally resilient? Why do you think that is?

Susan Isaacs

Full name: Susan Isaacs

Born: 1885

Died: 1948

Place of birth: Turton, Lancashire, England

Countries of residence: England

What she did: Isaacs extended the nursery education movement. The current high quality provision for early years education across the UK, would probably not exist were it not for the work of strong women, among them Susan Isaacs.

Influences on education today: The current emphasis on independence, and supporting independent learning is one of the most important legacies of Susan Isaacs. She has also been a major influence on the expansion of early years education in the UK and across the developed world, particularly for children from deprived backgrounds.

Theories and areas of work: Educational psychology, Psychiatry

Key influencers and followers: Jean Piaget, Sigmund Freud, Friedrich Fröebel, John Dewey

Key works: *Nursery Years* (1929), *Troubles of Children and Parents* (1948).

…play has the greatest value for the young child when it is really free and his own;
   Susan Isaacs, The Nursery Years: The mind of the child from birth to sixth years, 1971

Life, love, theory and research

Susan Isaacs, was born in Lancashire, England, where she lived with her father after her mother died when Susan was six. She left school early, spent some time abroad as a governess and then returned to England to teach. However, she had no qualifications so she enrolled on a teaching course for non-graduates and followed this by gaining a degree in philosophy, then training in psychoanalysis.

She then spent her working life as an educational psychologist, psychoanalyst and educator promoting the Nursery School movement alongside her work in psychoanalysis. Her published work emphasises the importance of independence which she maintained was the best way for children to learn. The most effective way for this to happen was through play, with the adult as guides.

In 1924, Isaacs was appointed as the head of an experimental school called Malting House School in Cambridge where she made extensive observations of children during her three years as head of the school. The children attending the school were aged from two to seven years old and were generally from more affluent families. At Malting House School, they were given freedom. They were encouraged rather than corrected or punished and they were helped by staff to be as independent as possible. The teachers were encouraged to observe the children closely and Isaacs referred to the children as her research workers. Adults were provided with a record card for each child where they could note significant events and behaviours, building up a picture of the child over time. By listening to and playing with the children, the adults could enter their world and be familiar with the things that were important to them.

The environment at Malting House School would be very familiar to practitioners today, with blocks, role play areas, books, beads, dressing up clothes and access to plenty of materials for creativity. Outside was a garden, with one of the first climbing frames for children of this age, a sand pit, tool shed and place for gardening. The children were regularly taken on local walks and visits, usually following their interests. One feature that encouraged independence was the opportunity to leave constructions and other games without pressure to 'tidy up', and children could return to these activities over long periods. Isaacs felt that this encouraged not just independence, but persistence and powers of attention. The children took responsibility for planning snack and mealtimes, setting tables, clearing everything away afterwards and washing up.

Isaacs was a devotee of the importance of play to children's education. She saw play as the vehicle for releasing anxieties, replaying experiences and coming to an understanding of the behaviour and actions of others. Play was the 'breath of life to the child, since it is through play activities that he finds mental ease, and can work upon his wishes, fears and fantasies so as to integrate them into a living personality (Isaccs, 1951). Nursery school experience could bring opportunities for social interaction and collaborative play, which was not always possible in children's own homes.

Despite the emphasis on independence and responsibility, the role of the adult was a key component at Malting House School. She believed that children needed to project their feelings and experiences onto their environment and on the people within it, including the adults. Practitioners should take the place of the parent and 'help them to be good'. The adults should also demonstrate good behaviour and set clear boundaries for their own and the children's behaviour.

Isaacs followed and promoted the work of Jean Piaget and Sigmund Freud and expanded on the work of Friedrich Fröebel and Dewey, but her initial enthusiasm for Piaget's work was later moderated by her criticism of his schemas and stages of development as, unlike in her research, he had not collected his information from children playing in a natural environment.

Isaacs' influence on early education has been significant, particularly in ensuring that play is at the centre of provision. Being a strong supporter of play as children's work, she was particularly interested in the way that fantasy and imaginative play could enrich learning, and in the role of social interaction in play. In both these aspects, children could express and develop their feelings. Her book *Intellectual Growth in Young Children* explained her views on imaginative play and contains the following:

> *What imaginative play does, in the first place is to create practical situations which may often then be pursued for their own sake, and this leads on to actual discovery or to verbal judgment and reasoning.*

(Isaacs, 1951)

However, she was not in favour of complete freedom or uncontrolled self-expression and emphasised that the adult, although primarily a guide in children's learning, should also set the standards for behaviour which she described as being the 'good/strict' parent.

Between 1929 and 1940 she was the 'agony aunt' for several English child care magazines, responding to readers' problems with advice for parents and practitioners on a range of early childhood issues.

In 1933 Isaacs became the first head of the University of London School of Education (now the Institute of Education) where she developed courses for practitioners working with young children. These focused on the need for adults to encourage independence and learning through play, although she always believed that parents are the child's first teachers. She was one of the first psychologists to integrate theory on child development with child-rearing and education, making these accessible to both practitioners and parents.

Isaacs had a real passion for education and her contribution came at a time when there was an interest in the difference that high quality early education could make to children's lives. She believed that attending nursery school should be a normal part of every child's early years – a place that mirrored home life while offering exciting new ideas and activities in the company of other young children, and that '*nursery school is an extension of the function of the home, not a substitute for it*' (Isaacs, 1952). The social benefits of nursery attendance were also seen as very important to her philosophy, and vital for children's development.

Isaacs died from cancer in 1948, at the age of 63.

Legacy and impact

Although she was working nearly a hundred years ago, Isaacs' methodology, and particularly the practical demonstration of her theories that she gave at The Malting House School feel very familiar to practitioners today. Her devotion to the power of play, her emphasis on independent learning, even the activities and resources she developed would fit in well in most early years settings at the beginning of the 21st century. Her use of indoor and outdoor spaces, her emphasis on role-play and creativity, and the central place of social development have all been incorporated into good early childhood education practice across the world.

The environment at the Malting House School contained elements that have now become permanent features of high-quality provision. Child-sized furniture, purpose built outdoor play equipment, a commitment to gardening and growing and a place for long-term projects remain ideals for modern provision.

Isaacs also raised the image of the early years practitioner to a new level, not just a minder of children, but a conscientious professional, observing and responding to children's needs. Her attention to the detail of the practitioner's role as observer, planner and supporter of children's learning is a model we still aspire to, and her expectation of meticulous record-keeping would delight the most diligent inspector!

Without her thorough and extensive work in collecting and presenting information based securely in practice we would not have an agreement, at least in principle, on the central themes of early education – freedom, independence and a focus on children's ability to make imaginary worlds where they can explore their feelings through play.

Influences on early years practice across the UK

Isaacs' influence on early education spreads beyond the provision of play and her model of nursery schooling has had a significant effect on the current curriculum documentation across the UK. As seen below, play is a central feature, highly valued for its contribution to learning.

England

In the 'Statutory Framework for the Early Years Foundation Stage', play is seen as central, and should be both planned and purposeful:

> *Play is essential for children's development, building their confidence as they learn to explore, to think about problems, and relate to others. Children learn by leading their own play, and by taking part in play which is guided by adults.*
>
> (DfE, 2014)

Wales

The documentation for Wales, the 'Foundation Phase Framework' contains the following commitment to the power of play in supporting learning, as a serious and demanding activity:

*Children learn through first-hand experiential activities with the serious business of 'play'
providing the vehicle. Through their play, children practise and consolidate their learning, play
with ideas, experiment, take risks, solve problems, and make decisions individually, in small and
in large groups.*

And

*For children, play can be (and often is) a very serious business. It needs concentrated attention.
It is about children learning through perseverance, attention to detail, and concentration –
characteristics usually associated with work. Play is not only crucial to the way children become
self-aware and the way in which they learn the rules of social behaviour; it is also fundamental to
intellectual development.*

(Welsh Assembly Government, 2015)

Scotland

In Scotland, the commitment to play, both child-initiated and planned by practitioners,
where the adults are available to support and extend their play is detailed in 'A Curriculum
for Excellence':

*Children play for much of the session in small groups, are free to move about and talk during
play and have high levels of adult support available for their emotional and learning needs.*

And

*When children are involved in self-directed play, staff have an opportunity to observe their
learning and, if appropriate, take it forward through sensitive intervention or using a more direct
teaching approach.*

(Learning and Teaching Scotland, 2007)

Northern Ireland

Finally, in the 'The Northern Ireland Curriculum Primary', there is a commitment to play in
these words:

*In the Foundation Stage children should experience much of their learning through well planned
and challenging play. Self-initiated play helps children to understand and learn about themselves
and their surroundings. Motivation can be increased when children have opportunities to make
choices and decisions about their learning, particularly when their own ideas and interests are
used, either as starting points for learning activities or for pursuing a topic in more depth.*

(CCEA; Northern Ireland; 2007)

Susan Isaacs

England

Independence, autonomy and active learning are also well-rehearsed when constructing a curriculum for the early years. The short examples included below give some flavour of the way these essentials have been incorporated across the UK. In supporting independent, active learning, the EYFS in England requires that practitioners take account of the Characteristics of Effective Learning, which are described as:

> In planning and guiding children's activities, practitioners must reflect on the different ways that children learn and reflect these in their practice. Three characteristics of effective teaching and learning are:
>
> - playing and exploring;
> - active learning; and
> - creating and thinking critically.

(DfE, 2014)

Scotland

Active learning in the Scottish Curriculum has a document dedicated to this aspect – 'Active learning in the Early Years' which says:

> Active learning is learning which engages and challenges children's thinking using real-life and imaginary situations. It takes full advantage of the opportunities for learning presented by:
>
> - spontaneous play
> - planned, purposeful play
> - investigating and exploring
> - events and life experiences
> - focused learning and teaching supported when necessary through sensitive intervention to support or extend learning.
>
> All areas of the curriculum can be enriched and developed through play. (Learning and Teaching Scotland, 2007)

Northern Ireland

In the Northern Ireland documentation for the primary years from 3–11, play and independent learning are promoted in these words:

It is important that children:

- have secure relationships with peers and adults;

- have opportunities to be actively involved in practical, challenging play-based learning;
- have opportunities to initiate play;
- have choice and exercise autonomy and independence.

(CCEA, 2007

Wales

And finally in the Foundation Phase curriculum for Wales, which covers the ages from three to seven, the themes are expressed in this way:

Motivation and commitment to learning is encouraged, as children begin to understand their own potential and capabilities. Children are supported in becoming confident, competent and independent thinkers and learners. They develop an awareness of their environment and learn about the diversity of people who live and work there. Positive attitudes for enjoying and caring for their environment are fostered. As their self-identity develops, children begin to express their feelings and to empathise with others. They experience challenges that extend their learning.

(Welsh Government, 2015)

If Isaacs could see the impact she has helped to bring about, she would surely see that her commitment to nursery education has resulted in initiatives that have gone far beyond her original aspirations.

Key guidance documents for countries in the UK

DfE, (2014) 'Statutory Framework for the Early Years Foundation Stage'.
Welsh Assembly Government, (2015) 'Foundation Phase Framework'.
Scottish Government, (2006) 'Curriculum for Excellence'.
CCEA, Northern Ireland, (2007) 'The Northern Ireland Curriculum Primary'.

Things to think about

- Isaacs insisted that her nursery practitioners kept detailed information about the children in their care. Do you think the current emphasis on assessment and record keeping is helpful?
- What are the most popular pieces of equipment indoors in your setting? Why do you think this is?
- What are the most popular in your outdoor area? Why do you think this is?

Susan Isaacs

- Isaacs thought that practitioners should 'mirror the role of the good/strict parent'. Do you think you are able to be that parent? What get in the way?
- Social development is a high profile aspect of the curriculum. What are the pressures when you are trying to support social development in your setting?

Ferre Laevers

Full name: Ferre Laevers

Born: 1950 (still living)

Place of birth: Belgian Congo

Countries of residence: Belgian Congo, Belgium

What he did: Ferre Laevers' contribution to early years education has, without doubt, been in observation, in the Leuven Scales for observation, which practitioners can use to identify high levels of self-esteem as well as the more usual levels of involvement.

Influences on education today: The Leuven Scales, which assess involvement through observation, are widely used by early years practitioners throughout Europe and beyond.

Theories and Areas of work : Child development

Key influencers and followers: Carl Rogers, Jean Piaget

Key works: *Process-oriented child tracking system for students* (1998) , *Involvement of Children and Teacher Style* (2003)

Development can only take place when children are actively involved, when they are actively involved with a high, non-stop degree of concentration, when they are interested, when they give themselves completely, when they use all their mental abilities to invent and make new things, and when this gives them a high degree of satisfaction and pleasure.

Ferre Laevers, Deep Level Learning and the Experiential
Approach in Early Childhood and Primary Education, 2005

Life, love, theory and research

Ferre Laevers was born in the Belgian Congo in 1950 but moved to Belgium when he was ten, and has lived there ever since. His major field of work is experiential education, influenced by Jean Piaget and Carl Rogers.

His most important contribution to educational theory has been in the field of child involvement in learning, and in the way that practitioners and teachers might be able to identify children's level of involvement, so they can match the activities offered to the individual child.

In 1976 Laevers began work with a group of pre-school practitioners to reflect on their current practice and find a way to make their work more effective. Between them they developed Experiential Education (EXE) a new way of working with pre school children. EXE sits between educational models that are focused on outcomes, and those that are focused on the context or means. The practitioners chose to develop a model that was situated between these, and built on the process of learning. The process of effective education, they thought, was built on two essentials:

- high levels of child involvement
- high levels of well-being.

Measuring involvement is not connected to any particular style of teaching, any subject or area of learning, or to any stage of development. Babies, pensioners, disabled children and university students can all become involved in learning. Csikszentmihayli calls this the state of 'flow', a state where optimal involvement and optimal learning take place. The learner is totally involved in the activity, concentrating, sometimes unaware of their surroundings or of time. Obviously no one could expect to be in this state during every activity, but it is the aim to be engaged and involved for as much of the time as possible. Laevers says: '*The 'state of flow' is sought actively by people. Young children find it most of the time in play.*' (2003) This activity is also described by Lev Vygotsky who named it the Zone of Proximal Development, and by Czicksentmiyhalyi, who defined flow (p 73).

The Leuven Scale for involvement was developed to capture just this state. At Level 1, the child is mentally, if not physically, absent; at Level 5, the child is totally absorbed and concentrating, often in the state of flow. Obviously, to make an accurate observation and allocate a level, the adult must almost get inside the child's mind, and of course, children are more likely to demonstrate the Level 5 descriptions in a high quality setting and with an imaginative and creative practitioner.

Well-being is closely related to involvement, as a state of well-being is almost always present when a person is in a state of flow. From the indicators reproduced below it is possible to look across the two scales and see that they complement each other, that well-being depends to a certain extent on high levels of involvement.

The Leuven Scales were developed at the Research Centre for Experiential Education at Leuven University, in the Netherlands, under the supervision of Laevers. Since their construction, the scales have been widely used in settings in Europe, the USA and other countries worldwide, and have made a significant contribution to the research of the Effective Early Learning Project (EEL) in England, where more than 5,000 adults learned to use the scale in observations of more than 50.000 children of pre-school age.

The scales, consisting of two sets of indicators, are used to evaluate and improve the environment for learning, particularly the involvement of the learner. They are applicable

The Leuven Scale for emotional well-being. Well-being is the extent to which pupils feel at ease, act spontaneously, show vitality and self-confidence. It is a crucial component of Emotional Intelligence and good mental health.	The Leuven Scale for involvement. Involvement focuses on the extent to which pupils are operating to their full capabilities. In particular it refers to whether the child is focused, engaged and interested in various activities.
Level 1: Extremely low The child clearly shows signs of discomfort such as crying or screaming. They may look dejected, sad, frightened or angry. The child does not respond to the environment, avoids contact and is withdrawn. The child may behave aggressively, hurting him or herself or others.	**Level 1: Low activity** Activity at this level can be simple, stereotypic, repetitive and passive. The child is absent and displays no energy. There is an absence of cognitive demand. The child characteristically may stare into space. N.B. This may be a sign of inner concentration.
Level 2: Low The posture, facial expression and actions indicate that the child does not feel at ease. However, the signals are less explicit than level 1 or the sense of discomfort is not expressed the whole time.	**Level 2: A frequently interrupted activity** The child is engaged in an activity but half of the observed period includes moments of non-activity, in which the child is not concentrating and is staring into space. There may be frequent interruptions in the child's concentration, but his or her involvement is not enough to return to the activity.
Level 3: Moderate The child has a neutral posture. Facial expression and posture show little or no emotion. There are no signs indicating sadness or pleasure, comfort or discomfort.	**Level 3: Mainly continuous activity** The child is busy at an activity but it is at a routine level and the real signals for involvement are missing. There is some progress but energy is lacking and concentration is at a routine level. The child can be easily distracted
Level 4: High The child shows obvious signs of satisfaction (as listed under level 5). However, these signals are not constantly present with the same intensity.	**4) Continuous activity with intense moments** The child's activity has intense moments during which activities at level 3 can come to have special meaning. Level 4 is reserved for the kind of activity seen in those intense moments, and can be deduced from the 'involvement signals'. This level of activity is resumed after interruptions. Stimuli, from the surrounding environment, however attractive cannot seduce the child away from the activity.
Level 5: Extremely high The child looks happy and cheerful, smiles, cries out with pleasure. They may be lively and full of energy. Actions can be spontaneous and expressive. The child may talk to him or herself, play with sounds, hum, sing. The child appears relaxed and does not show any signs of stress or tension. He or she is open and accessible to the environment. The child expresses self-confidence and self-assurance.	**Level 5: Sustained intense activity** The child shows continuous and intense activity revealing the greatest involvement. In the observed period not all the signals for involvement need be there, but the essential ones must be present: concentration, creativity, energy and persistence. This intensity must be present for almost all the observation period.

Ferre Laevers

for use with any age from the early years to late secondary school, although their use in early education has been much more extensive.

The indicators give five levels of involvement and five levels of well-being, and descriptions of the probable behaviour observed at each level. The process begins by using the indicators below to identify involvement and well-being for each child. These observations can be of individuals or small groups and take place over a period or about ten minutes:

If there are high levels of both well-being and involvement, the observer will know that high levels of both development and learning are present, and that these aspects can be promoted by the offer of further engaging activities.

Laevers suggests that it is unrealistic to expect the children to reach level 4 or 5 in every activity and that levels of both well-being and involvement fluctuate during the day so practitioners are advised to use the scales several times at different times of day and in different activities. Practitioners should use their first observations as a baseline, building on these over time, to establish a child's overall levels.

Laevers also worked with teachers to develop action points for engaging children further by improving the classroom environment. Some of these have been published and include these ten ways in which practitioners could improve the provision in their settings. These include rearranging the classroom, looking at resources, following children's interests, and using the results of observations to identify children with additional needs.

Observe children carefully, then respond, either with additional resources, changes to or removal of resources, or by finding out about, and involving yourself in the children's interests.

Legacy and impact

Since the development of the Leuven Scales, Laevers has been involved in work in Flanders and across the Netherlands to implement the Experiential Education (EXE) method, which is now well established. He also went on to develop indicators for an 'experiential' teacher style, involving three dimensions of teaching: stimulation, sensitivity and giving autonomy. Laevers has also developed an adult observation model to establish the level of teacher competence in EXE, during which they found that the practitioner was even more influential than they had thought, even more important than the space, the environment or the learning resources in raising levels of well-being and involvement.

Laevers has also been influential in the work of individual early years practitioners and their settings, encouraging them to evaluate their own effectiveness in order to improve practice. The scales are used regularly in many settings across Europe, both for research purposes and in the day-to-day work of nurseries and other settings. Laevers has also influenced local and national policy for early years education, where governments have taken note of the work of researchers when they are advising and evaluating practice or writing documentation.

Influences on early years practice across the UK

The major influence Laevers' work has had is in helping practitioners to look at the process of learning, not just the inputs and outcomes, or using simplistic developmental stages.

Of course, it is much less time consuming to use simple measures such as curriculum statements and goals for learning, but identifying the situations, activities and opportunities that result in flow offers a much richer picture, both of individual children and of the quality of the setting itself. There is no direct reference to the work of Laevers or the Leuven Scales in national documentation. However, there is a strong message about observation as the major vehicle for assessment in the documentation across the UK.

England

In England, assessment of the learning of individual children is a statutory requirement and is mainly informed by observation, although there is an increasing move towards national tests and assessments on entry and at the end of the Foundation Stage, as stated in the 'Statutory Framework for the Early Years Foundation Stage':

Ongoing assessment (also known as formative assessment) is an integral part of the learning and development process. It involves practitioners observing children to understand their level of achievement, interests and learning styles, and to then shape learning experiences for each child reflecting those observations.

(DfE, 2014)

Northern Ireland

Northern Ireland has a clear message that the process of learning is more effective than the simple product. 'The Northern Ireland Curriculum Primary' states:

Intrinsic to this is a recognition of the importance of process based learning, as opposed to product based, outcome driven learning, with observation based assessment, carried out in a unobtrusive way, as an ongoing and integral part of the learning and teaching process.

Learning is supported by adults when assessment is ongoing, formative and integral to learning and teaching. It is observation based, informs planning and is carried out in an unobtrusive way.

(CCEA, 2007)

Scotland

In Scotland there is a clear message in 'A Curriculum for Excellence' about the purposes and benefits of regular observation of every child by practitioners:

Staff also need time to observe children, in order to learn about their understanding and approach to learning. They can then plan appropriate next steps and gauge the level of support or challenge required.

(Learning and Teaching Scotland, 2007)

Wales

In the 'Foundation Phase Child Development Assessment Profile', the following guidance is provided:

Assessment is achieved by observing each child, either individually, in a pair or in a group, as they engage with the various kinds of resources provided in a setting. As far as possible, assessments are spontaneous and observe characteristics and behaviours that occur naturally in a setting.

(Young Wales, 2011)

It would be heartening to know that the time spent by the EEL project in observing children was not wasted. Their work in observing a huge number of children, using the Leuven Scales, has been influential in early years circles. It could make a real difference to the pressures on practitioners if it also focused the eyes of government ministers and inspectors on the process of learning, not just the product.

Key guidance documents for countries in the UK

DfE, (2014) 'Statutory Framework for the Early Years Foundation Stage'.
CCEA, Northern Ireland, (2007) 'The Northern Ireland Curriculum Primary'.
Learning and Teaching Scotland (2007) 'A Curriculum for Excellence.'
Young Wales, (2011) 'Foundation Phase Child Development Assessment Profile'.

Things to think about

- How do you make time to observe children's learning?
- How do you plan time for children to engage in the new experiences you offer, and talk through their own ideas?
- How much opportunity is there in your setting to observe and follow up on children's interests?
- Do you ever make time for children to continue their activities beyond the time you originally allotted?
- Does your training give you enough support in how, when and where to observe children, and record what you see?

Loris Malaguzzi

Full name: Loris Malaguzzi

Born: 1920

Died: 1994

Place of birth: Correggio, Italy

Countries of residence: Italy

What he did: Loris Malaguzzi helped parents to establish the world-famous Reggio Emilia Pre-schools and Infant-Toddler Centres in Northern Italy.

Influences on education today: Malaguzzi's influence has spread well beyond the schools in Italy, to permeate early education across the world. Settings where practitioners have read about the Reggio approach, or visited the Reggio schools, have made significant changes to the environment, establishing ateliers for creative activities, and maintained the project approach to learning.

Theories and areas of work: Socio-cultural, Child development, Linguistics

Key influencers and followers: Jerome Bruner, John Dewey, Jean Piaget, Les Vygotsky

Key works: *A journey into the rights of children* (1995), *Loris Malaguzzi and the Schools of Reggio Emilia* (2016)

The wider the range of possibilities we offer children, the more intense will be their motivations and the richer their experiences.

Loris Malaguzzi, The Hundred Languages of Children, 2011

Life, love, theory and research

Loris Malaguzzi was born, worked and died in Reggio Emilia, a city in Northern Italy, famous for its cheese, wine and the birthplace of the national flag. Reggio Emilia is also world renowned for its pre schools under the collective name of Reggio Schools.

For the whole of his life, Malaguzzi worked as an early years teacher, an interest which was ignited just after the end of the Second World War, when Malaguzzi, already a local primary teacher, met a group of mothers who were struggling to bring up their families without their husbands who had been killed or injured during the war. The idea these women came up with was to build and run their own school, as the local municipality was uninterested in the education of their children, concentrating entirely on the children of the rich.

The women asked Malaguzzi to help them to look after their children and he promised to work alongside the children themselves learning from them and teaching them himself. The first Reggio Emilia school opened in 1945 on the day after Liberation Day, and was financed by the selling of a German tank, nine horses and two military trucks. Other schools followed until the collective organisation covered a large area including the city of Reggio Emilia.

When the schools first opened, everyone helped; parents worked alongside Malaguzzi, either with the children or cooking meals, making or painting furniture, cleaning and maintaining the building. This support and involvement of parents became one of the principles of the first school and the others that followed. The community raised enough money to keep the schools running until 1963. During this time, Malaguzzi worked with Reggio teachers and others to present exhibitions of the children's work, which have been shown throughout the world. Books, films, collections of children's writings and drawings and other information are all now available in Reggio and other countries for enthusiasts' and students' use.

Malaguzzi believed that children use at least a hundred languages as they learn, of which talking, painting, writing, role-play, photography, sculpture, fabric work, natural materials such as wood, wire and metal, are just a few. He was interested in making sure that children used as many of these languages as they wanted to communicate their thoughts and feelings to the world. He was a truly innovative educator and an inspiration to all who worked with him and many others around the world, although interestingly, he was virtually unrecognised by Italians during his lifetime.

The principles which the schools follow include:

- Children are capable of constructing their own learning and should have some control over the direction it takes
- They must be able to learn by using all their senses
- Children are natural communicators and must have opportunities to form relationships with other children
- Adults are mentors and partners in children's learning
- The environment is the third teacher and must offer opportunities for children to explore materials and resources in all the ways they wish
- Documentation of children's thoughts and of the learning process is crucial for understanding what is important to children
- Parents and families are partners in the learning process.

Teachers in Reggio schools are valued as co-learners in the children's chosen learning journeys. They document children's learning in what other practitioners might understand as 'learning journeys': full of notes, photos, video and tape recordings. This information is used to make decisions on how to support children's interests and how these might be extended through sensitive adult interventions. The documentation is also used to locate the learning needs of individuals and groups, affecting the resources and activities offered each day. Malaguzzi said, *'What children learn does not follow as an automatic result from what is taught. Rather, it is in large part due to the children's own doing as a consequence of their activities and our resources.'* (1998)

Rather than being instructors, practitioners are expected to view the child as an apprentice to life. The adults identify interests arising in individuals and groups of children, and plan projects round these; projects which have no boundaries, perhaps beginning with a question posed by a child or a problem that needs to be solved. Staff turnover in Reggio schools has historically been low and children stay with the same teachers for the whole time they are at the school, thus emphasising continuity for adults, children and families.

In Italy, teachers in government-run preschools are very autonomous. They have few teaching guidelines or handbooks, curriculum documents or assessment objectives. They also have few opportunities for professional development. By contrast, teachers in Reggio Schools are well supported. They identify their own development needs and are given non-contact time for training, planning and the work associated with keeping the extensive documentation of each child's learning, discussing these with colleagues in order to identify children with similar interests who might work together, groups who may need particular skills practice and ideas for extending children's leaning, across and between age groups. Teachers believe in their own ability to respond appropriately to children's ideas and interests and they believe that children will be interested in things worth knowing about.

Reggio teachers also believe in the right of parents to be informed and productive members of the school team. Parents are welcomed, and are expected to be partners in their children's learning, taking their place at one corner of the learning triangle, with the children and the environment at the other two corners; these are the 'three teachers':

- The parents as the first teachers, later joined by other adults

- The child as the second teacher

- The environment as the third teacher

Parents are welcome at any time and many parents join the school committee. However, because nearly all Reggio parents work, most of the exchanges with parents take place at the end of sessions, usually in the early afternoon, when the children have had lunch and a rest during which time the practitioners are able to work on documentation, training and preparation. The teachers are available to talk to parents without pressure, and central to these discussions is the collection and display of the child's documentation. Learning and development are thus demonstrated to parents without the need for formal assessment or tests because observation is a constant activity.

Reggio schools emphasise the power of the environment to expand children's experiences. As shown above, teachers refer to the environment as 'the third teacher' and they take great care to make the setting stimulating and linked to children's current interests, with their work carefully displayed with enormous respect. Where possible, the resources used are of neutral colours and natural materials, such as wood, fabric and metal. Displays of plants, found objects, natural resources, flowers, shells, stones etc., ample daylight, and quiet places and spaces such as 'thresholds and corners' where children can pause and watch are all features of the schools.

The Reggio approach and the settings it is practised in are a tribute to the enthusiasm of one individual, working against the odds with a group of strong women to provide a unique collection of buildings, people and families, all dedicated to meeting the needs of very young children.

In the 1950s, Malaguzzi qualified as an educational psychologist and founded Reggio Emilia's municipal Psycho-Pedagogical Medical Centre where he worked for more than 20 years. In the 1960s, he worked with the city's administration to open municipal, government funded preschools and in 1963 the municipality began to take over the original Reggio Emilia preschools founded just after the war. Malaguzzi continued to manage this network of schools for several years as the Reggio approach became more well-known. In 2003 the municipality of Reggio Emilia decided to incorporate all the schools under local government, and the network of school services and toddler centres became an association called the *Instituzione Scuole e Nidi d'Infanzia* (Institution of Toddler Groups and Preschools). This meant that the Reggio preschools could still maintain their independent programmes and activities, but with support from the public sector government.

Today there are 13 infant and toddler centres and 22 preschools for children aged three to six. A large proportion of the children of the city of Reggio Emilia attend the preschools and they are now renowned across the world as examples of inspiring practice.

In all Reggio schools, and in those in other countries inspired by Maoaguzzi's practice, the children are participants in their own learning, helping to decide on topics and projects, using the community as a resource and getting involved in creative activities with the support of professionals and local artists. Children are encouraged to be independent, to solve problems and to work together on projects using adults as an additional resource.

Legacy and impact

During recent years, an increasing number of teachers and education experts from around the world have flocked to study Reggio's unique methods and attempt to apply them in their own countries. Malaguzzi and his team have promoted the Reggio approach through strictly managed visits by foreign practitioners to the schools, lectures on the history and philosophy of the approach, films, exhibitions and books.

In February 2006 the Loris Malaguzzi International Centre, a meeting place for educators and for professional development, opened in Reggio Emilia. The non-profit organisation of the Reggio Children, and The Loris Malaguzzi Centre Foundation was officially established on September 29th 2011 with the aim of promoting *Education and research to improve the lives of people and communities in Reggio Emilia and in the world.* (reggiochildrenfoundation.org)

It has always been a principle of the Reggio Schools that the unique method they had developed could not be exported. Like a plant, it can only flourish in the right soil. However, practitioners can take the essence of Reggio and build their own version which many enthusiastic practitioners have done in countries all over the world. *Taking Reggio Emilia Home* (1997), is an interesting and honest book in which Louise Boyd Cadwell, an American teacher, gives an account of the way that, after spending some time in Reggio, she adapted her own setting to adopt many aspects of the approach.

Schools and settings across the world have adopted some of the ideas of the Reggio methods and found that the creative and free-flowing nature has a beneficial effect on their own work. What they have brought back to their settings from visits to Reggio schools and from conferences, courses and books is that children can be strong and powerful individuals, managing their own learning with adults as an informed resource, and this has become an accepted ambition for practitioners who have an enthusiasm for the Reggio approach. Settings where the approach has been established without compromising the Reggio principles have the support of local education bodies and are celebrated in magazine articles and books.

In 2015, Howard Gardner was asked his opinion of the Reggio schools:

'I can say that my over 30 years of visiting Reggio have affected profoundly my understanding of young children, of their teachers, and of the possibilities of the pedagogical environment..... For me, and for others like my teacher Jerome Bruner, time in the Reggio preschools has opened our eyes to potentials that we had not appreciated before.'
(https:// howardgardner.com/2015/10/01/the-reggio-emilia-approach-to-education/)

Schools influenced by the approach have been established all over the world and there has been great interest from politicians, educators and higher education staff, intrigued by how the approach might influence their work.

Books and other resources for information and training are available in the UK, and conferences, training events and magazines can all help practitioners who are interested in exploring the approach. Replicas of furniture and resources, such as the 'triangular mirrors', dressing up trolleys, baskets and containers, screens and shelving, have become available although of course Reggio staff would say that the approach is about much more than furniture.

Influences on early years practice across the UK

The influences of the Reggio approach on documentation and practice in the UK have been subtle. None of the National Curriculum documents make direct reference to Reggio approaches or to any other national or international approaches or those from countries other than their own. The exception to this is Learning Scotland's booklet (see below). However, child-centred, active learning is a feature in many schools in the UK.

Scotland

In Scotland there has been a somewhat more overt recognition of the Reggio approach, and settings adopting the approach have been supported. Learning and Teaching Scotland have produced a booklet, 'The Reggio Emilia approach to early education', which covers the history and approach in some detail, thus implying that practitioners might take time to read about and perhaps be influenced by its contents.

Although there is no reference to any particular approach to learning in the National Curriculum documentation for Scotland, one can see a clear influence of practices such as those adopted in Reggio schools as well as other high quality providers. 'The child at the centre' documentation states:

> The child is at the centre of what we do in the early years. This is a critically important stage in the development and learning of children. Children are naturally curious and eager to find out about the world around them. We must build on their curiosity and enthusiasm to learn when we develop their learning environments, working outwards from their individual interests and needs.
> (HM Inspectorate of Education, 2007)

The National Curriculum for Scotland emphasises active learning from 3 to 18 years. This has provided helpful guidance on how teachers can provide learning in an active context throughout school life and across the whole age range. There is also an admission that a historical model of more 'systematic' instruction does not meet the needs of children under the age of seven in the 'Pre-birth to three' documentation:

> Whilst children's early experiences play an important part in shaping their future attitudes and dispositions, very young children are capable individuals in their own right, and, with appropriate support, can develop resilience to deal with many of life's challenges.
> (Learning and Teaching Scotland, 2010)

And in 'Building the Curriculum 2':

It (research) suggests that there is no long-term advantage to children when there is an over-emphasis on systematic teaching before 6 or 7 years of age.

(Scottish Executive, 2007)

England

In England, the guiding principles for the 'Statutory Framework for the Early Years Foundation Stage' are clear about how children should be supported, with maximum independence, and maximum support:

Four guiding principles should shape practice in early years settings. These are:

- *Every child is a unique child, who is constantly learning and can be resilient, capable, confident and self-assured;*
- *Children learn to be strong and independent through positive relationships;*
- *Children learn and develop well in enabling environments, in which their experiences respond to their individual needs and there is a strong partnership between practitioners and parents and/or carers; and*
- *Children develop and learn in different ways and at different rates.*

(DfE, 2014)

'Development Matters in the EYFS', includes the following statements about playful learning, an expression coined to describe activities which have been initiated by adults or children, but are carried out in a practical, active, 'playful' way:

Play is a key opportunity for children to think creatively and flexibly, solve problems and link ideas. Establish the enabling conditions for rich play: space, time, flexible resources, choice, control, warm and supportive relationships.

Children are born ready, able and eager to learn. They actively reach out to interact with other people, and in the world around them. Development is not an automatic process, however. It depends on each unique child having opportunities to interact in positive relationships and enabling environments.

(Early Education, 2012)

Northern Ireland

In Northern Ireland, there is very clear guidance in 'Understanding the Foundation Stage' on how the experiences offered to children must build on the child's interests, motivating them and ensuring they develop the positive attitudes to learning that an active approach should bring:

The learning experiences provided should reflect pupil's interests and the practical and informal ways in which pupils of this age learn. These experiences should be enjoyable and challenging,

Loris Malaguzzi

*and should motivate pupils and encourage them to adopt positive attitudes to school and
learning.*

(CCEA; Northern Ireland, 2006)

The documentation is also very clear about the role of the practitioner, which is described
in this way:

*Learning is supported by adults when: early years practitioners are committed, sensitive,
enthusiastic and interact effectively to challenge children's thinking and learning; planning is
collaborative, holistic, child focused and informed by observations of learning.*

(Understanding the Foundation Stage; CCEA; Northern Ireland, 2006)

Wales

In Wales, where the Foundation Phase covers the ages from 3–7, children can expect that
every effort will be made by practitioners to enable them to become active, confident,
independent learners as detailed in 'Foundation Phase Framework':

*Educational provision for young children should be holistic with the child at the heart of any
planned curriculum. It is about practitioners understanding, inspiring and challenging children's
potential for learning. Practitioner involvement in children's learning is of vital importance
particularly when interactions involve open questioning, shared and sustained thinking.*

(Welsh Government, 2015)

Practitioners should understand that being influenced by the Reggio approach, or any
other high profile approach to early learning, is not a cosmetic job. It is unfortunate that
some magazines and advisers think that a 'quick fix' approach can be used to implement
the Reggio approach. The following, rather simplistic advice was offered in an early years
magazine:

- *Place plants around your setting to bring the 'outside in'.*
- *Use unbreakable mirrors in creative ways to stimulate interest.*
- *Offer 'personal paper bags' for children to take home over weekends or vacations. Inside
each bag, suggest activities family members can do together.*
- *Invite family members to bring in real 'props' from their workplaces.*

Scholastic, Early Childhood Today – title 'Pioneers in Our Field:
Loris Malaguzzi – Founder of the Reggio Emilia Approach, 2001

Simply buying a few plants or paper bags, adopting a few random activities, or buying a
some 'Reggio inspired' resources will not turn a setting into a Reggio School. The approach

is not a simple adaptation of your environment, and for many practitioners, adopting the full Reggio approach will involve enormous change, particularly in adapting their own role. To do this means making changes in practice that would be challenging for the most committed community of practitioners, parents and children. Reggio practice is in the blood of the people who work there; practice which is as natural as breathing.

Key guidance documents for countries in the UK

HM Inspectorate of Education, (2007) 'The child at the centre'.
Scottish Executive, (2007) 'Building the Curriculum 2 (3–18); Active learning in the early years'.
Learning and Teaching Scotland, (2010) 'Pre-birth to three'.
DfE, (2014) 'Statutory Framework for the Early Years Foundation Stage'.
Early Education, (2012) 'Development Matters in the EYFS'.
CCEA, (2006) 'Northern Ireland Curriculum: Understanding the Foundation Stage'.
Welsh Assembly Government, (2015) 'Foundation Phase Framework'.

Things to think about

- How do you think you would be able to cope without any curriculum guidance or objectives for learning?

- How much of your time is available for following up on children's own interests? Why do you think this is?

- Reggio practitioners have many visits from practitioners from countries all over the world. How would you explain what you do to a visiting colleague?

- Projects and topics have had a variable amount of popularity in the recent past. Do you still plan topics for your group? How much are you able to link these to the interests of individuals and groups of children?

- Would you welcome the opportunity to work in a setting that followed a Reggio approach?

Loris Malaguzzi

Abraham Harold Maslow

> **Full name:** Abraham Harold Maslow
>
> **Born:** 1908
>
> **Died:** 1970
>
> **Place of birth:** Brooklyn, New York, United States
>
> **Countries of residence:** United States
>
> **What he did:** Maslow gave us the Hierarchy of Need, which we can use to establish children's (and our own) development towards self-actualisation, the highest level of human development.
>
> **Influences on education today:** Maslow's Heirarchy is still included in education courses for teachers and early years practitioners. It is also a key reference for other research, and for understanding behaviour in children.
>
> **Theories and areas of work:** Humanism, Psychology
>
> **Key influencers and followers:** Alfred Adler, Sigmund Freud, Mihaly Csikszentmihalyi
>
> **Key works:** *A Theory of Human Motivation* (1943), *Toward a Psychology of Being* (1968)

All the evidence that we have indicates that it is reasonable to assume in practically every human being, and certainly in almost every newborn baby, that there is an active will toward health, an impulse towards growth, or towards self-actualization.

Abraham Maslow, A Theory of Human Motivation, 1943

Life, love, theory and research

Abraham Maslow was born and raised in Brooklyn, New York, oldest of seven children, and the son of second-generation Russian immigrants to the USA. During his childhood, Maslow was deemed to be unstable and endured anti-Semitism from other children and even from his teachers. His relationship with his mother was poor and he had few friends, preferring to spend his time in the library. He attended one of the top high schools in Brooklyn and spent much time in physical exercise and training, believing that physical strength was the most important asset for a male.

After several failed attempts at gaining a higher level qualification, Maslow graduated from the University of Wisconsin with a degree in psychology. His master's thesis was titled 'Learning, retention, and reproduction of verbal material' but he thought this subject was so insignificant that he withdrew the thesis from the university library and destroyed it. However, after a time he agreed to resubmit it in two separate articles.

Just before the Second World War Maslow, now married to his cousin Bertha, and with two children, began to question the elements of psychology he had studied at college and started to develop his own theories. He began to study examples of self-actualising individuals – among them Abraham Lincoln and Albert Einstein – people who had achieved their potential to become exceptional human beings. This work was the beginning of a lifelong study of human potential and mental health. He adopted and adapted the work of others in the areas of hierarchy of needs, metamotivation, self-actualisation and peak experiences. This work was to form the basis of future developments in presenting new ideas for other psychologists to follow.

Maslow's thinking was original. He was different from previous psychologists in that they had been concerned with the abnormal or irregular. Maslow wanted to identify what was 'normal' or ideal, and what people need to live fulfilled and happy adult lives; the true meaning of mental health. This came to be referred to as 'Humanistic psychology' and its therapies were based on the idea that growth and healing will result from ensuring that people have the inner resources to 'heal' themselves, and the job of a psychologist is to remove the obstacles to this. Self-understanding and self-improvement are the answers.

Maslow is best known in education circles for his description of the hierarchy of needs, which was an exploration of the innate human needs that we all should satisfy if we are to get to the level of self-actualisation. He used a biographical analysis method to come to his views of the hierarchy by examining the biographies and writings of 18 people (including Abraham Lincoln, Albert Einstein, Aldous Huxley, Gandhi and Beethoven), all thought by him to be self-actualising individuals. From these biographies he constructed a list of the characteristics that he considered to define self-actualisation.

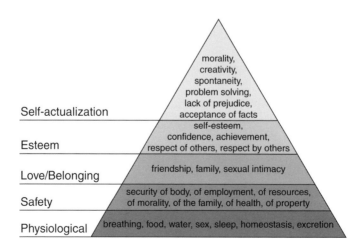

The hierarchy of needs was illustrated in this way, and should be read from the base of the pyramid. Each level of need builds on the one below, and can't be fully achieved until the level below has been fulfilled. However, the levels of the pyramid are not meant to be a fixed, rigid sequence and many of the needs may be present in a person at any one time. The boundaries between the levels should be seen as permeable.

In this interpretation the hierarchy the needs have been related to children, but they are equally applicable to adults.

- Physiological: At the bottom of the pyramid are the basic physiological needs of a human: food, water, sleep and sex. *Young children need nutritious food, water, plenty of sleep, shelter and a human touch. If they don't get these they will not thrive.*

- Safety: Next come the safety needs of security, order and stability. *Babies and young children rely mostly on adults to provide this for them, ensuring that they ride in car safety seats, are protected by childproofing such things as electric plug covers and stair gates, and are not put in danger of avoidable risks. Children who are abused, neglected or living in poverty are less likely to be able to fulfill this level of need.*

- Love and belonging: The third level explores our need for love and belonging – when a human has taken care of their own needs, they are ready to help others. *Young children need our unconditional love, the love of caregivers, room to play and explore and feeling of belonging with their siblings and peers.*

- Esteem: The fourth level is achieved when we feel satisfied with what we have achieved – this is the esteem level, where we need recognition from others. *As they develop, young children need our protection from behaviours that undermine their self-esteem, such as bullying, teasing or other discrimination. They need to feel respected and valued for themselves, given the skills to manage their own lives, and discipline that is positive rather than negative and punitive.*

- Self-actualisation: Next comes the cognitive, or self-actualising level, where Maslow sees humans as needing to stimulate themselves intellectually by independent learning. *At this level, growing children need to be encouraged to take up interests and hobbies, but not so many that they feel overwhelmed or under-skilled. They also need to be encouraged to engage in a wide range or activities such as reading for pleasure, writing, drawing and painting, dancing, playing games and sports etc, as aesthetic and cognitive aspects are included at this level. At this stage children will become 'self-actualising' by achieving their full potential and meeting their own goals.*

According to Maslow, as people achieve the level of self-actualisation, they will display a range of characteristics and many were identified in his book *Towards a Psychology of Being*. These characteristics and qualities included: *'Truth, wholeness, beauty, autonomy and perfection with nothing superfluous, nothing lacking, everything in its right place'.* (Maslow, 1968)

Abraham Harold Maslow

Maslow also recognised and identified what he referred to as peak experiences, profound moments of peace, love, happiness or understanding, and that self-actualising people have more of these experiences, which are akin to the moments identified by Csikszentmihalyi in his work on features of flow.

Of course, children will not always be able to display all these characteristics until they reach adulthood and many of us are prevented from achieving them because the circumstances of our lives, careers and family prevent us from reaching the final level. However, as seen below, the curriculum guidance for the EYFS relates to many of the principles Maslow identified and gives clear guidance on how these might be promoted.

Maslow worked for his whole life in the United States, achieving a reputation in adulthood as a major philosophical thinker, and inventor of a system that is widely used in education and in Humanistic psychology.

Legacy and Impact

The scientific methodology which Maslow used, particularly in establishing a hierarchy of needs, has been criticised by other researchers. His reliance on biographical research is notoriously prone to the bias of the researcher, and the fact that the sample was predominantly white and 100% male made it even more suspect.

Despite this criticism, since its construction in the late 1960s Maslow's work has been influential in many fields of work. During the 1960s and 1970s, the hierarchy was extended to give more status to cognitive and aesthetic needs, including them as the fifth and sixth levels in the diagram, pushing self-actualisation up to level seven. Both the five and the seven stage models have been applied in many different settings to ensure that employees remain motivated, including personnel management, project management and even in marketing, where appealing to basic needs such as hunger and thirst are used to market products.

It is also possible to apply the hierarchy of needs to situations such as floods or other disasters. As we watch the coverage of such events on TV, it is clear that the overriding priorities of aid agencies are to fulfill the first levels of need, providing water, food and shelter for those affected.

The work of Maslow has had a significant effect on education where his views have changed classroom practice to include a recognition and response to individual needs. Maslow's work is still studied in many teacher training institutions where the effect of such needs on young children is discussed. Practitioners and teachers know that a hungry, tired or neglected child will not learn and, particularly in the early years and primary stages of education, these needs are often met within the education setting. Breakfast clubs, mid-morning snacks and places where children can rest and be quiet are all common features of early years provision. Also, Maslow's research helps teachers move away from seeing learning as simply a response to the environment, helping us to understanding the complexity of human needs and how they affect the lives and learning of individual children.

Influences on early years practice across the UK

England

The 'Statutory Framework for the Early Years Foundation Stage' in England reflect the qualities Maslow identified in his work, emphasising the unique nature of each child, and recognising the need for practitioners to respond to their individual needs. The principles also identify some of the characteristics of self-actualisation such as independence, confidence and resilience:

Overarching principles

- every child is a unique child;
- children learn to be strong and independent through positive relationships;
- children learn and develop well in enabling environments; and
- children develop and learn in different ways and at different rates.

(DfE, 2012)

The EYFS also contains guidance on the Characteristics of Effective Teaching and Learning, and we can see the effect of Maslow's work throughout these in words such as 'playfulness, fun, joy, self-sufficiency, autonomy, independence', some of which are identified in this quote from the Statutory Framework:

In planning and guiding children's activities, practitioners must reflect on the different ways that children learn and reflect these in their practice. Within the three Characteristics of Effective Teaching and Learning are:

- *investigate* and experience things, and *'have a go'*;
- *keep on trying* if they encounter difficulties;
- *enjoy achievements*; and
- *develop their own ideas, make links* between ideas, and *develop strategies* for doing things.

(DfE, 2012)

Northern Ireland

In the section on Approaches to Learning in 'The Northern Ireland Curriculum Primary', the following description of children's needs is included:

It is important that children:

- *have secure relationships with peers and adults in a positively affirming environment;*
- *have opportunities to be actively involved in practical, challenging play-based learning in a stimulating environment;*
- *have opportunities to initiate play which capitalises on intrinsic motivation and natural curiosity;*
- *have choice and exercise autonomy and independence in their learning*
- *are given equality of opportunity to learn in a variety of ways and in different social groupings;*
- *are actively involved in planning, carrying out and reflecting on their work.*

(CCEA, Northern Ireland, 2007)

There are many words here that Maslow would recognise from his work on self-actualisation.

Throughout the early and lower primary years, the characteristics identified by Maslow have been embedded in practice to become a seamless part of the National Curriculum and the broader curriculum. They are now so familiar that it is difficult to think of early education without these principles.

Key guidance documents for countries in the UK

DfE, (2014) 'Statutory Framework for the Early Years Foundation Stage'.
CCEA, Northern Ireland, (2007) 'The Northern Ireland Curriculum Primary'.

Things to think about

- Did you study Maslow's work during your training? Has it had an effect on the way you work?
- How far do you think you have been able to move towards achieving self-actualisation in your life? Which of the characteristics identified by Maslow have you managed to achieve?

- Do you know anyone who appears to have reached the level of self-actualisation? Does this make them a better person? A better friend or colleague?

- Has working in education helped you to recognise needs in others?

- How do you and your colleagues incorporate the Characteristics of Effective Teaching and Learning in your work?

Rachel and Margaret McMillan

Full names: Rachel and Margaret McMillan
Born: Rachel: 1859, Margaret: 1860
Died: Rachel: 1917, Margaret: 1931
Place of birth: Westchester, New York, United States
Countries of residence: United States, Scotland, England
What they did: The McMillan sisters worked tirelessly to improve conditions for poor children and their families. Their names are revered in the nursery education movement, where they had their greatest influence.
Influences on education today: Every early years practitioner should thank these sisters for their tireless efforts to establish nursery schools and health clinics, particularly for deprived children.
Theories and areas of work: Child development, Pedagogy
Key influencers and followers: Rudolf Steiner, Jean Piaget
Key works: *The Life of Rachel McMillan* (1927), *The Nursery School*, (2009)

Educate every child as if he were your own

Rachel McMillan, Handwritten manuscript, 1924

Life, love, theory and research

Rachel and Margaret McMillan were born in New York State, spending their very early childhood in a house in the country, which Margaret remembered as 'a mere shelter in summer'. The stay in this house affected the sisters throughout their lives. Margaret said the house was '...*less a house than a roofed series of gateways opening on the wide sunlit world*' (Jarvis, 2014). However, the McMillan sisters had but a short time in their idyllic house in the country before their father and younger sister both died from scarlet fever in 1865 and their mother took them back to Inverness in Scotland to her family home.

When they left school, the sisters became involved in socialist politics and Margaret began to write and to contribute to the work of the Labour movement. In 1887 Rachel was introduced to Christian Socialism and read articles by William Morris and others who promoted this belief.

In the 1880s Margaret moved to London where Rachel later joined her. Margaret spoke publicly, talking at Speakers' Corner in Hyde Park which was most unusual for a well brought up woman and resulted in her dismissal from her job. Both Rachel and Margaret campaigned for women's rights to vote and while protesting about the way protesters for women's rights were treated in prison, they were physically assaulted by police. The sisters then moved to Bradford where they lived for ten years and Margaret contributed to the birth of the Parliamentary Labour Party in 1900.

Margaret continued to promote her ideas as a Christian Socialist and travelled across Yorkshire giving lectures on behalf of the Labour cause. During this time, she served on the Bradford School Board. This position gave her an opportunity to visit city schools where she was appalled at the state of poor children, and felt that it was a waste of effort to insist that children should go to school when they were struggling with hunger, poverty, infestation and dirt at home and school was no better. Margaret's work in Bradford resulted in the city becoming the first in the country to provide medical inspections, free or low cost school meals and school baths in some of the poorest areas. Sadly, in 1902, Margaret had to step down from the School Board when local authorities (to which women could not at that time be elected) took over responsibility for schools. She then left Bradford to live with Rachel in Bromley, Kent.

Rachel was working as a health inspector when Margaret moved in with her at the end of 1902. The sisters began to agitate for better conditions for poor children in Bromley, a district of London. Margaret served as manager on the board of a group of schools and the sisters led a deputation to parliament in 1906 to lobby for compulsory medical inspections for school children. They were successful in this, gaining not only a Bill in Parliament but a bursary of £5000 from a philanthropist which they used to open a clinic in Deptford in 1910. The clinic was an immediate success and money was found to expand it in 1911. The sisters remained in Deptford for the rest of their lives.

The next development started with a project to help poor girls in the locality. This was a camp in their garden where the girls could sleep, have nutritious breakfasts and hot baths. They later successfully established a boy's camp as well. The next venture was to open a school for children from 6 to 14 years of age where children could receive a more holistic education in the open air. Three teachers and 57 children worked together in this school.

Ever since opening the original camps, Margaret had dreamed of opening a baby camp, saying that:

We must open our doors to the toddlers, we must plan the right kind of environment for them and give them sunshine, fresh air and good food before they become rickety and diseased. (1919)

In front of the clinic was a muddy field, and the sisters persuaded the London County Council to let them use it for an outdoor school.

We asked for leave to use the site as an open-air nursery, and leave was granted. 'Only you can't have it long,' we were told, 'for we shall want it soon for building purposes'. (1919)

The outbreak of the First World War in 1914 helped the sisters to achieve this intention, as women were needed to work in factories to support the war effort, and needed somewhere to leave their babies. 'The nursery' and its associated training centre thrived during the war but turnover of staff and frequent risks of bombing took their toll on both sisters.

Rachel died on her 58th birthday in 1917, and Margaret renamed the nursery The Rachel McMillan Open Air Nursery in memory of her sister. It still bears her name today, and occupies the same site 100 years later.

It was a great sorrow to Margaret that it was only after Rachel's death that their work was recognised. Margaret received a CBE and a Companion of Honour medal for their contribution to early years education. She wrote about the nursery in her book, *The Nursery School*, published in 1919. In the introduction, she wrote:

The need for a book on this subject is certainly urgent. Not merely a few children, here and there, but hundreds of thousands are in dire need of education or nurture in the first years.

In 1922 Rudolf Steiner visited the school and praised the work of the sisters. His work in the Steiner-Waldorf Schools was instrumental in the way they set up their nursery, with a series of 'shelters' for different age groups and activities.

Margaret continued the work, serving on committees, notably the London County Council, where she was influential in gaining a grant for the Deptford Nursery which enabled a substantial expansion of the provision, increasing its numbers to 215. Queen Mary attended the opening of this extension in 1930. Margaret also worked with the newly established National Day Nursery Association, (NDNA), helping with its work in supporting and promoting nursery education in the UK.

In her later years, Margaret campaigned for a training college to be established to meet the needs of students wanting to work in Nursery Schools. The Rachel McMillan Training College was opened in May 1930, building on the training work the sisters had done at the nursery school. The college was a lasting tribute to Margaret and the pinnacle of her work of combining education and health for the very youngest children. The Rachel McMillan College moved into premises in Deptford in 1930 and in 1961 was taken over by the London County Council (LCC). The LCC created an annexe of the College on the New Kent Road which went on to merge with South Bank Polytechnic in 1976. The rest of Rachel McMillan College merged with Goldsmith's College in 1977.

Margaret died in 1931 leaving a legacy which is still very much alive today in the dwindling group of people who have been involved in and understand the importance of nursery education. A memorial college named after Margaret was erected in Bradford in 1952.

Legacy and impact

It is interesting to speculate how the progress of nursery education in the UK would have progressed without the dedication of the McMillan sisters. Their efforts, spanning 70 years, established high-quality provision for young children, which became the envy of many other countries. Establishing high quality, state-funded nursery schools in poverty stricken areas of great cities was a huge achievement for them, only equalled by their commitment to the training of the adults who worked in them. In her books, Margaret explored the state of practitioner training, saying of such training at the time '... *any kind of nice, motherly girl would do for a nursery-teacher' and that nursery schools were 'a dumping ground for the well-intentioned but dull women.'* (McMillan, 1919)

Her students worked in the nursery for the first year of their training, learning from hands-on experience before embarking on the study of the theory of education during their second and third years. In her book *The Nursery School* (1919) Margaret gave detailed guidance on everything needed to set up and run a nursery school, not only the staff and their training but the every detail of the buildings, for example:

> *There should be writing boards all along the walls, but even that is not enough. For children use the hand, as they use the voice or the tongue, not in mere lesson time, but all day long and in every kind of play or work. The occasion to use it is always arising, and being so we must make provision for a natural activity.*

There was also guidance about the nursery garden, with information about trees, walls, the greenhouse, herb and kitchen gardens, slopes and climbing areas, water, sand etc, and particularly ample space 'to move, to run, to find things out by new movement'.

There was also guidance on diet, clothing (including designs for embroidery for school clothing), what children of different ages need, the programme for the day and overtime, and how to ensure continuity and progress for the children. The practical guidance was followed by examples from the nursery day, and 'pen portraits' of individual children. The second part of the book was composed of detailed information for nursery teachers, from dental health to psychology. The sections were illustrated with photographs and line drawings.

This book was (and still should be) an invaluable source of information for setting up a nursery school, from building the walls to making clothing for the children. Of course, it is dated in language and the examples describe children from a different age, although they are are still familiar characters. Margaret left us a legacy of early years practice in her books which every practitioner, every manager, every college lecturer, every politician should read. She believed that teaching very young children was not a burden, but a pleasure:

> *The washing, the feeding, the training in table manners, the listening to toddlers, the talking to three-year-olds, were not drudgery, but illuminating, wonderful tasks, opportunities such as no*

one ever had before. They were done not as mere labour, but as a preparation for mental work, and not as only ministering to bodies, but as a means of finding how the instrument of mind, the brain, develops and is helped.

(McMillan, 1919)

Since the days of the McMillan sisters, the situation in the early years has changed dramatically. The legal status of early years education and the rapid growth of the entitlement to early years education for two and three year olds has resulted in the establishment of a wide range of early education settings – registered childminders, playgroups, day nurseries, preschools, children's centres, foundation stage units and classes for under fives in primary schools as well as the remaining nursery schools – and these have both enhanced and complicated the situation. In the recent past and through to the present, there is growing pressure in government that nursery education should be incorporated into primary schools and in many parts of the UK this has happened. Whether this is a response to the academy movement, where schools are removed from Local Authority control, it is not clear, but some cities are now forced by spending cuts to reduce nursery school provision to part-time only places, and in some authorities to close the nursery schools altogether. The result is that there are now fewer than 700 government funded nursery schools in the UK.

The McMillan sisters and the practitioners who worked with them made a huge and lasting difference to state funded early years education in the UK, particularly in the education and health of children in the poorest homes. Their model has been admired and adopted in countries across the world and has influenced such social programmes as Head Start in the USA, Te Whariki in New Zealand and programmes in European countries, some of which are open to all children, others targeting socially deprived families or areas of need.

Influences on early years practice across the UK

The McMillan sisters' effect on all aspects of early education is difficult to narrow down to just a few examples where their influence is evident within the current documentation. However, early years education in every country has its own aims and principles – the why and how of a commitment to education for the youngest children.

This section covers the stated aims and principles for early years education in each of the four countries of the UK.

Rachel and Margaret McMillan

England

In England, the 'Statutory Framework for the Early Years Foundation Stage' gives clear purposes for universal, state funded early years education from birth to five years of age. This purpose emphasises partnership between practitioners and parents, and the place of the EYFS in preparing children for future stages of education and for life. There is little acknowledgement of the importance of early years experiences for their own sake or any support for the conviction that the years between pre-birth and five have a unique nature. It is only in the emphasis on the Unique Child and their needs that the McMillan sisters would recognise their model of nursery education with its focus on the unique needs of the very youngest children.

> Every child deserves the best possible start in life and the best support that enables them to fulfill their potential. Children develop quickly in the early years and a child's experiences between birth and age five have a major impact on their future life chances. A secure, safe and happy childhood is important in its own right. Good parenting and high quality early learning together provide the foundation children need to make the most of their abilities and talents as they grow up.
>
> Four guiding principles should shape practice in early years settings. These are:
>
> - every child is a unique child, who is constantly learning and can be resilient, capable, confident and self-assured;
>
> - children learn to be strong and independent through positive relationships;
>
> - children learn and develop well in enabling environments, in which their experiences respond to their individual needs and there is a strong partnership between practitioners and parents and/or carers; and
>
> - children develop and learn in different ways and at different rates. The framework covers the education and care of all children in early years provision, including children with special educational needs and disabilities.
>
> (DfE, 2014)

Scotland

In Scotland all documentation emphasises that children's experiences start before birth, and that achieving individual potential should be at the heart of all learning. There is reference to the UN Convention Rights of the Child, and a strong commitment to the professional development of practitioners. The earliest provision, 'Pre-birth to three' still maintains its uniqueness in a separate, linked document:

This guidance reflects and supports Scotland's shared vision and commitment to developing a strategic approach to prevention and early intervention in tackling the significant inequalities in Scottish society. These priorities are set out in the Scottish Government's interrelated policy frameworks entitled The Early Years Framework, Equally Well, and Achieving Our Potential, all of which aim to build the capacity of individuals, families and communities so that they can secure the best outcomes for themselves.

The main aim of Pre-birth to 3: Positive Outcomes for Scotland's Children and Families is to promote continuing professional development. It will also:

- *facilitate effective partnership working for the benefit of every child*
- *build confidence, capability and capacity across the current workforce*
- *inform students engaged in pre-service training programmes*
- *provide a common reference source to promote reflection, debate and discussion*
- *share and inform ways in which staff support children and families*
- *improve and enhance evidence-informed practice.*

(Learning and Teaching Scotland, 2010)

Northern Ireland

In Northern Ireland, the documentation includes the need to follow children's interests and to plan flexibly to meet these. There are also useful descriptions of what the learning programme might look like:

Children learn best when they:

- *have opportunities to be actively involved in practical, open-ended and challenging learning experiences that encourage creativity;*
- *have opportunities to initiate experiences that capitalise on their individual interests and curiosities;*
- *are actively involved in planning, reviewing and reflecting what they have done;*
- *are involved in play that is challenging, takes account of their developmental stage and needs and builds on their own interests and experiences;*
- *have choice and exercise autonomy and independence in their learning, and are encouraged to take risks.*

(CCEA, Northern Ireland, 2006)

Rachel and Margaret McMillan

Wales

The aims and principles for the 'Foundation Phase Framework' in Wales echo those for the other three UK countries, emphasising that the purposes of education include reducing poverty, being safe, experiencing respect and developing emotional health.

> *We aim to ensure that all children and young people:*
>
> - *have a flying start in life and the best possible basis for their future growth and development*
> - *have access to a comprehensive range of education, training and learning opportunities, including acquisition of essential personal and social skills*
> - *enjoy the best possible physical and mental, social and emotional health, including freedom from abuse, victimisation and exploitation*
> - *have access to play, leisure, sporting and cultural activities*
> - *are listened to, treated with respect, and are able to have their race and cultural identity recognised*
> - *have a safe home and a community that supports physical and emotional well-being*
> - *are not disadvantaged by any type of poverty.*

(Welsh Government, 2015)

The combined efforts of the four governments of the UK have hopefully ensured the permanence of early years education across the whole UK but this universal entitlement may mean the sacrifice of the specialist nursery with its nursery trained teachers, nursery nurses, purpose built accommodation and specialised equipment. Nursery schools have a unique place in education history, particularly in the UK, which should be celebrated by remembering such founders as the McMillan sisters.

Key guidance documents for countries in the UK

DfE, (2014) 'Statutory Framework for the Early Years Foundation Stage'.
Learning and Teaching Scotland, (2010) 'Pre-birth to three'.
CCEA, (2006) 'Northern Ireland Curriculum: Understanding the Foundation Stage'.
Welsh Assembly Government, (2015) 'Foundation Phase Framework'.

Things to think about

- The McMillan sisters were committed to providing free education for poor children. How well do you think we are doing as a nation in eradicating poverty through education?

- The McMillan sisters were passionate in their belief that children can't learn unless they are healthy and well-nourished. Do you think it is the job of early education to deal with health issues?

- Margaret believed that early years settings should be like the children's homes – do you think this is possible? Do you think it is desirable?

- Do you think that there should be a place in the future for separate nursery schools?

- Have you ever visited a nursery school? What is special about a school that is just for nursery aged children?

Maria Montessori

Full name: Maria Montessori

Born: 1870

Died: 1952

Place of birth: Chiaravalle, Manche, Italy

Countries of residence: Italy, Spain, Netherlands

What she did: Maria Montessori worked with children with special needs, and brought this experience to her work with mainstream schools. She was one of the first to work with child-sized and specialised equipment, and to allow children freedom and choice, elements which we still try to ensure exist today.

Influences on education today: Montessori schools continue to flourish, and many of her principles have been incorporated into national guidance.

Theories and Areas of work: Medicine, Child development, Pedagogy

Key influencers and followers: Jean Itard, Edouard Seguin, Friedrich Fröebel, Johann Pestalozzi, Jean-Jacques Rousseau, Jean Piaget

Key works: *The Montessori Method: Scientific Pedagogy as Applied to Child Education in the Children's Houses* (1912), *The Absorbent Mind* (1949).

What is the greatest sign of success for a teacher thus transformed? It is to be able to say, "The children are now working as if I did not exist".

Maria Montessori, attributed in Winning Strategies
for Classroom Management, 2010

Life, love, theory and research

Maria Montessori was born, brought up and worked for most of her life in Italy. She had a very close relationship with her parents, particularly her mother, an educated woman who encouraged her daughter in all her efforts. Montessori was a good but not outstanding student, who worked hard and completed her school education with good results, particularly in science and mathematics. Her first ambition had been to study engineering at university, an unusual profession for a woman, but she changed her mind and decided to study medicine instead, an even more unusual choice for a young girl at the time.

In 1890 she enrolled at the University of Rome and graduated with a first class degree in 1892, which qualified her to enter a medical course the following year. She was not welcomed by all of the students and professors, receiving some hostility, and she was required to do her dissections and other work with the naked body after-hours and alone. In her last two years of training she studied pediatrics and psychiatry, working in children's wards and emergency centres to become an expert in pediatrics, graduating in 1896 as a doctor of medicine. She also visited asylums where she observed disabled children, an experience which enhanced her later work. She was thus the first woman in Italy to qualify as a medical doctor and after qualification, she worked at the university hospital and in private practice.

In 1897 Montessori moved to Turin where she worked to improve the education of disabled children. She became interested in children with additional needs, many of whom were considered to be 'ineducable', and became known for her lectures and educational input, where she was an advocate of women's rights and the education of children with disabilities. She was convinced that with the right support and frameworks, disabled children could and should be educated.

Montessori had one son, Mario, but she never married because she would have had to give up her profession if she did. Mario's father looked after him until he married another woman, at which point Montessori placed her son in foster care with a family living in the country, so she could continue her work. Mario remained in foster care until he was in his teens, when he was reunited with his mother and worked alongside her as an assistant in her work.

In 1900 she was invited to worked at the Orthophrenic School, which trained teachers in the teaching of children with disabilities. During this time she developed some of the resources and materials that she would later use in her own schools when she worked with mainstream children. The Orthophrenic School was very successful and attracted interest from the medical and educational professionals. The children in the school were from ordinary schools but considered to be 'ineducable'. However, some of these children later passed public examinations taken by mainstream children.

In 1901, Montessori enrolled in a philosophy course which included what we now call psychology, expanding this work with observations in schools and independent study.

In 1906, Montessori was invited to oversee the care and education of a group of children of working parents in a new apartment building for low-income families in the San Lorenzo district of Rome. She was interested in applying her work and methods to normal children so she accepted. The name *Casa dei Bambini*, or Children's House, was suggested to Montessori and the first *Casa* opened on January 6, 1907, enrolling 50 to 60 children between the ages of two or three and six or seven. Maria continued to work in her medical role during the period in which the school was getting established.

The first *Casa* just had a teacher's table, a blackboard, stove, small chairs and tables for the children and a locked cupboard where the specialist Montessori materials were kept. The children were encouraged to look after themselves and the classroom, dressing and undressing themselves, dusting, sweeping and gardening, as well as using the materials that Montessori had developed herself. Every one of these materials was developed after observing children selecting and using them without any prompting or help from an adult.

The materials included sorting, stacking and manipulating objects made of a range of materials and textures. Many of these objects were made of smooth polished wood, others were of enamelled metal, wicker and fabric. The children could also explore items from nature, such as pebbles, seashells and birds' nests. Some of the materials were aimed at teaching a particular skill, for example threading, tying shoelaces, doing up buttons etc. Others were mathematical, for example, using beads and blocks, and yet others were designed to help children with listening skills, such as wooden cylinders with moving contents.

These resources were specially designed to 'grow with the children', being open-ended and free from restrictions. For instance, the wooden cubes could be used for building and pattern making by a younger child, or by an older child for learning algebra. Other materials such as felt and wooden numerals and letters were added as children became ready for their use. The teaching part of the activities with these resources can be provided in several different ways:

- a teacher might demonstrate an activity to a small group or single child
- a child might give a 'lesson' to others
- children could learn by watching others use the same equipment
- the child might explore the materials freely.

Children then use the materials in the demonstrated activity or to explore other possibilities.

Montessori did not teach the children herself; this was done by the daughter of the building's porter, under her instruction. She observed the children as they used her materials noticing periods of deep concentration, repetitions of activities and a sense of order in the way children worked with the materials. When offered a free choice, she observed that children chose practical activities, such as gardening, block play, painting and the Montessori materials over the other toys provided. They did not seem to need rewards for their work, even sweets did not seem to tempt them and they seemed to be developing a self-motivated sense of self-control, again akin to Csikszentmihalyi's flow.

Based on these observations, Montessori began to develop the principles and resources that became hallmarks of Montessori Schools. These included:

- Child-sized furniture, light enough for children to move and rearrange themselves.
- Child level, open shelving so children could access their own resources.
- Real-life, but small sized household tools, such as brooms, dustpans, dusters, cooking utensils, gardening tools etc.

- Open-plan rooms where children could move about freely.
- A range of activities linked to the care of the environment such as pet care, flower arranging, cooking etc.
- Outdoor facilities.

These facilities were not used at the time in schools, where it was more common for children to sit at school desks and use such things as slates and chalks. Children were instructed, and independent access to toys and other equipment was virtually unknown. Montessori believed that children should work with 'real' objects but scaled down so they suited the size of young children's hands and bodies.

Working independently enabled children to be more confident, reaching higher levels of autonomy and understanding. Treating the children as individuals was another principle of Montessori's work, enabling her to help each child to fulfill their potential. She constantly reviewed her materials, removing those with less appeal to the children and adding new ones. Her commitment to fostering independence led her to experiment with allowing children free choice in some periods of the day.

The daily programme at the *Casa dei Bambini* would be very familiar to practitioners today, with periods of adult-led activities, some free choice, songs, stories and conversations. Time was spent outside, in gardening or group games and 'gymnastics', but 'tidy up time' was a much more 'deep clean' process, with dusters, mops, brooms and dustpans, much more than just 'picking up the bricks and hanging up the dressing up clothes'.

The role of the adult was seen as observer and director of children's development. Teachers in these settings operated at what Montessori described as 'the margins', observing and intervening from the edge of children's activity, not the centre.

Her influences were Friedrich Fröebel, Jean-Jacques Rousseau and Johann Pestalozzi, and she advocated Fröebellian methods for teacher training, emphasising learning from nature and following the child's interests. Her central principle was 'first educate the senses, then the intellect', and she devised a method for teaching that depended on this principle, so *'looking becomes reading, touching becomes writing'* (Montessori, 1916). Her Children's Houses became unique learning environments, and their example has become an international feature of Montessori education.

In 1909, Montessori wrote her first book, *The Method of Scientific Pedagogy Applied to the Education of Children in the Children's Houses*, which described her observation and teaching methods. More Children's Houses were opened, and further training courses for teachers were held in Rome. Montessori methods were adopted in some other countries, including Switzerland where the methods replaced Fröebellian methods in orphanages and kindergartens, and at this time, she decided to give up her medical practice to concentrate on the schools and her increasingly demanding educational work at home and abroad.

Montessori methods spread rapidly and by 1912 private Montessori schools had also opened in the UK, France, Argentina, Australia, China, India, Japan, Korea, Mexico, Switzerland,

Syria, the United States and New Zealand. Montessori methods were increasingly being adopted in government funded school systems and increasing numbers of countries were adopting the whole method into their mainstream schools. Translations of her works were widely available in a range of languages and *The Montessori Method* became a bestseller.

Maria embarked on world wide lecture tours, three in the USA, and including one where a glass-walled classroom was exhibited so the public could see how the method worked in practice with 21 children. She returned to Europe in 1915 and moved to Barcelona, continuing her lecture tours and training sessions. She also opened a small group of schools supported by the Catalan government, developed materials for children up to the age of 11 and provided training in the use of these. However, the Catalan government wanted her to make a public statement of her support for Catalan independence and when she refused, funding was withdrawn from her projects. In 1936 she left Spain permanently.

Between the World Wars, the Montessori method became tainted when she was closely associated with Mussolini who funded schools and training while his Fascist regime was in power. After she spoke in defence of peace, Mussolini put Montessori and her son under surveillance and so they left Italy and Montessori activities were ended there in 1936. Maria and Mario moved to Amsterdam where they continued to produce materials although Maria was increasingly involved in the peace movement.

In her later life she visited and stayed in India, and was interned there at the beginning of the Second World War because she was an Italian. During her final years she moved between Italy, Amsterdam and India continuing to lecture and write about her methods until she died in the Netherlands aged 81.

Although so well-received and seemingly universally approved, Montessori was not without her critics. Education reformer John Dewey wrote a dismissive and critical book and The National Kindergarten Association was also critical. They said that Montessori methods were too rigid, leaving little time for creativity, imagination or social interaction. They also resented the tight hold she held over the production of her materials.

Legacy and impact

Montessori schools have been established in many countries, particularly in the Netherlands where by the mid-1930s there were more than 200 Montessori schools in the country. The Montessori Society moved permanently to Amsterdam.

As the Montessori method spread across the world and practitioners and teachers bought and read her books, Montessori's ideas were incorporated into mainstream and special schools practice. The Montessori movement in America broke up after the criticism of her methods by John Dewey and the National Kindergarten Association mentioned above, but there are still many schools in America which claim to use the method even though some have no Montessori trained teachers or relevant materials.

Montessori education has been popular in the UK ever since she came to lecture here in 1919, and the Montessori Association continues to work to promote her methods. In order to be a true Montessori school the establishment must have trained staff and follow a Montessori programme, using Montessori resources. Because the Montessori name is not well protected by trademark law, anyone can set up a school and put 'Montessori School' on the sign but that does not make them a Montessori school.

The Montessori (England) website includes information about the way it ensures that all schools affiliated to the association really are true to the aims and principles and practices of Montessori, and still meet the criteria for good or outstanding schools as judged by Ofsted.

Despite some criticism, Montessori continues to be an enduring influence in early years education across the world, even though her methods have not been adopted across all government controlled early years establishments in any country.

Influences on early years practice across the UK

Montessori's materials and methods have had a great influence on practice and on resources used in our early years settings. Because Montessori was very careful to preserve the rights for production of her own specialist resources, they are as closely linked with her methods as those used by Reggio Schools. However, many of the specialist resources she produced have since been replicated by others, so it is difficult to untangle whether a set of stacking beakers, or a child-sized dustpan and brush is a specialist Montessori teaching resource or a toy bought from a high street toy shop. What makes the difference is the way the practitioner uses the resources in a structured environment, with his or her specialised knowledge and training.

Because none of the UK countries have adopted the Montessori method whole sale, there is no reference to these in the documentation produced by governments. However, Montessori methods and principles are comparable and in many places compatible with the principles and practices recommended to early years practitioners in the UK. If we use her principles (which have been condensed here), we can make links with the UK documentation. Montessori principles include respect for the child, a recognition that children can and do educate themselves (autoeducation), that there are sensitive periods in development and that the adult has the role of guide and mentor.

After some initial reservations about the national guidance for the early years in England, and having carefully compared their own principles with those of the EYFS, the Montessori Association recommends to its member schools that they should adhere to the legal requirements of the EYFS (2012). In their 'Guide to the early years foundation stage in Montessori settings', the Association acknowledges the compatibility between the two sets of curriculum guidance:

'The principles underlying the EYFS are ones with which Montessorians are very familiar and which they endorse that children learn to be strong and independent through positive relationships; that they learn and develop well in enabling environments; and that they develop and learn in different ways and at different rates.'

(Montessori Schools Association, 2012)

If practitioners just looked at the paperwork, the resources on the shelves, the organisation of the space, indoors and outside, or the planning, they would find few differences between the early years setting in a Montessori school and their own. The difference is subtle but important and mainly consists of the freedom of the child to follow their own interests for as long as they wish and the closeness with which the adults observe and plan for the next steps for each individual. This difference is summed up in an article by Rob Gueterbok on the Montessori website:

'Within this space there are very few limits to the child's freedom and decision-making. A child is shown a variety of activities, is free to choose what to do, and for how long. Through detailed observations of his choice and use of activities, further individual lessons are offered, giving him an increasing range of materials to explore. Children are free to use an activity until they decide to put it away. They are free to choose when to be active, when to rest and watch, when to look at a book, to go outside, to have a drink or prepare some fruit.'

(www.montessorisociety.org.uk)

The nearest approach to the Montessori day in a non-Montessori setting is sometimes referred to as 'free flow', where children are free to move about as they please, following their own interests or getting involved in activities planned by others. However, in most settings, the balance of adult and child initiated activity is different, with a varying degree of control by the practitioner but little possibility for the child to be given so much control of their own learning.

The principles of the Montessori approach are summed up on their website www. montessorisociety.org.uk/montessori/montessori-principles in the following words:

The Montessori approach to education rests on the premise of supporting the tendencies and sensitivities of each individual as they present themselves as different developmental needs at each stage of development. This can be summarised in the following way:

- *An environment that serves the particular needs of the child's stage of development.*
- *An adult who understands the developmental needs of the child and acts as a guide to help the child find his natural path of development.*

- *Freedom for the child to engage in his own development according to his own particular developmental timeline.*

This description would be recognised by every early years practitioners wherever they work. The focus on the relationship between children and adults is a universal feature, present in every document worth implementing. The difference is in how the principles are interpreted.

> ## Key guidance documents for countries in the UK
>
> Montessori Schools Association, (2012) 'Guide to the early years foundation stage in Montessori settings'.

Things to think about

- Montessori has proved to be one of the most influential thinkers in education. Can you see any sign of her work in your own setting?
- How much freedom do the children in your setting have? Have you worked out the balance between child-initiated and adult-directed activity? Don't forget to include story time, circle time, registration and all those other activities where the children have no choice.
- What do you think is the ideal balance between adult control and child freedom in an early years setting?
- Have you ever visited or worked in a Montessori school? What were the key differences about it?

Ivan Pavlov

Perfect as the wing of a bird may be, it will never enable the bird to fly if unsupported by the air. Facts are the air of science. Without them a man of science can never rise.

Ivan Pavlov, article in *Science* magazine: 'Request of Pavlov to the Academic Youth of His Country', 1936

Life, love, theory and research

Ivan Pavlov was born in Russia, the eldest of 11 children. He enjoyed his childhood, playing, gardening and helping to look after his brothers and sisters. He could read by the time he was seven but a fall from a wall prevented him from attending school until he was 11.

He was educated at a local seminary but did not complete his studies, deciding in 1870 to leave his intended career in the church to attend the University of St Petersburg. Here he studied physics, mathematics and natural sciences, graduating with a qualification in natural sciences. Pavlov went on to study at the Imperial Academy of Medical Surgery and followed this by graduating from the Medical Military Academy in 1879 with a gold medal award for his research work.

Pavlov had already studied the circulatory system and for his doctorate he expanded this work into investigation of the nervous system, gaining another qualification in 1883. Once his studies were completed, Pavlov worked in Germany for some time where he began his studies of the behaviour and digestive systems of dogs. This interest in dogs was to continue for the rest of his life and to be his most significant contribution to science.

Pavlov returned to St Petersburg in 1886 and remained there for the next 30 years. During this time, he concentrated on his work on the digestive system which eventually resulted in him winning the Nobel Prize in Physiology or Medicine in 1904. He investigated the digestive systems of dogs and later of children, partly by devising an external salivary gland so he could collect and analyse salivary excretions and responses to different foods. He became interested in the way that dogs began to salivate before the food was actually in their mouths and embarked on a long-term study of this behaviour, resulting in his work on conditioned and unconditioned responses.

The observation of dogs over long periods of time was a new way of working as Pavlov and his team needed to keep the animals alive and in good health in laboratory kennels in order to make the research valid. His kennels were among the first laboratory kennels to be managed in the interests of the animals as well as the interests of science. Before this, animals were usually experimented on by vivisection.

Pavlov's work on dogs, particularly the conditioned response theories he developed, provide context for current discussions on education. Pavlov's methods systematically found that dogs will salivate at feeding times, even before they could see or taste their food and this reflex could be influenced by adding a sound (a buzzer or bell) or a visual stimulus to the experiment at the same time as the food is given.

	Stimulus type	Response	Response types
Before conditioning			
Food only	Unconditioned Stimulus (UCS)	**Salivation**	Unconditioned, reflexive (UCR) natural response
Bell or other stimulus only	Neutral Stimulus (NS)	**None**	None
During conditioning			
Bell +Food	UCS	**Salivation**	UCR
After conditioning			
Bell only with NO FOOD	Conditioned Stimulus (CS)	**Salivation**	CR

Pavlov knew that there are some things that a dog does not need to learn. For example, dogs don't learn to salivate whenever they see food. This reflex is 'hard wired' into the dog. However, if he made a sound or showed a visual stimulus at the same time as the food is given, gradually over time, the dog would begin to salivate when it heard the sound or saw the image, even before seeing or smelling the food. As he continued the work, Pavlov found that the dogs would salivate when they saw or heard the trigger, even when no food was offered. The influence on education came when a link was made between Pavlov's experiments using this manipulation of events or stimuli before a specific behaviour to produce salivation in dogs, much like teachers manipulate instruction and learning environments to produce positive behaviours or decrease maladaptive behaviours.

Although Pavlov's work was essentially in the learned behaviour of dogs, many have made the link between his work and learning in humans. The educational practice of conditioned response training has been particularly evident in the handling of behaviour (behaviour modification), where a child's behaviour is observed in the now familiar ABC method:

- A is the antecedent – what happened before the incident (such as a temper tantrum)
- B is the behaviour itself – described in detail
- C is the consequence – what happened after the behaviour (what the adult did, how the child responded, any sanctions or punishments).

The adults will use the 'antecedent' information to find out whether the behaviour is triggered by any particular activity, time of day or anything else, which might be preventable. For example:

Following observations, the practitioners in the nursery found that Brian's tantrums often happened when he was asked to stop what he was playing with to come for group time, or to let another child have a turn with a toy.

If they looked at their 'behaviour' observations, they found that:

At this time, Brian would throw things, stamp and shout, sometimes endangering other children's safety.

The information from observation was used to construct a 'consequence', a programme where a Brian knew that the response to his tantrums would be:

'If you throw a tantrum, I (your teacher) will take you to a quiet place to sit on your own for five minutes. After five minutes you will clear up any mess made during the tantrum and apologise to any other child you have hurt or upset.'

If these processes are used systematically, the child begins to understand 'what will happen if…' and begins to modify their behaviour. This method has been referred to as 'Behaviourism'. These types of procedures have been thoroughly researched and found to be effective in reducing behaviour problems in classrooms. Behaviour modification has also been compared with the use of medication and has been found in many studies to be the more effective of the two.

The term 'Pavlov's dogs' has been used as a term to describe a conditioned response in humans and so has become an understood 'shorthand' for unconditioned or even conditioned responses.

Legacy and impact

Strategies developed from Pavlov's work became known as 'conditioning', and were a key component in behaviourist approaches, many of which are still used today, not just in behaviour management techniques and in everyday classroom management but in family education programmes where parents are trained to use these methods, which can include use of a 'naughty step'.

Pavlov's work had a significant effect on psychologists and particularly on those who believed in the power of behaviour and instinct over reason. What happens before an event is likely to affect our behaviour during and after the event and sometimes we are not even aware of the way we have been influenced. Pavlov's work on conditioning also influenced the way humans perceive their own behaviour and learning processes and his studies of conditioning continue to be central to modern behaviour therapy. Bertrand Russell, the British philosopher, was an enthusiastic advocate of Pavlov's work, as was Aldous Huxley in his book *Brave New World*, where conditioning is used to change society.

Simplified methods based on Pavlov's work are used by many practitioners and teachers in early years settings although there are still some reservations about their effectiveness if the practitioner has not been adequately trained in the use of such methods. A consistent approach and a common response from all the adults working with the child, both in the setting and at home, are central to any successful programme and it is vital that parents understand and agree with any rewards or sanctions applied, particularly if the plan is to be applied at home as well as in the setting. Simply using the 'naughty step' approach randomly to suit the adults will not only give an inconsistent message but will undermine any subsequent attempt to use a behavioural approach.

There have been some recent attempts to popularise behavioural approaches through television, social media and on the Internet. However, these attempts are rarely successful as they require professional support and consistent approaches for all concerned.

Influences on early years practice across the UK

The links with Pavlov and the resulting behavioural therapies and treatments have influenced guidance in schools and settings, particularly in the documentation for special needs support. Behaviour management bridges the domains of mainstream and special education and many practitioners in the early years have successfully managed children with emerging needs as well as those whose needs have been identified but have not yet been met.

The quotes below from the UK documentation focus on managing children with behavioural problems and in involving parents in the process.

England

In England, there is mention of managing behaviour as part of the Personal Social and Emotional Development area of learning. There is also very helpful documentation which supports practitioners and their managers working in settings across the spectrum. In the EYFS Statutory Framework for all settings and schools in England, the following references make a clear link between behavioural methods within mainstream groups, including the need for a corporate approach to managing behaviour, and the importance of praise.

> 'Development Matters in the EYFS' states: 'Practitioners should have agreed procedures outlining how to respond to changes in children's behaviour.'

> (Early Education, 2012)

And the 'Statutory framework for the EYFS' includes:

Early Learning Goal

Children talk about how they and others show feelings, talk about their own and others' behaviour, and its consequences, and know that some behaviour is unacceptable. They work as part of a group or class, and understand and follow the rules. They adjust their behaviour to different situations, and take changes of routine in their stride.

> (DfE, 2014)

In the 'SEND Code of Practice' for English schools, there is more detailed advice on managing children's behaviour if it becomes more problematic. This guidance emphasises the importance of clear processes and involvement of all staff, and the parents of the child:

> *…using a carefully designed system of behaviour targets drawn up with the child and linked to a reward system which, wherever possible, involves parents or carers.*

- *ensuring that all staff coming into contact with the child are briefed on potential triggers for outbursts and effective ways of heading off trouble at an early stage*

- *drawing up a contingency plan if there is an outburst in class, for example, identifying with the child a key helper who can be called to remove the child from the situation.*

(DfE/DoH, 2015)

More recently, the UK government has provided a document for settings and schools which has a specific focus on managing behaviour within the broad spectrum of mental health. The first quote is one of many examples in the document entitled 'Mental health and behaviour in schools', giving case study information from individual schools:

Widden Primary School has a 'rainbow room', a small, quiet and calm room where staff can take individual children and small groups to get ready for the school day, talk about concerns and worries or to calm down if something has upset or angered them. All the children are supportive and keen to use it and the school works hard to make sure it is not seen as a time out or naughty room. There is no stigma and all of the children like being made to feel unique. The school has seen benefits in terms of attendance, well-being and achievement.

The strongest evidence supports prevention/early intervention approaches that include a focus on:

- *regular targeted work with small groups of children exhibiting early signs of anxiety, to develop problem-solving and other skills associated with a cognitive behavioural approach; and*

- *additional work with parents to help them support their children and reinforce small group work. Such work is likely to be especially effective when the parents are themselves anxious and the children are younger.*

(DfE, 2015)

Northern Ireland

In Northern Ireland, 'Understanding the foundation stage' contains the following advice for practitioners:

It is also important that adults are:

- *sincere, fair and honest with children;*
- *patient, allowing time for children to adjust to the setting (transition);*
- *consistent and have a positive approach to behaviour management.*

(CCEA, Northern Ireland, 2006)

In the guidance for early years practitioners supporting children with special needs, and particularly for supporting children with behavioural difficulties, the Northern Ireland Government suggests the following in 'Extended Early Years Special Educational Needs (SEN) Supplement', which has a direct link with the behavioural approaches resulting from Pavlov's research on conditioned response:

A positive approach, which is focused on social and emotional wellbeing with logical consequences will help the child to develop self management of their behaviour.

(Northern Ireland Department of Education, 2012)

Of course, no-one would suggest that education should become simply training, and that children should be treated like Pavlov's dogs, but it is evident that children do respond to plans which have clear outcomes and an opportunity to copy positive models:

Practitioners should:

- *Have consistent and clear protocols and procedures established and used by all members of staff.*

- *Make sure the children have a clear understanding of rules, which should be backed up with visual reminders. Don't have too many rules.*

- *Pick up on positives and establish yourself as the focal point of interest and authority.*

- *Use praise effectively.*

(Northern Ireland Department of Education, 2012)

Scotland

In Scotland, the document 'Pre-birth to 3' contains the following advice for practitioners:

All staff have a key role to play in understanding and managing the behaviour of babies and young children. Children often experience strong emotions and do not always have the capacity to regulate these emotions for themselves.

Very often, children's behaviour is their way of communicating a need and is reflective of their developmental stage and not meant to be intentionally challenging.

(Learning and Teaching Scotland, 2010)

Wales

Guidance in Wales includes direct reference to the ABC method described above.

The Antecedent-Behaviour-Consequence (ABC) chart is used to collect information through observing information about the events that are occurring within a child's environment.

A = *Antecedent: what happens before the behaviour occurs.*

B = *Behaviour: the observed behaviour.*

C = *Consequence: the positive or negative results of the behaviour.*

Ivan Pavlov

Once the practitioner has collected the information, they are advised to use problem solving approaches and the guidance offers a range of questions for practitioners to ask themselves. These include identifying when, where and why the behaviour occurs, what the triggers are and what alternative behaviours could be suggested to the child. Once these questions have been answered, a systematic approach to managing behaviour can be implemented, to include:

- clear descriptions of the undesirable behaviour

- clear sanctions, understood by the child

- any rewards, and how these can be achieved

- links with parents (where deemed appropriate).

'Practical approaches to behaviour management' (Welsh Government; 2012) provides an extremely informative and practical document on behaviour management techniques in detail, giving examples of how practitioners and teachers can respond to a range of classroom behaviours that disrupt learning for the child and for others. This document would be a helpful addition to any staffroom bookshelf.

Key guidance documents for countries in the UK

Early Education, (2012) 'Development Matters in the EYFS'.
DfE/DoH, (2015) 'SEND: Code of Practice.'
DfE, (2015) 'Mental health and behaviour in schools: Departmental advice for school staff.'
Northern Ireland Department of Education, (2012) 'Extended Early Years Special Educational Needs (SEN) Supplement.'
Welsh Government (2012) 'Practical approaches to behaviour management in the classroom: a handbook for classroom teachers in primary schools.'
Learning and Teaching Scotland, (2010) 'Pre-birth to three.'

Things to think about

- Pavlov's experiments on dogs were very influential. Some people think it is inappropriate to use evidence from animal research in education. What do you think?

- Have you ever used the ABC method for managing behaviour? What happened? What are the advantages and disadvantages of the method?

- What are appropriate sanctions for children in the early years?
- Which behaviours do you find most difficult to handle? Why do you think this is?
- Some children's behaviour is very challenging. Do you think you have had sufficient help in knowing what to do when a child in your group is badly behaved?

Johann Heinrich Pestalozzi

Full name: Johann Heinrich Pestalozzi

Born: 1746

Died: 1827

Place of birth: Zurich, Switzerland

Countries of residence: Switzerland

What he did: Pestalozzi's was committed to establishing schools that follow practices described in Rousseau's instructive novel *Emile*. These principles include child-initiated learning, an interest in physical sciences, and a commitment to the natural world.

Influences on education today: Pestalozzi's influence can be seen in early years settings everywhere, including the commitment to learning out of doors, and the focus on the children and their interests. Two centuries after his death, there are still Pestalozzi schools in many countries, and his name is synonymous with child-centred learning.

Theories and areas of work: Pedagogy, Child development

Key influencers and followers: Jean-Jacques Rousseau, Friedrich Fröebel, Maria Montessori

Key works: *How Gertrude Teaches her Children* (1801), *The ABC of Sense Perception, Lessons on the Observation of Number Relations* and *The Mother's Book* (all 1803).

The circle of knowledge commences close round a man and thence stretches out concentrically.

Johann Heinrich Pestalozzi, The Evening Hour of a Hermit, 1780

Life, love, theory and research

Johann Pestalozzi was born and died in Switzerland and did much of his work there, although his influence went far beyond the Swiss borders. His family experienced poverty throughout his life and he was one of seven children although, as was common in his time, four died in childhood.

Originally brought up to join the clerical profession, he became an enthusiastic educator and particularly an educational reformer, whose work influenced education practice across his country and then across Europe and the United States. After dropping out of university, Pestalozzi started his own school on his farm, working there with his wife for 30 years and teaching their own son alongside the children of destitute families. During this time, Pestalozzi read Jean-Jacques Rousseau's *Emile* which affected him deeply. He was very impressed by an education which stayed near to nature, rather than in a school. Sadly, due to shortage of money, the farm school at Neuhof closed.

After the Napoleonic Wars, Pestalozzi gained permission to start another school at Stans, to educate the children of the village whose houses had been burned to the ground by French soldiers. This school, always short of money, gave him a chance to observe the way poor children could learn in a caring and supportive environment. However, following mistrust of the villagers, the school was closed, and Pestalozzi was moved by the government to a school in Burgdorf castle where he was successful in using his own methods to teach a small group of children.

He had already written one novel – '*Leonard and Gertrude*' – and in 1801 he published '*How Gertrude Teaches her Children*.' The book was written as 14 letters from Pestalozzi to his friend Heinrich Gessner, explaining Pestalozzi's philosophy of education. His purpose in these letters was to show that, by reducing knowledge to its elements and by constructing a series of psychologically-ordered exercises, anybody could teach their children effectively. Reading about Gertrude and her children put Burgdorf on the map and visitors flocked to observe Pestalozzi the innovative educator. Since his reading of *Emile*, he had followed the naturalist philosophy of Jean-Jacques Rousseau, and worked to extend this philosophy, focusing on the teacher's work in schools rather than Emile's tutor working with a single child. He constructed a series of simple, psychologically ordered exercises so teachers, tutors and parents could teach their children effectively by following them. His principles for teaching included:

- Beginning with the concrete object before introducing abstract concepts
- Beginning with the immediate environment before moving to what is distant and remote
- Beginning with easy exercises before introducing complex ones, proceeding gradually, cumulatively, and slowly.

A romantic at heart, Pestalozzi thought that education theory should be broken down into its constituent parts, ensuring that teachers attended equally to *the head, the hand and the heart – to intellectual, physical and emotional development*. The children learned weaving, painting and woodwork as well as reading and writing. Pestalozzi argued that, instead of just dealing with words, children should learn through activity and through using things, and his theory of *Anschauung* (having sensory experience of concrete objects before learning through words) resulted in children learning to read, write and calculate much more easily than children who began direct teaching of reading and writing at an early age. Pestalozzi designed an elaborate series of graded object lessons by which children examined minerals, plants and animals and human-made artefacts found in their environment.

In Pestalozzi's schools, children were free to pursue their own interests, self-motivated activity was recognised and supported, and children were encouraged to find their own answers to questions rather than relying on the teacher to answer. Schoolwork was considered by Pestalozzi as a way to train physical dexterity, promote efficiency and encourage mutual helpfulness. He argued that children should learn through activity and observing things. They should be free to pursue their own interests and draw their own conclusions. Parents should also be encouraged to educate their children using familiar objects available in their homes.

Pestalozzi's philosophy was based on the concept of four spheres of influence. Three of these spheres were considered to be 'external' to the learner: home and family, vocation and individual self-determination and society, state and nation. The final sphere was the learner's 'inner sense', implying that once education has satisfied basic needs, the individual experienced inner peace and a keen belief in God. Pestalozzi goes beyond Rousseau in that he sets out some concrete ways forward, based on research. He tried to reconcile the tension, recognised by Rousseau, between the education of the individual (for freedom) and that of the citizen (for responsibility and use).

There was interest from Europe and the United States in Pestalozzi's methods, which were child-centred and took into account children's individual differences, encouraged self-chosen activity and perception by the senses. Pestalozzi worked to adapt the teaching of ancient languages (Latin, Hebrew and Greek) to primary teaching, exploring how a child's mother tongue could assist in learning these languages. With his colleagues, Pestalozzi also constructed a curriculum for physical education, exercise and outdoor activity, and linked this education of the body to his theories of general, moral and intellectual education.

Further political problems necessitated a move from Burgdorf to Yverdon castle in 1804. In this location, the school model flourished: staff and children lived in the village. Children who could not pay the fees were admitted for nothing and parents were kept informed through regular updates from teachers. The natural environment was very important and children were involved in walks, swimming, gardening, raising animals and growing food. The school was successful for 20 years but constant financial problems led to the closure of the institute in 1825 and Pestalozzi returned to Neuhof where he lived until he died in 1827.

Pestalozzi never managed to achieve his dream of a perfect education but he did inspire many others who followed and went onto implement his philosophy.

Legacy and impact

Pestalozzi had a great influence on Friedrich Fröebel, who worked for a time with Pestalozzi at Yverdon before setting up his own kindergartens which were modelled in many ways on Pestalozzi's work.

As with many pioneers, Pestalozzi never really saw his dreams come to fruition but his ideas had been planted in the fertile soil of the educators who visited his schools, taking his ideas back to their own schools and systems in Europe, the United States and beyond, particularly in countries where child-centred education for young children was beginning to become accepted, allowing all children a time for childhood, for exploration, for self-selection of materials and in following their own interests.

Throughout the 19th and 20th centuries, early years practitioner's and teacher's practice has reflected the principles of Pestalozzi. These include:

- free choice in learning
- hands-on experiences
- real objects
- outdoor learning (including gardening and physical development)
- problem solving and exploratory approaches
- experiencing new materials and resources in play, before being asked to use them in an adult led task.

If Pestalozzi could visit our schools nowadays he would be pleasantly surprised by how many changes to early education have been implemented in the intervening years. However, he would also be surprised that in countries where his principles of child-centred learning have been implemented, there is also an undue emphasis on tests and reports as measures of children's success. Maybe we should now take time to evaluate the ways in which we have supported some of his theories while ignoring those we feel are less important.

Pestalozzi's name lives on, not only in educational theory but in the foundation established in his name. A Pestalozzi training school has been established in Zurich, and there are schools all over the world named after him – including those in Switzerland and Germany, Greece, South America. Pestalozzi Villages in Switzerland and the UK have been established to house war orphans and give them opportunities to study in the UK, and the Pestalozzi- Fröebel-Haus in Berlin continues to train nursery school teachers. The projects of the Pestalozzi Foundation have benefitted well over 300,000 children and adolescents in Switzerland and abroad.

Elizabeth Mayo (1793–1865), a British teacher, was inspired by Pestalozzi's methods and was credited with promoting the formal education of infant teachers. Mayo was the first woman in Britain to be employed to train these teachers.

Influences on early years practice across the UK

As stated above, Pestalozzi's approach has been embedded in early years practice across the world. We all espouse the belief that 'child-centred' learning, choice and free access to resources are at the heart of what we do. We are also aware of the way the pressures of inspection, self-evaluation, reporting to parents, and even assessments based in observation of individuals can divert even the best practice.

Pestalozzi had a great commitment to nurturing equally *the head (intellectual development), the hand (physical development) and the heart (emotional development)* and this has led to an emphasis on these areas of learning. In all four countries, these areas of learning (Physical Development, Personal Social and Emotional Development, and Communication, rather than 'reading and writing') have become more important than others.

The statute and guidance for the four countries of the UK all include references to Pestalozzi's principles, if not his name.

England

In England, the 'Statutory framework for the EYFS 'states:

Three areas are particularly crucial for igniting children's curiosity and enthusiasm for learning, and for building their capacity to learn, form relationships and thrive. These three areas, the prime areas, are:

- *communication and language;*
- *physical development; and*
- *personal, social and emotional development.*

(DfE, 2014)

In 'Development Matters in the EYFS' adults are advised to:

- *Build in opportunities for children to play with materials before using them in planned tasks.*
- *Establish the enabling conditions for rich play: space, time, flexible resources, choice, control, warm and supportive relationships.*
- *Encourage children to describe problems they encounter, and to suggest ways to solve the problem.*
- *Provide something that is new and unusual for them to explore, especially when it is linked to their interests.*

(Early Education, 2012)

Throughout the documentation for the EYFS, there is an emphasis on child initiated learning and in activities that may have formerly been seen as part of the role of the adult. These include planning and monitoring their own activities, changing strategy if needed and learning how to review how well their approach works.

Scotland

In Scotland, in the document 'Building the curriculum', the emphasis is again on hands-on, explorative learning, which 'engages and challenges children's thinking' (Scottish Executive, 2007) It takes full advantage of the opportunities for learning presented by:

- spontaneous play
- planned, purposeful play
- investigating and exploring
- events and life experiences
- focused learning and teaching.

There is also a clear recognition of the dangers when an overcrowded curriculum forces out exploration and active learning:

> …it suggests that there is no long-term advantage to children when there is an over-emphasis on systematic teaching before 6 or 7 years of age. A key message is that approaches to fostering learning need to be flexible to take account of the needs of the child, and will change as children develop.
>
> (Scottish Executive, 2007)

Northern Ireland

In Northern Ireland, practitioners are reminded in 'Understanding the foundation stage' that:

> Children learn best when they:
> - have opportunities to be actively involved in practical, open-ended and challenging learning experiences that encourage creativity;
> - have opportunities to initiate experiences that capitalise on their individual interests and curiosities;
> - are actively involved in planning, reviewing and reflecting what they have done;
> - are enabled to express themselves by creating images, sounds, movements, structures and invented stories;
> - are involved in play that is challenging, takes account of their developmental stage and needs and builds on their own interests and experiences;
> - work in stimulating environments and have access to a range of resources;
> - develop secure relationships with peers and adults;
> - have choice and exercise autonomy and independence in their learning, and are encouraged to take risks.
>
> (Northern Ireland, 2006)

Wales

In Wales the principles are neatly summed up in the following quote from the Welsh Government's useful guidance 'Play/Active learning overview for 3 to 7 year olds':

Children's learning is most effective when it arises from first-hand experiences, whether spontaneous or structured, and when they are given time to play without interruptions and to reach a satisfactory conclusion.

(Welsh Government, 2008)

Key guidance documents for countries in the UK

DfE, (2014) 'Statutory Framework for the Early Years Foundation Stage'.
Early Education, (2012) 'Development Matters in the EYFS'.
Scottish Executive (2007) 'Building the Curriculum 2 (3–18); Active learning in the early years'.
CCEA, (2006) 'Northern Ireland Curriculum: Understanding the Foundation Stage'.
Welsh Government (2008) 'Play/Active learning Overview for 3 to 7-year-olds'.

Things to think about

- What do you think Pestalozzi would say if he came to your school and watched your approaches to active learning?

- Pestalozzi was committed to providing activities for the head, the hand and the heart. Can you identify activities that feed all three of these needs?

- How could you make more time and space for children to explore and experiment with self-chosen resources?

- Do you always give children time to explore new resources before using them in an adult-led activity?

- Do you agree that Physical, PSED and Communication should be the most important areas of learning?

- If you are still a student, do you think you will be incorporating Pestalozzi's philosophy in your work when you complete your training?

Jean Piaget

Full name: Jean Piaget

Born: 1886

Died: 1980

Place of birth: Neuchatel, Switzerland

Countries of residence: Switzerland, France,

What he did: Piaget's work has been among the most influential in shaping educational and medical practice. His work in observing children's development resulted in his schedule of schemas, and in his writing on children's stages of development.

Influences on education today: The staged development model has had a significant effect on the education and care of young children across the world. Much of the guidance for practitioners advises using Piaget's stages of development for planning and assessing learning. However, recent developments in neuroscience have resulted in some criticism of these rigid stages, implying that a more flexible approach to development should be implemented.

Theories and areas of work: Constructivism, Developmental psychology

Key influencers and followers: Lev Vygotsky, Jerome Bruner, Konrad Lorenz

Key works: *The Language and Thought of the Child* (1926), *The Child's Conception of the World* (1928), *The Child's Construction of Reality* (1955).

If you want to be creative, stay in part a child, with the creativity and invention that characterizes children before they are deformed by adult society.

Jean Piaget, quoted in Critical and Creative Thinking:
A Brief Guide for Teachers, 2015

Life, love, theory and research

Jean Piaget was born in 1886 in Switzerland. He worked in his own country for his whole life and died there in 1980. He considered himself to be a 'genetic epistimologist' (the study of the origins of knowledge) and he was the first to look in depth at this line of research. His main interest was how one comes to know things, and Piaget felt that the difference between humans and animals was the fact that humans are able to reason through abstract symbolism. His study focused on how people develop cognitively from birth throughout their lives and for his purposes he established four primary stages of development.

Piaget's early love and the focus of his early studies were molluscs (snails and shellfish) and he published his first paper on this subject when he was in his late teens. However, a chance opportunity to move to France and be involved in standardising Burt's test of intelligence influenced his eventual choice to work with children, particularly his own and the children of friends, to observe the ways that children learn. He undertook his first experimental studies of the growing mind while he was employed at the Binet Institute in the 1920s where his job was to develop French versions of questions on the Binet intelligence tests, previously only available in English.

It was while he was helping to mark some of the Binet tests that Piaget noticed that young children consistently gave wrong answers to certain questions. Piaget did not focus so much on the fact of the children's answers being wrong but that young children consistently made types of mistakes that older children and adults did not.

Throughout his adult life, Piaget's one goal was to answer the question 'how does knowledge grow?' and he concentrated his work on observing a group of children from birth to adolescence. The main benefit derived from these studies was that Piaget learned through direct observation how intellectual operations are prepared by sensory-motor action, long before the appearance of language. He began his work by observing young children in their natural activities without asking questions or being involved in the child's play. As he worked, he modified his methods by providing specific objects that the children could explore and manipulate themselves.

One of Piaget's most famous studies focused on the abilities of younger children to discriminate between groups of objects. He began by taking children of different ages and placing two lines of pennies, one with the coins in a line spread apart and the other with the same number of pennies placed more closely together.

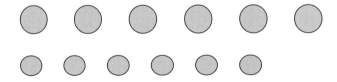

He found that:

- children aged between two and a half years and three years and two months could correctly discriminate the relative number of objects in the two rows
- children aged between three years and two months and four years and six months would identify a longer row, even with fewer objects to have 'more'
- after four years and six months they again discriminate correctly.

He conducted other experiments where children were asked to estimate the volume of liquid in different sized containers and identical dough balls, one of which was rolled into a 'sausage' in front of the child. The same results were found in each case, children of different ages had different abilities to conserve number, volume and quantity – conservation is defined as the ability to retain information in the face of change.

Before these experiments, the development of younger children had not been studied in any depth and it was thought that if a four year old could not 'conserve' quantity, then a younger child presumably could not either. However Piaget's results show that children younger than three years and two months have quantity conservation but as they get older they lose this ability and do not recover it until four and a half years old. Research also showed that children develop explicit understanding by the age of five and as a result the child will count the objects to decide which has more.

Having collected this information, Piaget changed his method of study by modifying the direction of conversation to objects that children could manipulate themselves. He discovered that children up to the age of 12 did not believe in the constancy of material quantity, weight and volume of a lump of modelling clay. He had also discovered from his own children that between the ages of six to ten months, they did not possess the notion of constancy and permanency of an object which had disappeared from view. He believed that there must be successive stages in the development of ideas of constancy, and these could be studied in concrete situations rather than solely through language. Piaget was interested in the thought processes that underlie reasoning and felt that younger children answered differently from their older peers due to the fact that young children reasoned differently.

This was a significant development in psychological research and although Piaget's work was later criticised and in some cases disproved (see Margaret Donaldson p 89), his pioneering work was influential, and in many countries is still the basis for work in child development, health and education.

In 1921, Piaget was invited by Edouard Claparede to become the director of research at the Jean-Jacques Rousseau Institute in Geneva and in 1925, Piaget took the chair of philosophy at the University of Neuchatel as he wanted to work in the field of inductive and experimental psychology. It was at this time that he began to call himself a genetic epistemologist, working on how children think and why they think the way they do. He was not interested in how well children could read or calculate, he was much more interested in how they think and how fundamental concepts such as time, mass, justice or number developed. He also observed children's development and was the first scientist to make a systematic study of children's growth in thinking as well as their physical growth. Much of his information was gathered from observations of his own three children and this information was taken to his laboratory for further testing by asking other children questions and recording their answers, particularly during their thinking and reasoning. He showed that young children think in strikingly different ways from adults.

He became intrigued with the reasons children gave for their wrong answers to the questions that required logical thinking. He believed that these incorrect answers revealed important differences between the thinking of adults and children. According to Piaget, children are born with a very basic mental structure (genetically inherited and evolved) on which later learning and knowledge is based.

To Piaget, cognitive development consisted of a repeated reorganisation of mental processes. As the child grows, they revisit learning and build on previous knowledge. Children continually construct an understanding of the world around them, then they explore the differences between what they already know and what they discover in their environment. This, he thought, explained how children grew, became more knowledgeable and more able to think logically. He referred to this repeated visiting of activities and experiences, constructing the building blocks of knowing as schemas or schematic play. Piaget described a schema as 'a cohesive, repeatable action sequence possessing component actions that are tightly interconnected and governed by a core meaning'. (Piaget, quoted in Educational Psychology Bruce Tuckman, 2010)

A toddler may have a 'cat' schema – understanding that cats are furry, walk on four legs, have a tail. However, when they apply this schema information to other animals, they obviously won't call a snake a 'cat', but they may mistake a dog for a cat and call it 'Kitty'. They may also mistakenly identify the postman as 'Daddy' because daddy is a man and all men are therefore 'Daddy'. Piaget proposed that children adjust to the world through adaptation of ideas and information, gradually understanding that not all fruit are 'apples', and not all men are 'Daddy'. As a child gets older – his or her schemas become more numerous and elaborate but very young children can become confused when they use schematic information to try to make sense of what they see.

In 1953, Piaget described three kinds of intellectual structures which he called:

- **Behavioural, or sensorimotor schemas:** organised patterns of behaviour that are used to represent and respond to objects and experiences. *These are the schemas we see in babies and toddlers as they repeatedly perform an action such as filling and emptying containers or transporting objects in prams and barrows.*

- **Symbolic schemas:** internal mental symbols (such as images or verbal codes) that children use to represent aspects of experience. *These might include using a brick as a hairbrush or a counter as money.*

- **Operational schemas:** internal mental activity that a child performs on objects of thought. *The child can now understand that different sizes of container may make the same amount of liquid look different, or that spreading a line of pennies out does not mean more pennies.*

As he amassed observational information and asked questions of older children to find out how they were thinking, he set out his findings in his theory of the stages of development. Every child passes through these stages in the same order and, Piaget maintained, is never in two stages at once. Most children passed through all the developmental stages but some never could because of limits to their thinking. Thinking also develops through these stages of development even though some children may need to stay longer at an earlier stage. He assigned an age range to each stage of development, but these do not always apply.

Piaget's stages of development are:

Stage of Development	Approximate age range	Key feature
Sensorimotor stage	0–2 years	Object permanence
Preoperational stage	2–7 years	Egocentrism
Concrete operational stage	7–11 years	Conservation
Formal Operation stage	11 years+	Abstract reasoning

(Piaget, 1952)

Piaget's stages of development are internationally known and used in education, health and psychology, particularly when making developmental assessments and identifying children with developmental delays. Their use continues today, even though there is considerable doubt that these stages are as strictly defined as Piaget believed.

Piaget was the pioneer researcher to examine children's conversations in a social context where children were comfortable and spontaneous, starting from examining their speech and actions, and developing his observations to include direct questioning. However, he did realise that it was difficult to know whether children are telling the truth when we ask them what they are thinking. There is the same conundrum when observing children in conversation with dolls or soft toys – do they really believe the toy is alive, or are they just pretending?

Piaget remains the most influential figure in modern child development research and many of his ideas are still considered accurate, including the basic notion of qualitative shifts in children's thinking over time, the general trend toward greater logic and less egocentrism as they get older, the concepts of assimilation and accommodation, and the importance of active learning by questioning and exploring.

In 1955, Piaget created the International Centre for Genetic Epistemology, and was its director until his death in 1980.

Legacy and impact

Piaget did not explicitly relate his theory to education although later researchers have explained how features of Piaget's theory can be applied to teaching and learning. Practitioners and teachers who follow Piaget's thinking will focus on the child as an individual learner, exploring the world and adding new knowledge to their previous experience and understanding. Their curriculum is 'child-centred' and the planning is linked to the needs and stages of development of individuals and groups within a class. Educators are flexible, and allow the child's interests and abilities to affect the curriculum, which will alter to incorporate these, with exploration and creativity central to their methods.

Piaget has been uniquely influential in the formation of educational policy and teaching practice. His work was at the centre of the Plowden Report (1967) on primary education, which had a great influence on the curriculum in the UK and elsewhere. Discovery learning, where children learned through doing and exploration, was promoted. This view transformed the primary curriculum in the years after the publication of the report. Active learning, play, creativity, problem solving and exploration all echo Piaget's work, and remain at the heart of early years and primary practice throughout the UK and beyond.

The effect of this pressure resulted in schemes of work for subjects which followed a staged approach, with concepts and curriculum content taught when children have reached the appropriate stage of cognitive development. This has resulted in a translation of Piaget's 'staged approach' into an 'age-related' approach where concepts are introduced at a particular age, rather than when individual children are ready.

The role of the teacher is to facilitate learning, rather than as a direct 'teacher', focusing on the ideal situation where:

- The process of learning is valued, rather than the outcome (process, not product)
- Learning progresses through discovery
- Collaborative approaches are widely used (group learning, where children help each other)
- Problem solving approaches are encouraged (rather than asking closed questions which only have one correct answer)
- Assessment is by observation during the learning process, so teachers can plan appropriate activities for future sessions.

Since his death, Piaget's research methods have come under scrutiny and the validity of using such small samples of children has been questioned. This sample consisted of Piaget's own children and the children of close friends. Piaget also worked alone, so the results of his observations may not be completely reliable, as there was no corroboration of his findings. Working with another researcher would have given his work more credibility.

Piaget's theory of schemas has also been criticised because his definition of a schema referred to an internal process, which cannot be directly observed. Other psychologists have redefined schemas and have included those behaviours, which are more visible, particularly in very young children. Recently schemas have come to be defined as:

'Schemas are patterns of linked behaviours, which the child can generalize and use in a whole variety of different situations.'

(Bruce, 2014)

'A schema is a pattern of repeated actions. Clusters of schemas develop later into concepts.'

(Athey, 1990)

Many schemas are observable in young children, and these include:

- **Transporting** – A child may carry all the bricks from one place to another in a bag, or the sand from the tray to the home corner in a bucket.
- **Enclosure/containing** – A child may fill up and empty containers of all kinds, climb into large cartons, sit in the tunnel or build 'cages' with blocks.
- **Trajectory** – Diagonal/vertical/horizontal – A child may drop things from their cot or chair, make arcs in their spilt food with their hand, or climb up and jump off furniture.

Different schemas may be observed in different children. This group of visible schemas is usually seen in infants and toddlers, and although some children never exhibit a single schema, others may adopt a schema which they explore for months or even years, even into adulthood. For example, many adults may still use a handbag to extend a continuing collecting schema or continue their interest in moving objects by pursuing sports and games involving balls and bats.

Vygotsky, Bruner and Donaldson all believed that children's development was not subject to rigid stages at all. They preferred to see development as a continuous process, and there was even some research in the late 20th century questioning Piaget's view that all humans progressed through all the stages of development. This later research also found that many adults, even university students, may never develop as far as Piaget's 'formal operational stage'.

More recently, psychologists and neuroscientists have produced evidence that there are really no easily defined 'critical stages' in development when children are open to specific concepts. Instead, there may be 'sensitive periods' for learning particular skills, and this is particularly the case for learning to communicate. Piaget maintained that children's language developed from action, but Vygotsky argued that language and thought develop together – our ability to reason is an outcome of our desire to communicate, not a result of interaction with the material world.

Because Piaget's theories are based upon biological maturation and stages, the notion of 'readiness' was important in his thinking. Readiness governs when certain information or concepts should be taught. More recently, the concept of 'readiness' has been challenged as it is sometimes used as an excuse to allow children to stagnate at a particular level. If practitioners and teachers are given permission to allow children to cross the rigid age barriers they can embark on learning which is stimulated by their interest or ability, not purely their age.

Because Piaget concentrated on the universal stages of cognitive development and biological maturation he failed to accept that individual children develop in different ways. Across the range of normal development individual children, those from the same family or identical twins, will not only pass through the stages at different speeds but may cover the stages in a different order, even missing some stages altogether.

It is taking some time for educators to catch up with current research into cognitive development and those who work to produce national guidance in the early years are among these. There is now some admission that the stages of development have 'permeable boundaries' and that children may move through them at different rates but the staged approach is still evident when national standards for different age groups are used to identify success or failure in very young children. Parents are offered booklets such as 'What happens when' which contains developmental criteria for six stages of development across seven areas of the curriculum. Parents need information about their children's learning, but do they really need to know what their six month old baby should be doing in expressive arts and design?

Influences on early years practice across the UK

Piaget has had a massive effect on educational theory and practice and although some of his ideas are now being challenged, his stages of development in particular have provided the backbone for curriculum guidance in many countries across the world for decades. In the UK, the four different countries place slightly different emphases on Piaget's work.

England

In the 'Development Matters in the EYFS' guidance in England, there are six 'stages of development' each covering an overlapping age range with statements for the areas of learning at each stage. There are cautions about treating these stages too rigidly, and the following statement appears at the bottom of every page in the guidance:

> Children develop at their own rates, and in their own ways. The development statements and their order should not be taken as necessary steps for individual children. They should not be used as checklists. The age/stage bands overlap because these are not fixed age boundaries but suggest a typical range of development.

> (Early Education, 2012)

It is unfortunate that this caution is not included in 'What happens when'. The introduction to the EYFS document contains the following advice on using a flexible approach to the statements in each section, emphasising that individual children will follow a unique pathway which must be recognised by practitioners:

Development Matters might be used by early years settings throughout the EYFS as a guide to making best-fit judgements about whether a child is showing typical development for their age, may be at risk of delay or is ahead for their age.

(Early Education, 2012)

In assessment processes, the 'Statutory Framework for the Early Years Foundation Stage' states:

It (assessment) involves practitioners observing children to understand their level of achievement, interests and learning styles, and to then shape learning experiences for each child, reflecting those observations.

(DfE, 2014)

However, the documentation in England does also contain the following requirement, urging practitioners to ensure that all children reach the Expected Level of Development by the time they leave the Reception year:

Early years providers must guide the development of children's capabilities with a view to ensuring that children in their care complete the EYFS ready to benefit fully from the opportunities ahead of them.

(DfE, 2014)

This part of the Statutory Framework is somewhat contradictory to the principles of good early years practice in insisting that all children 'must' complete the EYFS curriculum by the time they enter statutory schooling in the September following their fifth birthday. Piaget would be among the first to say that this is impossible, given the range of development across a year group, the month of a child's birth and the natural differences in rate of development across any group of children.

Scotland

In Scotland, the document 'Pre-birth to three', although making no mention of specific stages of development or of Piaget's theories, advises practitioners to take into account the development of individual children when planning and evaluating the curriculum:

Environments and resources which are skilfully planned and organised, with challenge and risk in mind, can be flexible and appropriate to suit each child's interests and unique stage of development.

Staff should avoid limiting choices and experiences for children based on past experience and preconceived ideas. They should recognise children's abilities and potential abilities and should have high expectations, believing children to be competent individuals.

(Learning and Teaching Scotland, 2010)

The guidance in 'Experiences and outcomes (3–18): The Scottish Curriculum for Excellence' is very clear that practitioners must take into account children's individual stage of development, and that these stages do not have age boundaries. For instance, the guidance for Mental, Emotional, Social and Physical Wellbeing contains a set of outcomes, which are common to all four Levels of the Scottish Curriculum from early years to the end of secondary education:

The statements of the experiences and outcomes themselves describe national expectations of learning and progression from the early to the fourth curriculum level, during the period from the early years to the end of S3. They do not have ceilings, to enable staff to extend the development of skills, attributes, knowledge and understanding into more challenging areas and higher levels of performance.

Many of the experiences and outcomes span two or more levels; some are written to span from early to fourth because they are applicable throughout life. All of these should be revisited regularly in ways which take account of the stage of development and understanding of each child and young person and are relevant and realistic for them.

(Learning and Teaching Scotland)

Northern Ireland

In Northern Ireland, the requirements for teaching stated in 'The Northern Ireland Curriculum Primary' are presented in key stage groups, emphasising that children may take two or more years to cover the material in the programme of study. The guidance on Thinking Skills and Personal Capabilities gives additional freedom for practitioners and teachers to develop individual approaches that meet the needs of their current group of children.

The Northern Ireland Curriculum sets out the minimum requirement that should be taught at each key stage. The Thinking Skills and Personal Capabilities Framework allows teachers to teach the knowledge, skills and understanding in ways that suit individual pupils' ability.

(CCEA, Northern Ireland, 2007)

In the Foundation Stage practitioners have freedom to plan the curriculum to follow children's needs and interests. 'Understanding the Foundation Stage' says:

It is important that children:

have opportunities to be actively involved in practical, challenging, play-based learning in a stimulating environment, that takes account of their developmental stage/needs (including Special Educational Needs) and their own interests/experiences.

(CCEA, Northern Ireland, 2006)

Wales

In Wales, guidance on observation and planning make clear reference to the developmental stages of the children:

> Owing to the range of individual differentces in development it is important that observation informs planning in order that each child's needs are met appropriately .
>
> (Learning and Teaching Pedagogy, Welsh Government, 2008)

The document 'Play/Active overview for 3 to 7 year olds' learning advises practitioners working in Wales that play opportunities should not just be provided in a haphazard way, and that practitioners should be knowledgeable about the stages of development in children's play so they can provide support through additional materials, ideas for developing play and the stimulus of adult company as play partners. There is also an emphasis on understanding the way children might move through stages, taking individual paths that may involve repetition, slowing, speeding up or even missing a stage altogether:

> Children develop at different rates and some will move through the different stages more quickly/slowly than others. It is also important to be aware hat children reach plateaux and will move back and forth along the learning continuum. A great deal will depend on the children's previous experiences.
>
> (Welsh Government, 2008)

The developmental stages of play identified in the Welsh document are different from Piaget's stages, but are influenced by his work, and the continuing need of some practitioners for frameworks which can help them to understand what children are learning:

Stage	Description of behaviours
solitary	children play alone; little interaction with other children, often absorbed in their own activities.
spectator	children observe their peers; usually they just watch and don't join in.
parallel	the child plays alongside other children; initially it will appear that children are playing together but on closer observation it is evident that they are playing separately
partnership/ associative	children play together, interaction between children is developing and they enjoy playing with the same activities and equipment.
cooperative/ group	children play in group situations and share outcomes from their play; often the play will be intricate and detailed.

It is evident from these few examples, that planning led by a model of stages of development is still very much evident in the curriculum across the UK. The emphasis on rigid, age-related criteria has in some cases been softened by acknowledging the need for flexibility in certain areas of the curriculum, and for individual children.

Key guidance documents for countries in the UK

Early Education, (2012) 'Development Matters in the EYFS'.
DfE, (2014) 'Statutory Framework for the Early Years Foundation Stage'.
Learning and Teaching Scotland, (2010) 'Pre-birth to three'.
Learning and Teaching Scotland; (document not dated) 'Experiences and Outcomes, 3–18: Curriculum for Excellence'.
CCEA, Northern Ireland, (2007)'The Northern Ireland Curriculum Primary'.
CCEA, (2006) 'Northern Ireland Curriculum: Understanding the Foundation Stage'.
Welsh Government (2008) 'Play/Active learning overview for 3 to 7-year-olds'.

Things to think about

- Piaget recommended the use of rigid stages of development, which every child should go through. What do you think?

- The guidance for the EYFS in England has much more information about the detailed outcomes for each development stage. Do you find this level of detail useful?

- In some UK countries, there is more flexibility in planning the curriculum to meet individual needs. What do you think about the differences across the guidance for different countries?

- Piaget also developed a theory that children used schemas to make sense of the world. Do you use information about children's current schemas to plan activities and offer additional resources?

- If there was sufficient evidence to undermine Piaget's stages of development, what do you think would replace them?

Carl Rogers

Full name: Carl Rogers
Born: 1902
Died: 1987
Place of birth: Oak Park, Chicago, United States
Countries of residence: United States
What he did: Rogers expanded earlier work on self-image and self-esteem in young children. He also promoted child-centred learning.
Influences on education today: Rogers' central themes of child-centred learning, and the crucial effect of encouraging high self-esteem in children, have both had a lasting effect in underpinning both the curriculum and the practice of teaching and learning.
Theories and areas of work: Humanism, Psychology
Key influencers and followers: Alfred Adler, Friedrich Nietzsche, Abraham Maslow
Key works: *On Becoming an Effective Teacher* (2014,) *Freedom to Learn* (1969)

When I look at the world I'm pessimistic, but when I look at people I am optimistic.
Carl Rogers, quoted in Early Childhood Education: History, Philosophy and Experience; Nutbrown, 2014

Life, love, theory and research

Carl Rogers was born in Chicago, the fourth of six children. From his early teens he lived on a farm, and his first qualification was intended to be a degree in agriculture. However, he changed course to study religion and, as part of his studies, spent six months in Beijing studying comparative religions.

Following his graduation, Rogers moved to New York continuing his studies with a PhD in Psychology at Columbia University. He worked at Ohio State University before returning to Chicago in 1945. In 1957, he returned to teach at the University of Wisconsin, moving to California (La Jolla) in 1964 where he remained until his death, working in psychotherapy and writing. He referred to himself as a humanistic psychologist who agreed with many of the theories of Abraham Maslow, adding that for a person to grow, they need an environment that provides them with:

- genuineness: openness, self-disclosure
- acceptance: being seen with unconditional positive regard
- empathy: being listened to and understood.

With these three conditions, a person could grow and achieve their ambitions – become self-actualising.

As with Sigmund Freud, Rogers' theories were based in clinical research, collecting information as he worked with his patients. Unlike Freud, he believed that people are basically good, with mental health as a normal process and mental illness as an aberration of human behaviour. His central theory was based in something that Maslow would recognise – a single force of life which he called the actualising tendency of living beings – a built-in tendency in all living things to work towards a state of actualisation (achievement of their potential) – to make the best of their lives. His belief was that all living things seek love, safety, air, water, and food, and humans develop new scientific creations, new medicines and works of art because it is in human nature to do the very best we can. The same instinct also drives plants and animals to strive to grow through concrete, survive in desert conditions and bring up their young under extreme pressures. Even ecosystems such as deserts and forests have the ability to self-actualise. When one insect or animal fails, another takes its place, adapting to fill the gap. Forests recover from fire and drought, and river valleys overcome the effects of floods.

Rogers maintained that humans recognise what is good for them – love, affection, attention, nurturing, positive self-regard, self-esteem, self-worth, a positive self-image. Animals and humans, if left alone will eat what is good for them, and even babies appear to be able to manage a healthy intake, if left to choose what they eat. However, Rogers maintained, humans have learned to like things that are bad for them – chocolate, tobacco, alcohol, sugar – and this may prove fatal for the human race. As our technologies, societies and cultures devise ever more complex solutions to our problems, there is a benefit, but also danger of disaster. The very things we invent and nurture may come back to destroy us. The current debate about the harm done by sugar is one example.

We are also ruled by the society we live in – we are rewarded by a sweet when we have eaten our broccoli, a game when we have finished our 'work', even love and affection when we behave appropriately. Rogers called this conditional positive regard. When we don't have positive self-regard, living up to the expectations we have for ourselves, or others have for us, we fall into what Rogers called incongruity or what other psychologists call neurosis. The balance between our own self-actualisation and external expectations is out of synch.

Rogers' approach states that the human self (in adults and children) has three components, with features unique to each of us:

Self worth (or **self-esteem**) – what we think about ourselves. Rogers believed feelings of self-worth developed in early childhood and were formed from the interaction of the child with the mother and father. As the child grows older other adults and children affect the child's feeling of self-worth. Children need to start their lives with unconditional positive regard in the form of love from their parents. Children who do not have this will not do well at school or in life. Some children grow up in a situation where positive regard is always conditional on their behaviour, or over-strict rules and no-one ever gives them unconditional love for being themselves. Living with entirely **conditional positive regard** leaves the child thinking that they are not loved for themselves, but on condition that he or she behaves in ways approved of by their parents or carers.

Self-image – how we see ourselves, which is also important to good psychological health. Self-image includes the influence of our body image on inner personality. At a simple level, we might perceive ourselves as a good or bad person, beautiful or ugly. Self-image has an effect on how a person thinks, feels and behaves in the world.

Ideal self – this is the person who we would like to be. It consists of our goals and ambitions in life, and is dynamic and forever changing. The ideal self in childhood is not the ideal self in our teens or late 20s, or even in adulthood.

In order to achieve self-actualisation, we all need to balance these three components and maintain a good level of self-worth, a positive self image and a realistic view of the person we would like to be. Failure to keep this balance will precipitate feelings of failure and in extreme cases, mental illness.

Like Maslow, Rogers developed his own descriptions of a self-actualised person: a person with a balanced view of their own worth, and an honest appraisal for their own image and personality. This self-actualised person … :

1 **is open to experiences**: the opposite of defensive, able to accept reality, including one's feelings. The hard part, of course, is distinguishing real feelings from the anxieties brought on by conditions of worth.
2 **is existentialist**: living in the here-and-now, not in the past or the future – the one is gone, and the other isn't anything yet. The present is the only reality we have. Mind you, that doesn't mean we shouldn't remember and learn from our past. Neither does it mean we shouldn't plan or even daydream about the future; just recognise these things for what they are: memories and dreams, which we are experiencing here in the present.
3 **trust feelings**: feelings, instincts and gut-reactions are paid attention to and trusted. People's own decisions are the right ones and we should trust ourselves to make the right choices, although this does not mean 'Do whatever you feel, regardless of others.'

Carl Rogers

4 **feels free**: it is irrelevant whether or not people really have free will. We feel very much as if we do, but of course, we are not free to do anything we like. I will not be able to fly like Superman however much I want to but Rogers says that the fully-functioning person acknowledges that feeling of freedom and takes responsibility for their own choices.

5 **is creative**: creative thinking and risk taking are features of a person's life. A person does not play safe all the time. This involves the ability to adjust and change and seek new experiences. If you feel free and responsible you will act accordingly, and participate in the world. A fully-functioning person can become self-actualising through creativity in the arts or sciences, through social concern and parental love or simply by doing one's best at one's job.

Rogers is best known for his work in therapy which he referred to as client-centred and described as 'just like helping a child to ride a bike' – you can't explain how to do it, you just hold onto the saddle until you feel they are ready, then you take your hand away and let go. If they fall, so be it, you just have to take the risk – if you don't, they will never learn. A client must learn to be independent of their therapist as a child needs eventually to live without their teachers or parents.

Legacy and impact

One of the greatest influences on education of Rogers' work was in child (or learner) - centred teaching which has its roots in Rogers' client-centred therapy. His book *Freedom to Learn* (1969) was devoted exclusively to this concept, and has been reprinted several times. *On Becoming an Effective Teacher* (2013) started by Rogers and completed after his death by Harold Lyon and Reinhard Tausch, elaborated on Rogers' work during his later years and since his death.

Rogers had the following five hypotheses about learner-centred education:

1 *A person cannot teach another person directly; a person can only facilitate another's learning.* The focus in a person centred approach is on the child. What the child does is more important than what the teacher does.

2 *A person learns significantly only those things that are perceived as being involved in the maintenance of or enhancement of the structure of self.* The child will select those things that are most relevant to them, so relevancy to the student is essential for learning. The students' experiences become central to the activity.

3 *Experience, which would involve a change in the organisation of self, tends to be resisted through denial or distortion of symbolism.* Being open to consider concepts that vary from one's own is vital to learning and gently encouraging open-mindedness is helpful in engaging the child in learning.

4 *The structure and organisation of self appears to become more rigid under threats, and to relax its boundaries when completely free from threat.* An open, friendly environment in which trust is developed is essential.

5 *The educational situation which most effectively promotes significant learning is one in which threat is reduced to a minimum and differentiated perception is facilitated.* (Rogers, Client Centred Therapy, 1951). Frequent interaction with the children will help achieve this goal. The adult should be prepared to be a mentor who guides, rather than the expert who tells.

Child-centred approaches are now accepted and promoted across the world although the current obsession with data and testing is stretching the boundaries of this approach. It is very difficult to equate this approach with one where unreasonable expectations by managers and governors result in imposition of heavily adult-centred sessions for part of the day, even with very young children, subjecting them to irrelevant content taught in a style inconsistent with the descriptions given by Rogers.

Influences on early years practice across the UK

The term 'child-centred' is used freely throughout the developed world to describe early years education where children have some choice in what, where and who they play with. However, this method is often far from the child-centred approaches Rogers would describe – a situation where the practitioner is mentor.

The constraints of centralised curriculum guidance have resulted in anxiety and a tendency in some settings to over-formalise the curriculum. The ethos of traditional early education where children were genuinely free for at least part of the day to engage in activities entirely self-chosen and with the adult as an additional resource, mentor and co-player has been stifled.

However, there are still some shining examples in every country of the UK where child-centred learning still exists, where practitioners have defended and are promoting this way of working. These include:

- **Nursery schools** (sadly reducing in number every year) where nursery teachers work with nursery nurses, both trained on specialised early years courses maintain the theory and practice of the early educators.
- **Children's Centres** where practitioners have held firm on the principles of child choice.
- **Forest Schools** where children spend long periods (and sometimes all day) outside, following their own interests whatever the weather.
- **Some infant and primary schools** where practitioners are supported by managers who have the vision to understand which methods work best in early education.

Carl Rogers

If we refer to the official government documentation for each country, we will find the rhetoric of 'child-centerdness'. It is a pity that often the rhetoric of policy does not match the reality of what inspectors and data interrogators want.

England

In England, the 'Statutory framework for the EYFS' places a high regard on the unique individual, stating that:

The EYFS seeks to provide:

- quality and consistency in all early years settings, so that every child makes good progress and no child gets left behind;

- a secure foundation through learning and development opportunities which are planned around the needs and interests of each individual child and are assessed and reviewed regularly.

(DfE, 2014)

These guiding principles are included, which should shape practice in early years settings. One of these is:

Every child is a unique child, who is constantly learning and can be resilient, capable, confident and self-assured

and

Practitioners must consider the individual needs, interests, and stage of development of each child in their care, and must use this information to plan a challenging and enjoyable experience for each child in all of the areas of learning and development.

(DfE, 2014)

However, there is a clear inference that, as children move nearer to statutory school age, the style of teaching and learning will swing towards a more adult-directed approach ready for primary education. The same framework also includes the following:

Early years providers must guide the development of children's capabilities with a view to ensuring that children in their care complete the EYFS ready to benefit fully from the opportunities ahead of them.

(DfE, 2014)

'Completing the EYFS' means meeting the age-related expectations – the 17 Early Learning Goals – set out in the framework. There is much discussion about the relevance and content of these goals, and whether they disadvantage some children, particularly the youngest 'summer born' in the year group, some boys, and children who have moved more slowly through the stages of their development:

> *Practitioners must indicate whether children are meeting expected levels of development, or if they are exceeding expected levels, or not yet reaching expected levels ('emerging').*
>
> (DfE, 2014)

Northern Ireland

The guidance in 'The Northern Ireland Curriculum Primary' includes the following text on methods that enhance children's motivation in the Foundation Stage:

> *Motivation can be increased when children have opportunities to make choices and decisions about their learning, particularly when their own ideas and interests are used, either as starting points for learning activities or for pursuing a topic in more depth.*
>
> (CCEA, Northern Ireland, 2007)

And in 'Understanding the foundation stage':

> *Children learn best when they:*
> - *have opportunities to be actively involved in practical, open-ended and challenging learning experiences that encourage creativity;*
> - *have choice and exercise autonomy and independence in their learning, and are encouraged to take risks.*
>
> (CCEA, Northern Ireland, 2006)

These laudable aims should put children on the path towards self-actualisation, as long as experiences at later stages of education do not reverse the process.

Scotland

In Scotland the child is valued at the centre of the education process, as stated in 'Building the Curriculum 2 (3–18)':

> *The child is at the centre of what we do in the early years.*
>
> *This is a critically important stage in the development and learning of children. We must build on their curiosity and enthusiasm to learn when we develop their learning environments, working outwards from their individual interests and needs.*
>
> (Scottish Executive, 2007)

A level 5 example of practice from 'The child at the centre: self-evaluation in the early years) describes child-centred learning in the early years in Scottish settings:

Our children enjoy and are actively involved in learning through play. They are fully engaged, highly motivated and interact well during activities. In our centre, activities sustain children's interest, help them make decisions, solve problems and develop independence. Children can plan and initiate their learning experiences. They exercise choice and take increasing responsibility for their own learning. Our children are treated with equality, fairness and respect. Almost all children are making very good progress and achieving well. They have formed friendships with other children and are increasingly able to cooperate with them and take turns. Our centre uses imaginative and appropriate methods to ask children about their learning. Our staff listen to children and act upon their views and interests. Children feel successful and are confident, and they can contribute appropriately in our centre. They feel valued, safe and secure.

(HMIE, Scotland, 2007)

Wales

In Wales there is an emphasis on play and child-initiated learning which would also fit well with Rogers' philosophy. Unlike the other countries of the UK, the guidance for the Foundation Phase in Wales covers the period from three to seven years of age. In the 'Foundation Phase Framework':

Educational provision for young children should be holistic with the child at the heart of any planned curriculum. Practitioner involvement in children's learning is of vital importance particularly when interactions involve open questioning, shared and sustained thinking.

(Welsh Government, 2015)

In 'Play/Active learning', the Welsh Assembly Government makes strong statements about the importance of play, and learning that is initiated by the children themselves:

Children's learning is most effective when it arises from first hand experiences, whether spontaneous or structured, and when they are given time to play without interruptions and to reach a satisfactory conclusion.

(Welsh Government, 2008)

'Play/active learning' goes on to say that, as well as being an important part of children's learning, the children as well as the adults who work with them should be involved in the planning and organisation of the learning environment, a statement that confirms their place at the centre of provision – bringing Carl Rogers' pupil-centred theory right into the 21st Century.

Things to think about

- Rogers thought the child should be at the centre of everything we do. Is this easy or difficult to achieve?

- How often do you consider how you are maintaining or improving self-image and self-respect in the children in your care? Do you involve them in these discussions, so they can build a realistic ideal self for themselves?

- Being a practitioner in the early years is not easy at the moment. How do you maintain your own self-image and self-respect when there are so many pressures?

- Do you believe Rogers' view that '*A person cannot teach another person directly; a person can only facilitate another's learning*'? *How does this affect your work?* (Client-Centered Therapy, 1951) If you are a student, how would you ensure that you followed this principle?

Jean-Jacques Rousseau

Full name: Jean-Jacques Rousseau

Born: 1712

Died: 1778

Place of birth: Geneva, Switzerland

Countries of residence: Switzerland, France, England

What he did: One of the earliest pioneers in early education, he was one of the first to question existing methods and promote a child-centred approach, which followed children's interests. He described these in his instructive novel *Emile*.

Influences on education today: Rousseau's *Emile* is still in print and widely referred to in training and education. Child-centred education methods, similar to those of Friedrich Fröebel, Maria Montessori and other leaders in early education, have continued to influence practitioners, trainers and pedagogues to the present day.

Theories and areas of work: Child development, Philosophy

Key influencers and followers: Johann Pestalozzi, Mary Montessori, John Dewey

Key works: *Emile,* or *On Education* (1762)

We are born weak, we need strength; helpless, we need aid; foolish, we need reason. All that we lack at birth, all that we need when we come to man's estate, is the gift of education.

Jean-Jacques Rousseau, Emile, 1762

Life, love, theory and research

Jean-Jacques Rousseau was born in Geneva in 1712. Sadly his mother died only days after his birth and his only brother, older than him, ran away while Rousseau was still a boy. He was brought up for his first few years by his father, a watchmaker, learning to read from the romantic novels left by his mother and then in Greek and Roman texts including *Plutarch*, which he read to his father as he made watches. His father's temper proved to be a problem for both father and son when Rousseau's father had an argument with a local businessman. He avoided legal action by leaving Geneva and his son, who rarely saw him again.

An uncle took Rousseau in, educated him alongside his own son and when he was 13 he was apprenticed to an engraver, which he did not really enjoy. He left Geneva in 1728 for Annecy where he became involved with Mme Louise de Warens who persuaded him to give up his own religion and become a Catholic. This conflict with religion followed Rousseau for the rest of his life as he lived in a time when religious persecution was common and different sects dominated different countries and even different regions in a single country. Rousseau was driven to move across Europe, not just for his religion, but also because of his difficulties relating with others and because he sometimes got into legal and political tangles.

During the next few years he earned money from teaching and doing secretarial work, continuing his relationship with Mme de Warens, who eventually became his lover and 'the love of his life' although he never married her. However, he soon decided he wanted to take up a career in music and he left for Paris in 1742, where he worked in the French Embassy in Paris and Venice. In Paris, he met and moved in with Therese Lavasseur, who he also never married though they had five children, all of whom Rousseau and Therese left at the Paris orphanage for foundlings. When Rousseau began to write about education, the abandonment of his children became a source of criticism used by those who disagreed with him. Later in life he tried to locate his eldest son but sadly failed to find him.

In Paris, Rousseau became associated with the philosophers Condillac and Diderot, working on articles for Diderot and d'Alembert's *Encyclopedie*. In 1750 he published his first widely read paper, the '*Discourse on the Arts and Sciences*', as an entry to the Academy of Dijon's essay contest. Winning the Academy's prize began Rousseau's writing career and his national reputation. While in Paris, he also composed an opera, *The Village Soothsayer*, which was performed for King Louis XV who loved it and offered Rousseau a lifelong pension to work in the court. Surprisingly, Rousseau refused the King's offer and turned away from writing music until very late in his life.

The central claim of Rousseau's discourse was that human beings are basically good by nature but are corrupted by historical events that affect their current civil society. Men differ from animals in their capacity for free will and their potential perfectibility. As they began to live in groups and families, humans also began to experience family love which Rousseau saw as the greatest source of happiness known to humanity. While men were natural, free and untrammelled by society they could be happy but as soon as they settled and began to own land, they became aware of what others thought of them, valuing the good opinion of others over their own self-esteem. He described these two sorts of happiness as *amour de soi* (a positive self-love and natural desire for self-preservation), and *amour-propre* (pride).

Rousseau's praise of and love for nature is a theme that he returned to again and again throughout his life, including in his work on the philosophy of education, *Emile*, published in 1762. This work proved to be the most influential book on education since Plato's *Republic*, causing so much controversy in France that the French authorities immediately banned it. Despite this, and even though Rousseau had to leave Paris as a result, *Emile* has had a significant effect on education, particularly the education of young children. The book has been translated into many languages and is still in print.

The major point of controversy in *Emile* was not in his philosophy of education. It was Rousseau's arguments against traditional views of religion that led to the banning of the book. *Emile* is unique because it is written as part novel and part philosophical treatise. The book is written in first person with the narrator as the tutor, describing his education of a pupil from birth to adulthood, including a section on religion and belief.

Before Rousseau's influence, education was very formal, heavily influenced by religion and not very enjoyable for the pupils. Rousseau brought a new view that children are very different from adults – being innocent, vulnerable, slow to mature – and entitled to freedom and happiness – in other words, children are naturally good and should be supported and helped, rather than beaten into submission. Central themes of Rousseau's education theory include the notion that education is about helping children – and at the time this meant boys – to reason and to think for themselves, not just follow the thoughts and ideas of the teacher. Children should be educated to maintain their own self-esteem within the pressures of society.

Emile, like all children in Rousseau's ideal society, was educated in the country, experiencing a series of activities organised by his tutor, following his interests and expanding his knowledge by exploring the world. He would learn to differentiate right from wrong by seeing the consequences of his actions, not through punishment. The tutor's role was to plan activities, support Emile's interests and explorations, and ensure that Emile was safe.

Rousseau was an early advocate of 'developmentally appropriate' education; activities should be matched to the age and stage of development of the child, and he divided child development into three stages:

1 **Stage 1: Infancy (from birth to about two years).** This stage finishes with the weaning of the child.
2 **Stage 2: 'The age of nature' (from 2 to 12).** The stage when children are guided by their own emotions and impulses, is the age of nature, when children are given what Rousseau called negative education – no moral instruction, no verbal learning, no religious instruction, and no constraints on time – '*Do not save time, but lose it … The mind should be left undisturbed till its faculties have developed*'. (Emile, 1762). The emphasis at this stage should be on the five senses and in Book 2 of *Emile*, Rousseau describes how each of his senses should be developed. Interestingly, the child is not allowed access to any books in this stage.
3 **Stage 3: Pre-adolescence (12–15).** The stage of the 'noble savage' when reason starts to develop and the boy grows into a man. At this stage, the child's urge for activity and physical strength increases and it becomes the tutor's or teacher's role to translate this high level of activity into sustained concentration. The only book Emile is allowed is Robinson Crusoe – the story of a solitary, self-sufficient man, the model of man that Rousseau seeks to form.

4 **Stage 4: Puberty (15–20).** By the time he is 15, with what Rousseau thought were the dangerous emotions of adolescence, and the challenges of moral issues and religion. At this stage Emile is to be gradually introduced to community life and to sexual and moral development. It was this part of the book that got Rousseau in so much trouble with the religious authorities.

Rousseau recommended that children should engage in a practical activity such as woodwork to ensure that they were prepared for adulthood. By 16, a boy would be ready to be introduced to a suitable girl. The intention would be that marriage would mean a 'nuclear' family with the father working and the mother at home looking after the home and children, and providing early education. So the last book of *Emile* introduces us to Sophie, and his education of, and relationships with women in general. Rousseau maintained that although gender differences run deep, men and women are complementary – 'The man should be strong and active; the woman should be weak and passive; he one must have both the power and the will; it is enough that the other should offer little resistance'. (Emile, 1762)

Sophie's training for womanhood up to the age of ten would have involved physical training for grace and the dressing of dolls, leading to drawing, writing, counting and reading, and the prevention of idleness. After the age of ten, there is a concern with adornment and the arts of pleasing others, religion and the training of reason.

Rousseau's philosophy of education does not involve specific techniques to ensure that pupils will absorb information and concepts. A better explanation is that the child's character should be developed to have a sense of self worth and morality, allowing the child to be virtuous even in the unnatural society in which he lives. Emile begins to learn important moral lessons from infancy, through childhood, and into early adulthood.

His education relies on the tutor's constant supervision, although the tutor must sometimes manipulate the environment in order to teach difficult moral lessons about humility, chastity, and honesty. As well as moral education, Emile is taught about love, women and relationships. Rousseau says that women are not inferior to men, just different (a new and revolutionary opinion at the time), and that although men are stronger and more capable in some ways, women are more clever. Although they should be submissive to their husbands, they excel in practical reasoning which they use to manage their lives and their families.

After the banning of Emile and another of his books, published at the same time, Rousseau fled from France and returned to Switzerland but continued to find difficulties, both with the Swiss authorities and his friends. He spent much time there trying to justify his views at a time when the Enlightenment was in full swing, and his personal relations with friends and colleagues were often strained.

Rousseau continued to write throughout the rest of his life and some of his books, such as *Julie*, a sentimental novel, and *Reveries of a Solitary Walker*, with their emphasis on nature, were very popular, and influenced the thinking of the late 18th century Romantic Naturalism movement in Europe. He spent time in England at the invitation of David Hume, where he was a popular focus for society. However, a combination of gossip, trickery and paranoia prompted a return to France and short periods in several locations.

Rousseau moved frequently, never settling for long in one country, as he was always at odds with friends and hosts, including an accusation of heresy, and defending his views on philosophy and religion. He finally returned to France and lived in relative quiet until his death following concussion brought on by a bizarre late night collision with a Great Dane in a dark street. This accident resulted in neurological damage and Rousseau suffered from epileptic seizures until his death two years later, when he suffered a massive stroke brought on by the accident and a series of subsequent falls. Until the time of his death, he was attempting to explain and justify his controversial views.

Legacy and impact

Rousseau has been praised and blamed for his so-called modern 'child-centered' approaches. Good or bad, the theories of educators such as Rousseau, his near contemporary Johann Heinrich Pestalozzi and later, of Montessori and John Dewey, have directly influenced modern educational practices. Many modern methods do have significant practices and theories in common with those of Rousseau.

Learning out of doors, a focus on natural objects, a staged approach and child centred learning are all as integral to early learning as they were to Emile. An investigative, problem solving approach is almost universal, where adults plan the environment and offer activities while the child is able to select the way they learn. Thinking skills and metacognition are words we often use to describe the aims of activities and in the best settings and schools, adults do act as mentors or guides, leaving the child to learn, observing them to see what interests them and following up these observations in further sessions.

Rousseau's thoughts on the roles of men and women are also still discussed today. The notion of 'not better or worse, just different' has echoed down the decades to inform current discussions about the roles of men and women. Rousseau would be surprised to see how society has moved on and perturbed to see the direction some emancipators have taken. Universal education for all, and particularly the education of girls and women, is something many of Rousseau's contemporaries could not even have dreamed of. In a life story of Rousseau, written in 1967, Will Durant sums up his work with the following questions:

> How did it come about that a man born poor, losing his mother at birth and soon deserted by his father … left to wander for twelve years among alien cities and conflicting faiths … had more effect upon posterity than any other writer or thinker of that eighteenth century?

> (Durant, 1967)

Influence on early years practice in the UK

In his book *Emile*, Rousseau began a discussion on education which has continued ever since. The notion that children should begin to think, to ponder and to enquire was something new in Rousseau's time, challenging previous methods of teaching, rocking not only the teaching profession but religious leaders and even those who wanted to keep women in the home.

Child-centred education, sexual equality and a reasonable attitude to religious education in schools has improved immensely in recent years, although there is still a long way to go before equality is a fact.

Nature and education in the open air were central themes in the early chapters of the book where *Emile* is young and experiencing life exploring the outdoor world. These are still familiar components of the early years curriculum and we all understand their benefits, particularly for children who do not have the opportunity to roam free in their spare time, or who are living in cramped conditions. The green and blue of grass and sky are powerful stimuli to the imagination and to learning.

Scotland

Across the UK, outdoor learning is promoted but the guidance in Scotland, where many Forest School settings flourish, has developed a specialism in the philosophy and the practice of outdoor learning that would surely impress Rousseau. The first group of quotes are from 'Pre-birth to three', Scotland's guidance for practitioners working with under threes:

> From the earliest days, children can experience the joy of physical activity through play
> both indoors and outdoors and in all weathers. Play and movement are essential for brain
> development as it is often through play that babies and young children learn about themselves,
> others and the world around them.

> Being outdoors has a positive impact on mental, emotional, physical and social wellbeing.
> The outdoors, which refers to the immediate environment attached to the setting, the local
> community and beyond, can provide opportunities for participating in new, challenging and
> healthy experiences. Most staff in early years settings understand that they have an important
> responsibility to ensure that regular and frequent outdoor experiences are integral to everyday
> practice for all children.

> For many children, opportunities to be, or play, outdoors are few and far between. Staff in early
> years settings therefore have an important responsibility to maximise outdoor play experiences

for children as it may be the only time they have to play freely and safely outside. Many staff teams recognise the great outdoors as a rich resource and strive to use it as creatively and positively as possible. They often discover, too, that outdoor play does not necessarily mean purchasing expensive equipment, as the natural environment itself contains a whole range of materials which can be adapted, explored and enhanced in a variety of ways. High quality provision ensures that outdoor play extends beyond the outdoor area belonging to the early years setting and into the local and wider community.

Outdoor play in particular can also be a major contributor to outcomes around physical activity and healthy weight. Developing play spaces, and play opportunities for children and removing barriers to play is therefore a priority.

(Scottish Government, 2008)

The Scottish curriculum 'Building the curriculum 2 (3–18): Active learning in the early years' builds on 'Pre-birth to three', by including an entitlement to learning out of doors at all ages:

The outdoor learning environment offers motivating and different opportunities for learning. Most establishments provide safe, secure outdoor spaces where children have regular outdoor play, fresh air and exercise. The sights, sounds and smells of the outdoors, the closeness to nature, the excitement most children feel, the wonder and curiosity all serve to enhance and stimulate learning.

(Scottish Executive, 2007)

The document 'Curriculum for Excellence through outdoor learning', the last in this group of commitments, gives some details of the expectations for the youngest children in Scotland. Children in Scotland experience the lowest temperatures out of doors of any country in the UK but some of the first UK settings to function totally out of doors, such as the Secret Garden Nursery (www.secretgardenoutdoor-nursery.co.uk/) have successfully opened there.

Outdoor learning connects children and young people with the natural world, with our built heritage and our culture and society, and encourages lifelong involvement and activity in Scotland's outdoors.

There are associated health benefits to learning outdoors. Research indicates that the use of greenspace or 'green exercise' improves health. In particular, learning outdoors generally results in increased levels of physical activity. In addition, interacting with greenspace (walking, gardening, etc) improves emotional wellbeing and mental health.

(Learning and Teaching Scotland, 2010)

Northern Ireland

Freedom is a word much used in relation to Rousseau and his work and this is reflected in documentation by referring to the concept of play and child-initiated learning. In Northern Ireland, the emphasis on thinking skills is explored by ensuring an active, play-based curriculum, and the documentation: 'Thinking skills and personal capabilities for Key Stages 1 and 2' goes on to advise Foundation Stage practitioners:

> Self-initiated play helps children to understand and learn about themselves and their surroundings. Motivation can be increased when children have opportunities to make choices and decisions about their learning, particularly when their own ideas and interests are used, either as starting points for learning activities or for pursuing a topic in more depth.
>
> In order to develop children's skills and capabilities across the whole curriculum, teachers will need to provide frequent opportunities for pupils to think and do for themselves.
>
> (CCEA, 2007)

Thinking Skills and metacognition, Emotional Intelligence and Personal Capabilities are all concepts Rousseau would have understood and these also fit well with his concepts of love of others and experience of the natural environment. These words are on the lips of most educationalists and many practitioners who are adapting their practice to allow children more ownership of their learning, and the move is reflected in national documentation for settings and schools across the UK. For instance, in Northern Ireland, the documentation is particularly helpful, influenced by the work at Belfast University on Thinking Skills in Primary Education (*www.journeytoexcellence.org.uk*).

This work has resulted in he inclusion of specific guidance for the development of Thinking Skills and personal Capabilities.

> Thinking skills are tools that help children to go beyond the acquisition of knowledge to search for meaning, apply ideas, analyse patterns and relationships, create and design something new and monitor and evaluate their progress.
>
> **Being Collaborative, Being Sensitive to Others' Feelings, Being Fair and Responsible** *This strand enables your pupils to engage in collaborative activities and to make the most of their learning when working with others. To do this, pupils must develop the confidence and willingness to join in, have the social skills required for working in face-to-face groups, show empathy, and develop a more general social perspective.*
>
> (CCEA, 2007)

Wales

In Wales, the 'Foundation Phase Framework' includes the following references to thinking skills:

Educational provision for young children should be holistic with the child at the heart of any planned curriculum. It is about practitioners understanding, inspiring and challenging children's potential for learning. Practitioner involvement in children's learning is of vital importance particularly when interactions involve open questioning, shared and sustained thinking.

Developing thinking

…the processes of planning, developing and reflecting…enable children to think creatively and critically, to plan their work, carry out tasks, analyse and evaluate their findings and to reflect on their learning, making links within and outside the setting/school. The processes of developing thinking, namely plan, develop and reflect, should not be seen as a set style of learning and teaching. Each process does not have a specific place in a task. The three processes should be interchangeable.

(Welsh Government, 2015)

England

In England, Thinking Skills are included in the Characteristics of Effective Learning as Creative and Critical Thinking, a strand that crosses the whole curriculum as specified in the 'Statutory framework for the early years foundation stage'. Practitioners are expected to provide opportunities where children can:

Have their own ideas

- Thinking of ideas
- Finding ways to solve problems
- Finding new ways to do things

Make links

- Making links and noticing patterns in their experience
- Making predictions
- Testing their ideas
- Developing ideas of grouping, sequences, cause and effect

Choose ways to do things

- Planning, making decisions about how to approach a task, solve a problem and reach a goal
- Checking how well their activities are going
- Changing strategy as needed
- Reviewing how well the approach worked (DfE, 2014)

Within the guidance to adults, the 'Development Matters in the EYFS' document includes the following guidance to practitioners for supporting the thinking process:

- Use the language of thinking and learning: think, know, remember, forget, idea, makes sense, plan, learn, find out, confused, figure out, trying to do.

- Model being a thinker, showing that you don't always know, are curious and sometimes puzzled, and can think and find out.

- Always respect children's efforts and ideas, so they feel safe to take a risk with a new idea.

- Give children time to talk and think.

- Value questions, talk, and many possible responses, without rushing toward answers too quickly.

- Sustained shared thinking helps children to explore ideas and make links. Follow children's lead in conversation, and think about things together.

- Give feedback and help children to review their own progress and learning.

(Early Education, 2012)

It would be interesting to bring Rousseau back, or even to magically create a real version of Emile, and observe his responses to current education practice. They might see parallels with some aspects from their lives over 200 years ago.

Key guidance documents for countries in the UK

Learning and Teaching Scotland, (2010) 'Pre-birth to three'.
Scottish Executive, (2007) 'Building the Curriculum 2 (3–18): Active learning in the early years'.
Learning and Teaching Scotland (2010) 'Curriculum for Excellence through outdoor learning'.
CCEA, (2007) 'Thinking skills and personal capabilities for Key Stages 1 and 2'.
Welsh Assembly Government, (2015) 'Foundation Phase Framework'.
DfE, (2014) 'Statutory Framework for the Early Years Foundation Stage'.
Early Education, (2012) 'Development Matters in the EYFS'.

Things to think about

- Rousseau's devotion to nature is a theme that ran through his entire life and we all say that the outdoor environment is an essential part of our provision. How well do you use your outdoor area?

- How much do you agree with Rousseau's statement that the teacher should be there just to plan and keep the child safe?

- Men are not better or worse than women, just different – do you agree?

- Emile had no access to books until he was beyond 12 years of age and then only had Robinson Crusoe. What do you think of this suggestion?

- Do you think your training (or professional development) has enabled you to reflect on the methods of such significant educators as Rousseau, Montessori or Fröebel?

Lev Vygotsky

Full name: Lev Vygotsky

Born: 1896

Died: 1934

Place of birth: Moscow, Russia

Countries of residence: Russia

What he did: Vygotsky introduced us to theories including the Zone of Proximal Development (ZPD), and the influence of the More Knowledgeable Others (MEO), expanded on the concept of scaffolding, and reinforced the importance of play and self talk.

Influences on education today: Vygotsky's concepts, although they were not published in the West until after his death, have had a significant influence on thinking in early education. The concept of the Zone of Proximal Development and scaffolding learning through practice and mastery approaches are now firmly embedded in the practice of most teachers and practitioners in pre-school and early education.

Theories and areas of work: Constructivism/Socio cultural, Psychology

Key influencers and followers: Jean Piaget, Jerome Bruner, Loris Malaguzzi, Urie Bronfenbrenner

Key works: *Thought and Language* (1986), *The Collected Works of L. S. Vygotsky* (1987)

In play, the child is always behaving beyond his age, above his usual everyday behaviour; in play he is, as it were, a head above himself.
    Lev Vygotsky, quoted in Early Chilhood Education; Rebecca Staples New, 2006

Life, love, theory and research

Although this Russian born psychologist and educational thinker died at the young age of 37, and some of his work has not even now been translated from the Russian, he has had a significant effect on educational theory and practice, both within and outside the Soviet Union.

Vygotsky was born in Western Russia, in Belarus, into a non-religious middle class Russian Jewish family and his father was a banker. He experienced both private and public education and was admitted to Moscow University as a result of a 'Jewish Lottery', which set a 3% quota of Jewish entrants to university. He originally wanted to study humanities and social sciences but his parents insisted that he studied at the Medical School. However, after the first term, he changed course and transferred to study Law. He graduated from Moscow University with a law degree, and returned to Belarus to teach.

Little information is available about his life during the German occupation and the Civil War and in 1917 he was invited to return to Moscow to become a research fellow at the Psychological Institute in Moscow. By this time he was already married to Roza Smekhova.

By 1925 he had written two books – *Pedagogical Psychology* and *The Psychology of Art* but neither was published until the 1960s. Vygotsky lived his whole life in Russia and all his writings were originally in Russian, many of them not translated or read in the West until the 1980's, long after his death.

In 1925 he also made his only visit abroad to London to attend a congress on the education of the deaf. He returned from this visit with recurring symptoms of tuberculosis, which he suffered from for the rest of his life, and which eventually caused his death.

Vygotsky spent 1926–1930 leading a research programme investigating the development of higher cognitive functions of logical memory, selective attention, decision-making and language comprehension. He worked with his students to research these behaviours from three different angles:

- The **instrumental angle**, studying the ways in which humans use objects as aids to memory and reasoning.
- The **cultural-historical angle**, studying the ways in which human development is shaped by different social and cultural patterns of interaction.
- The **developmental angle**, studying how children acquire higher cognitive functions during their development.

Over the ten years of his work in psychology, Vygotsky showed a wide interest in aspects of cognitive development, particularly in children. Unlike many psychologists he rarely conducted research – his investigations were entirely theoretical, focused on constructing the best possible theory of the transfer of knowledge and concentrating on two major areas:

1 **Instrumentalism** – the mechanistic, and simple view of development that had been previously accepted, in which he tried to understand the ways in which humans use objects as aides of mediation in memory and reasoning

2 **Cultural mediation and interpersonal communication** – the way a child internalises knowledge through self-communication, using language to learn how to

think. This was a more holistic view, dealing with 'knowing how' to do things – how to ride a bike, get dressed, climb a tree etc. including social norms which are initially out of the reach of the child, and how these can gradually become learned.

Vygotsky came to believe that cultural norms and behaviours are much more easily adopted if the child can 'talk themselves through' the activity or behaviour and try it out on their own terms. These accepted processes, some as simple as putting on a coat, may initially involve alternative attempts such as having the coat on upside down, inside out, or even back to front, before s/he learns for him/herself the accepted way of doing it. This may be why some children continue to put their coat on in a non-standard way. Vygotsky named this 'trying out' stage of learning 'appropriation' – the learner appropriates (takes ownership of) the behaviour. Practitioners who have watched a child learning to tie a shoelace will recognise the stages of appropriation as the child tries different ways of making the laces behave in the way he or she has seen adults do.

The principles of Vygotsky's thinking are:

- Children construct their own knowledge
- Development cannot be separated from social context
- Learning can and often does lead development
- Language plays a central role in mental (cognitive) development.

Vygotsky's theory suggests that development depends on interaction with people and the tools that the child's culture provides to help them form their own view of the world. Children acquire the ways of thinking and behaving that make up a culture by interacting with more knowledgeable people, and social interaction will lead to ongoing changes in a child's thoughts and behaviours. Of course, the actual thoughts and behaviours will vary between cultures.

Vygotsky believed that children learn in three ways:

- **imitative learning**, where one person tries to imitate or copy another
- **instructed learning** which involves remembering the instructions of the 'teacher' and then using these instructions to self-regulate
- **collaborative learning**, which involves a group of peers who strive to understand each other and work together to learn a specific skill.

The major elements of Vygotsky's theories, and those for which he is remembered and admired are:

The Zone of Proximal Development (ZPD)

What a child can do today with assistance, she will be able to do by herself tomorrow. Vygotsky observed that when children were tested on tasks on their own, they rarely did as well as when they were working in collaboration with an adult, even though the adult gave them very little help with the activity except to talk them through the task. It was by no means always the case that the adult was teaching them how to perform the task but the process of engagement with the adult enabled the child to refine their own thinking or performance to make it more effective. The development and use of language (both silent and vocal *self-talk*) and the articulation of ideas was central to their learning and cognitive development.

When a child is engaged in learning about the world he/she is involved simultaneously in two different levels of development:

- Level 1 – the 'present level of development'. This describes what the child is currently capable of doing without any help from others.

- Level 2 – the 'potential level of development'. What the child could potentially be capable of with help from other people or 'teachers'.

The gap between present and potential development, is what Vygotsky described as the zone of proximal development or ZPD, and the ZPD must contain two features:

1 **Subjectivity** – the two (or more) individuals begin a task with different understandings of how to approach it, and only after time together, eventually arrive at a shared understanding.
2 **Scaffolding** – a change in social support occurs over the course of a session, and through discussion, observation and questioning, the gap between the present and potential level of development closes. This process is called scaffolding. If scaffolding is successful, a child's mastery level of performance changes, increasing their performance on a particular task.

Vygotsky's believed that, through help from other more knowledgeable people, a child can potentially gain new knowledge or skills, and that if scaffolding occurs during the activity, the child will learn more quickly. In this model, the knowledge must be appropriate for the child's level of comprehension – if it is too complex or difficult, or the gap between what is known, the ZPD and the new knowledge is too big, the child will fail to understand or move to the next level.

The involvement of More Knowledgeable Others (MKO)

Vygotsky was convinced that moving into the ZPD involves contact with people with more knowledge than the child, and Vygotsky called these people More Knowledgeable Others (MKO). MKOs can be teachers and other adults, parents or family members, and Vygotsky includes other, more knowledgeable children. These companions can unlock the ZPD by discussion, demonstration, modeling or otherwise introducing the child to new knowledge.

Some people think Vygotsky would include computers in the list of MKOs as long as they contain more knowledge about the subject in hand than the learner. Others dispute the inclusion of computers, insisting that human language is an essential feature of scaffolding, and computer responses, particularly for young learners, do not have the possibilities of language nuance of the human brain and adult language.

Scaffolding

When an adult (or MKO) provides support for a child, they adjust the amount of help they give depending on the child's progress. For example, a child who is first learning to ride a bicycle might need help from training wheels, a MKO's hand on the back of the saddle and the MOK talking through the skills needed – 'Keep your feet on the pedals, keep pedalling, hold on to the handlebars, brake!' etc. As the child becomes more proficient and confident, they will need less support, including the removal of the training wheels. Eventually the MKO will merely show support by running or walking alongside the bike. The MKO scaffolds the child's learning until the child can ride the bike unaided.

Vygotsky referred to this progression of levels of help as scaffolding. It draws parallels from real scaffolding for buildings – a support for construction of new material (the skill/information to be learnt), which is removed once the building is complete (the skill/information has been learnt).

Self-talk or private-talk

Vygotsky placed great importance on the value of language, and maintained that there are two different roles for language, both vital for cognitive learning and thinking:

- Transmitting information – 'Language is the main means by which adults transmit information to children.'
- As a tool for learning – 'In itself, language becomes a very powerful tool for intellectual adaptation.' Vygotsky; Thought and Language; 1962

Without language, he maintained, humans are not able to think and there is a close link between the acquisition of language and the development of thinking. He maintained that there are three sorts of speech involved in learning any language:

1. **Social speech**, external communication, used to talk to others, discuss and question (typically from the age of two)
2. **Private speech**, or self-talk, which is normal for very young children, directed inwardly, to the self, usually when they are playing and learning (typically from the age of three). Vygotsky maintained that children often cease to verbalise aloud, or reduce the sound to a whisper as they get older, and become better at 'silent inner speech'
3. **Silent inner speech**, which describes the way that private speech 'goes underground', becoming inaudible from the outside, instead becoming a thinking tool, used to think and remember, and serving an intellectual function (typically from the age of seven).

An important feature of self-talk, or private-talk is that it enables children to begin to be their own more knowledgeable other (MKO) and can use this technique to begin problem

Lev Vygotsky

solving and decision making for themselves. Vygotsky believed that children who engaged in large amounts of self-talk are likely to be more socially competent than children who do not use it extensively. Self-talk is not just an accompaniment to the child's activity, it can act as a tool to support and extend cognitive processes.

Many of us continue to use self-talk, even as adults, and particularly when attempting a difficult task. Somehow, providing ourselves with a commentary on what we are doing can be very helpful!

Internalising these monologues, and therefore becoming a verbal thinker, is a stepping-stone to higher levels of thinking.

Authentic activities

An element of the concept of ZPD is the recommendation that effective learning and teaching would be more effective in 'authentic' activities that mimic real life. For example, a child should not be taught to write as an abstract skill, rather through purposeful tasks such as writing a letter. All activities should create an urge to acquire the new learning and move on into the new ZPD.

Play

Although it is not so well known, Vygotsky's work on play and children's games is also important. He thought that children develop many abstract thoughts by exploring them through play. He gives an example of a child of around three years of age who desperately wants to ride a horse but can't have one. The child realises that an outlet for her desire might be though imaginary play so she finds a broom and straddling the handle, she 'rides' round the garden, making 'clocking' sounds and slapping her own thigh as she imitates a rider. Vygotsky calls the broomstick a pivot to the child's imagination. He thought that babies and very young children are not able to express their thoughts through imaginary play, and play of this sort is totally absent in animals – play, and particularly 'pretend' play, is a feature that is uniquely human. (Vygotsky, 'Play is imagination in action', *Thought and Language*, 1962).

Practitioners provide pivots in many activities and resources in their settings. These include small world animals and vehicles, home play with clothing and props, and puppets. Wheeled toys, gardening and other outdoor activities also provide pivots for children's imaginations as they play out their experiences.

Vygotsky and Piaget

There was, and still is, a tension between the theories of Piaget and those of Vygotsky. The conflict was over whether concepts for the next developmental stage should be offered or even taught before children reach the next developmental stage, in order to help them to move into that stage.

Opposing Vygotsky's zone of proximal development, Piaget believed that, unless the child has already achieved the appropriate stage of development, they should not be exposed to the next level of learning. His stages of development were rigidly defined and although they were broad in age span, he insisted that children must go through them in the correct sequence. Children's development must necessarily precede their learning.

Vygotsky believed that it was entirely possible for a child to 'roam freely' across development stages, not necessarily visiting them in the strict order described by Piaget. He felt that children might be in different stages of development in some aspects (say physical development and language development) but not others.

There is also a major difference between the two psychologists in the development of language. According to Piaget, language depends on thought for its development (i.e. thought comes before language). For Vygotsky, thought and language are separate systems from before birth, only merging at about three years old when the child can produce verbal thought, as opposed to simple imitation of adult speech – cognitive development results from an internalisation of language (i.e. thought is dependent on language).

Vygotsky's theory of the development of thinking and reasoning was also very different from that of Piaget. His constructivist view recognised the importance of the growth of the mind, not just the body and the brain. In this approach the focus shifts from the teacher to the learner, who is actively involved in his/her own learning. Learners are encouraged to work collaboratively, to explore and investigate, and to use the adults and other children as mentors and supports to their learning.

Social, not simply biological factors are crucial to learning, and society plays a big part, giving children the support they need to avoid failure. For instance, a parent will help a child to succeed in dressing him/herself. The parent turns clothes the right way out, patiently shows the child how to do up buttons, zips, shoelaces. They show their child tricks they learned from their parents – placing clothes on a chair before lifting them over their head, putting the hood of their coat on their head before slotting their arms inside etc.

Vygotsky argued that the social environment could also help the child's cognitive development, as it is an important factor which helps the child to adapt culturally to new situations when needed. Both Vygotsky and Piaget agreed on the importance of finding out how children master ideas and then translate them into speech.

Vygotsky felt that the social context around learning was an important factor for children, and that human mental activity is the result of social learning – culture is the primary determining factor for acquiring knowledge. As children master tasks they will engage in social and cooperative dialogues with others, and this led Vygotsky to believe that acquisition of language is the most influential feature of a child's life and that the social context will result in highly variable development depending on the child's cultural experiences in the environment. Piaget, on the other hand, thought that children act independently on the physical world to explore and discover what it has to offer and this contact overrides social contexts, following a natural line where the child progresses through prescribed stages of development.

Piaget remained convinced that biological factors are in control throughout a child's development. The two psychologists never met as Vygotsky died before Piaget even had the opportunity to read his books, and if they had met, maybe they would have found that their interest in child development provided an ideal arena for their discussions. Piaget, on reading Vygotsky's books after his death, wrote the following:

Although my friend A. Luria kept me up to date concerning Vygotsky's sympathetic and yet critical position with respect to my work, I was never able to read his writings or to meet him in person, and in reading his book today, I regret this profoundly, for we could have come to an understanding on a number of points.

(Jean Piaget, Comments on Vygotsky's critical remarks concerning The Language and Thought of the Child, and Judgment and Reasoning in the Child, 1962)

Vygotsky died from a return of his tuberculosis in 1934. After his death, many of his ideas were initially repudiated by the Soviet Government of the time but were kept alive by his followers and students. After the end of The Cold War Vygotsky's works were revealed and his influence has pervaded psychology and pedagogy across the world, so that his books and theories have attained a stature equal to that of other major theorists. Sadly, our knowledge of Vygotsky's theories remains incomplete and some of his work still remains untranslated.

Legacy and impact

Vygotsky's approaches have been adopted widely across the world and in many countries children are now used to working in small groups, pairs and even alone on projects and topics that may cover several subjects of the curriculum, or areas of learning. This style of working enables children to work together, providing freedom to use self-talk, and to be each other's 'more knowledgeable others'.

Vygotsky's central belief was that ability was not entirely inherited but is dependent on the support of the society in which the children grow up. If a child is able to gain access to his/her own ZPD, and stay in this zone, he/she will succeed. It is therefore the teacher's job to identify for each child where their current ZPD is and provide activities and support to match. Scaffolding is at the heart of a discovery approach where the individual child can follow their own interests at their own speed. It is difficult with large numbers of children in a group to maintain their knowledge of every child's ZPD in every area of activity. Practitioners need to be observant, and vigilant, and spend as much time as they can in direct contact with children as they learn, providing the support of a more knowledgeable other (MKO), and scaffolding children's learning.

Teachers' assessments in some schools use Vygotsky's descriptions, with checklists of 'cannot yet do', 'can do with help', and 'can do alone'. These teachers accept that children's learning moves on at unpredictable rates, and their role is to find each child's next ZPD.

In his Philosophy for Children programme, which is devoted to thinking skills and creativity, Matthew Lipman has been influenced by Vygotsky's theories, and Carol

Dweck has used her reading of Vygotsky to support her thinking in the Growth Mindset programme, which focuses directly on children's perceptions of their own learning abilities, helping them to develop positive attitudes and a collaborative approach.

ZPD has become a well-understood concept in early years education, where practitioners all over the world are encouraged to scaffold and support children's learning rather than 'teaching at them'. There is also wide agreement that the society in which children are brought up has a far bigger effect on them than was previously believed.

Influence on early years practice in the UK

The notion of a ZPD is both welcomed and well recognised by early years practitioners. The sensitive intervention of practitioners as they work alongside children has been a central feature of good practice since early education practice first became an established feature in western society. The balance of child-initiated and adult-led activities is a frequent focus of discussion among practitioners, and they are always searching for the most effective proportions of each.

Scotland

In 'Pre-birth to three', the Scottish Government has espoused Vygotsky's principles by making direct reference to them in the framework for the youngest children. This document gives practitioners a direct link to his work, as well as giving useful support to their practice, by describing the process of scaffolding:

> Bruner (1986) built on Vygotsky's ideas and proposed that adults should support children by 'scaffolding' their learning through play. He explained that children can be supported in this way to move from where they are to their next level of understanding and learning. Scaffolding represents the purposeful interactions between adults and children that enables children to progress beyond their independent efforts. When scaffolding children's learning, the focus ideally stems from the interests and desires of children and it requires staff support, interaction, guidance, use of language and practical activity.
>
> (Learning and Teaching Scotland, 2010)

England

In England, the current requirements for practitioners focus almost entirely on ensuring that the balance of child-initiated and adult-directed activity moves towards more adult direction by the time children enter statutory schooling at the age of five. While acknowledging that children's learning depends on their freedom to choose the resources and places where they will play and learn, the current Framework and Guidance also emphasises that the adults role is more than ensuring safety and company. The purpose of government funded early years education must result in ensuring that children are 'ready' for school. The 'Statutory framework for the early years foundation' states:

Each area of learning and development must be implemented through planned, purposeful play and through a mix of adult-led and child-initiated activity. Play is essential for children's development, building their confidence as they learn to explore, to think about problems, and relate to others. Children learn by leading their own play, and taking part in play which is guided by adults.

(DfE, 2014)

In a previous guidance document, 'Learning, playing and interacting', produced in 2009, the following statement eloquently describes the adult role in scaffolding learning. Although this document now has the status of guidance, rather than statutory requirement, it does contain a very clear description of supporting the child into and on from their current ZPD:

It is through the active intervention, guidance and support of a skilled adult that children make the most progress in their learning. This does not mean pushing children too far or too fast, but instead meeting children where they are, showing them the next open door, and helping them to walk through it. It means being a partner with children, enjoying with them the power of their curiosity and the thrill of finding out what they can do.

(DCSF, 2009)

The concept of meeting children where they are, showing them the next open door, and helping them to walk through it makes the process clear and visible.

In the current EYFS Framework for England, the inclusion of detailed descriptions of the Characteristics of Effective Learning relates directly to the principles of Vygotsky in social contact, problem solving, thinking skills and working with MKOs:

Three characteristics of effective teaching and learning are:

- **playing and exploring** – children investigate and experience things, and 'have a go';
- **active learning** – children concentrate and keep on trying if they encounter difficulties, and enjoy achievements; and
- **creating and thinking critically** – children have and develop their own ideas, make links between ideas, and develop strategies for doing things.

(Learning, Playing and Interacting, Good Practice in the Early Years Foundation Stage; DCSF. 2009)

Northern Ireland

In Northern Ireland there is a national emphasis on thinking skills and there is now a central document relating to the incorporation of these called 'Thinking skills and personal capabilities of Key Stages 1 and 2', with descriptions of the behaviour of adults:

- Draw attention to the processes of learning and not just the products;
- are more likely to engage pupils in active rather than passive learning;
- Enable pupils to go beyond the mere recall of information and to develop deeper understanding of topics;
- Create positive dispositions and habits for learning; and they provide a new range of criteria against which pupils can evaluate their progress in learning.

    Essentially, they enable pupils to learn how to learn.

(CCEA, 2007)

There is also a public and welcome acknowledgement of a move away from the 'empty vessels' model of education:

Developing TS&PC requires an approach to teaching that extends beyond traditional didactic methods. To develop skills and capabilities, pupils need to be thoroughly engaged with their own learning, be given opportunities to practise their skills, to reflect on their achievements, and to recognise their strengths and weaknesses. Pupils cannot be considered as empty vessels to be filled; they should be viewed, instead, as active makers of meaning.

(CCEA, 2007)

…and in the Curriculum for Excellence in Scotland, there is a strong emphasis on collaborative learning – working with Vygotsky's MKOs, and emphasising that such learning can often be more effective than intervention by an adult:

Much effective learning is social, and teaching and learning amongst peers can sometimes be even more effective than when it is offered by an adult.

(Scottish Executive, 2007)

Wales

In Wales the 'Foundation Phase Framework' spans the years from 3 to 7, and has an emphasis on play and practical activities. There is direct reference to scaffolding as an essential tool for practitioners, who need to be able to tell the difference between a child who needs adult help to move through their current ZPD, and a child who can manage this alone:

Practitioners need to be aware of when it is appropriate to intervene sensitively to extend the children's learning and challenge their problem-solving and thinking skills, and when to allow the children to come to satisfactory conclusions on their own.

It is also important that practitioners should support/scaffold *children's learning when they are struggling with an activity or when they will not succeed without practitioner intervention. Once the children have succeeded with the activity the practitioners can then withdraw their support.*

(Welsh Assembly Government, 2015)

The influence of Vygotsky and other psychologists such as Bruner has resulted in their inclusion in major research projects as well as in national guidance. One long-term research project, 'Effective Provision of Pre-school Education (EPPE) Project', introduced a new concept for practitioners, and a description of the process of children's learning. This concept, now known as 'sustained shared thinking' was evidenced as one of the most effective tools for learning, and was a feature of the most effective settings included in the research project.

Effective pedagogy includes interaction traditionally associated with the term 'teaching', the provision of instructive learning environments and 'sustained shared thinking' to extend children's learning.

(Sylva et. al., 2014)

Sustained shared thinking is defined in the EPPE documents as:

Sustained shared thinking' occurs when two or more individuals 'work together' in an intellectual way to solve a problem, clarify a concept, evaluate an activity, extend a narrative etc. Both parties must contribute to the thinking and it must develop and extend the understanding. It was more likely to occur when children were interacting 1:1 with an adult or with a single peer partner and during focussed group work.

(Sylva et. al.,2014)

The concept of sustained shared thinking and Vygotsky's ZPD and MKO have been adopted in settings across the UK and beyond, improving children's experiences, and influencing practice, practitioner training and the evaluation of effectiveness by early years inspectors.

Things to think about

- Vygotsky maintained that children need the support of MKOs. These people are not necessarily trained practitioners. How often do you observe other children in the role of MKO in a group of other children?

- It's not easy to abandon the traditional 'teaching' role of the adult and stand back so children can move forward at their own pace. Are you a good MKO yourself? Do you always intervene at the right moment, or do you sometimes jump in too soon?

- How much time are you able to allocate in the planned programme for sustained shared thinking?

- Are you a 'Piagetian', believing that children pass through ordered stages of learning, and that thought comes before learning? Or are you a 'Vygotskian', believing that individual children learn in a more random way, not through defined stages, and need to learn language before they can use it to think?

- Most practitioners have learned about Vygotsky after their original training. If you are still a student, how do you think his theories will help you in your future work?

APPENDIX 1: Other influential thinkers

Simon Baron-Cohen (1958–)

Specialisms: autism, gender

Baron-Cohen works at Cambridge University focusing on autism and particularly the reason why so many boys are found to have the condition. He believes that Asperger's syndrome represents the extreme male brain, and, having worked with Uta Frith, he also believes that autism is a heritable condition, saying that '*In essence, some geeks may be carriers of genes for autism: in their own life, they do not demonstrate any signs of severe autism, but when they pair up and have kids, their children may get a double dose of autism genes and traits. In this way, assortative mating between technical-minded people might spread autism genes.*' (2013). In 2001 he developed the Autism Spectrum Quotient, a set of fifty questions that can be used to help determine whether or not an adult has symptoms of autism.

Sarah-Jayne Blakemore (1974–)

Specialisms: neuroscience in education, brain development and learning

Sarah-Jayne Blakemore is Professor of Neuroscience at the Institute of Cognitive Neuroscience, University College London. Her specialism is in social cognition and decision-making, particularly in adolescence. She is currently Head of the Development Group at the UCL Institute of Cognitive Neuroscience which focuses on the development of social cognition and decision-making in adolescence. Recommended book: *The Learning Brain* (co-authored with Uta Frith, 2005) and recommended paper: *Blackmore & Frith 'The implications of recent developments in neuroscience for research on teaching and learning.*' (Institute of Cognitive Neuroscience, 2011).

Ann Brown (1943–1999)

Specialisms: memory, metacognition, learning to learn

Ann Brown was born in England. After university, she spent her adult life in the United States, working on how metacognitive strategies such as mnemonics can help children to learn and remember. She and her colleagues developed the theory of cognitive-social learning, based on Vygotskian theory, where the learner is the active constructor of their own learning. This theory promotes critical thinking and other metacognition and higher language skills such as reading, writing, argument and collaboration. Guided assessment methods present children with problems just one step beyond their existing competence (the Zone of Proximal Development) and then provide help as needed for the child to reach independent mastery.

Edward de Bono (1933–)

Specialisms: thinking skills, lateral thinking

Born in Malta, but educated in Canada and in England, Eduard de Bono is famous for his work on lateral thinking. He published a book *Children Solve Problems* (1972) that suggested that children should be encouraged to use skills which they are born with, but is often ignored or suppressed in schools. His 'Six Thinking Hats' problem solving process provides a framework to help people think clearly and thoroughly by directing their thinking attention in one direction at a time – white hat facts, green hat creativity, yellow hat benefits, black hat cautions, red hat feelings and blue hat process. Contributors put on and take off hats as they think about and solve problems.

Noam Chomsky (1928–)

Specialism: language development

The child of immigrant parents, Noam Chomsky was born, raised, educated and worked in the United States. The school he attended as a child followed John Dewey's philosophy of reduced competition, and allowing pupils to follow their own interests. The basis of Chomsky's linguistic theory is in biolinguistics – the belief that language is heavily influenced by our genes, and an evolutionary process of humans that makes language different from the communication of animals. Chomsky believes that the unique nature of humans means that the baby will almost certainly develop the ability to speak and understand language, but a kitten never will. Chomsky's theory proposed that language consists of both surface structure, which 'faces out' and is represented by spoken utterances, while deep structure 'faces inward' and expresses the basic relations between words and conceptual meaning. However, more recently Chomsky has abandoned this theory in favour of one consisting of structures of 'Plastic (pliable) cerebral circuits'.

Marie Clay (1926–2007)

Specialisms: Pioneer of the Balanced Literacy Model and inventor of the Reading Recovery Programme

Born in New Zealand, Marie Clay became an international leader in the study of children's reading development. Her methods of teaching reading and written language swept through the English speaking nations in the years since she developed them in 1983, when it was implemented in all New Zealand schools. Reading Recovery was developed as a means of improving the motivation of low achieving 6 year olds so they achieved a level appropriate to their chronological age. The programme calls for close observation of the child by the teacher to design lessons that constantly build on what a child already knows and takes them to the next level (a process very much like that advised by Vygotsky). Children are then surrounded by a language-rich environment and encouraged to choose reading books that help them to follow their personal interests. During the 1970s and 1980s a Reading Recovery programme was funded by the UK government, but the method was costly, and is now one which individual schools must fund themselves. Reading Recovery was incorporated into Every Child a Reader, which aimed to eradicate the 'tail' of non-readers in primary schools by using Reading Recovery. However, the Every Child a Reader (ECaR) project has now been discontinued.

Uta Frith (1941 –)

Specialisms: autism, ASD, reading development

Uta Frith works at research level in cognitive neuroscience, but her major goal is to make neuroscience relevant and accessible to the general public. Her aim is to discover the underlying cognitive causes of neurological disorders particularly Asperger's syndrome and autism, and to link them to behavioural symptoms as well as to brain systems. She was one of the first neuroscientists to recognise autism as a condition of the brain rather than the result of cold parenting.

Neil D. Fleming (1939 –)

Specialism: learning styles, VARK

Neil D. Fleming is a teacher from New Zealand, who began asking questions about learning styles, and why different people learn better using different styles. His work has resulted in the Visual, Auditory, Reading/writing and Kinesthetic (VARK) approach to learning. He has been the main author of the VARK books available online on his website. Prior to his work, a Visual, Auditory, Kinesthetic (VAK) approach to learning was in common usage, promoted by accelerated learning. There is no conclusive evidence that this method works, but those who favour it maintain that they can get results by using it, and some governments have approved its use in schools.

Elinor Goldschmeid (1910 – 2009)

Specialism: nursery education, treasure baskets, heuristic play

The fourth of seven children, brought up in rural Gloucestershire, Elinor Goldschmeid was a pioneer of early childhood care and education. She trained at the Fröebel Institute in London, and her first job was at the progressive school Dartington Hall in Devon. She had a profound influence on practice across the world, but particularly in the UK. Her major claims to fame are the introduction of Treasure Baskets and Heuristic Play – collections of tactile objects for babies and toddlers to explore – and the role of the key person – the adult in the setting with whom the child will have most contact. Both these processes were described and explained in *People Under Three* (2003), and in her collection of videos, which were filmed in her nursery.

Alison Gopnik (1955 –)

Specialisms: the development of the brain in babies and very young children

Alison Gopnik is an American expert in cognitive and language development. Her books, including *The Scientist in the Crib: What Early Learning Tells Us About the Mind* (1999), and *The Philosophical Baby: What Children's Minds Tell Us about Truth, Love*, and *The Meaning of Life* (2009) both telling, in very accessible language, the story of her work with very young babies and toddlers.

Usha Goswami (1960 –)

Specialism: Educational neuroscience, dyslexia

A researcher and professor of Cognitive Developmental Neuroscience at the University of Cambridge, Usha Goswami is a developmental psychologist. Her work is mainly concerned with reading development, and dyslexia as a language disorder rather than a visual disorder. She is currently researching whether or not reading poetry, nursery rhymes, and singing can be used to help children with dyslexia. In January 2003 she moved to the University of Cambridge where she currently works as the director for the Centre for Neuroscience in Education. Her work has influenced practice in the early years through her books and scholarly but readable reports on neuroscience and education, for example 'Children's cognitive development and learning'. (Cambridge Primary Review Trust, 2015).

Vivian Gussin Paley – (1929 –)

Specialisms: observation, imagination in children

A lifelong teacher in the early years in the United States, Vivian Gussin Paley has spent time researching how young children think, imagine and recall their experiences. Her records of conversations with children, and the stories they tell her have been recorded in many books, all with idiosyncratic titles such as *The Girl with the Brown Crayon* (1997), *You Can't Say You Can't Play* (1993), and *The Boy Who Would Be a Helicopter* (1991). These books, all inspired by children's imaginative play, have had a great influence in the United States and in the UK, where practitioners want to extend opportunities for children to imagine and tell stories in free play.

Lilian Katz (1932 –)

Specialisms: early learning, STEM in early years

Lilian Katz, born and raised in England and educated at Stanford University, is an expert in early learning, and has been so for many years. Her work has been mainly in child development, children's minds, and parent education, through lecturing in education, work with early childhood associations, books and articles. Her most recent work is to raise the profile of science, technology, engineering and maths (STEM) in the early years; 'STEM in the early years' is available from ecrp.uiuc.edu/beyond/seed/katz.html

John Locke (1632 – 1704)

Specialism: cognitive development

John Locke influenced Jean-Jacques Rousseau and many other Enlightenment philosophers. His *Theory of Mind* is often thought to be the origin of modern concepts of identity. Locke's view was that at birth, the human brain is a blank slate (*tabula rasa*), with no knowledge and no innate ideas. Knowledge can only be gained through experience derived from direct sensation, with the experiences of parents, society, education and the world written on it.

A S Neill (1917 – 1973)

Specialism:

Delegating ownership for decision making about the running of a school, their participation in lessons, and the content of the curriculum to the children

Alexander Sutherland Neill known as A. S. Neill, was a Scottish educator and author known for his school, Summerhill, which adopted methods commonly referred to as a 'free school' philosophy. During the early years of the school's work, children had complete freedom from adult coercion, attended lessons when and if they wanted to, and contributed to a self-governing 'moot' where adults and children made decisions about the running of the school, including the food, punishment, and what was taught. Neill felt that children were innately good, and that they became virtuous and just naturally, when allowed to grow and be happy without adult imposition of morality. Neill's practice provided children with space, time, and empowerment for personal exploration, and with freedom from adult fear and coercion. In the 1950s, Neill published his writings in a book *Summerhill*, which attracted a great deal of attention, and a TV programme followed. Neill died in 1973 and the school is now led by his daughter.

Steven Pinker (1954 –)

Specialism: language development

Canadian born, cognitive scientist, psychologist and linguist, Steven Pinker has the skill of making scientific information accessible to lay people as well as the scientific community. His books cover children's language acquisition – how they learn verbs, learn about the past tense of English verbs, and learn the many irregular forms of the English language. He argues that language is an instinct, shaped by natural selection and passed on in our genes. His books include *The Language Instinct* (1994), *The Blank Slate* (2002) and *The Better Angels of our Nature* (2011). He is currently working on a style guide to help writers to make their writing more accessible to the reader, particularly in scientific and academic writing. Pinker believes that the sexes are not identical because human nature is the result of 'two overlapping distributions'.

Bhurrus Frederic Skinner (1904 – 1990)

Specialism: cognitive development

American psychologist, behaviourist, and author, commonly known as B. F. Skinner, who worked at Harvard University from 1958 until 1974. He considered that free will was an illusion. Human actions, he said, were dependent purely on previous actions (stimulus/response). This gave rise to the stimulus/response view of development, where a human responds to the stimulus, and if the consequences of an action are undesirable, the action will not be repeated; if the consequences are desirable, it will – the principle of positive or negative reinforcement. Skinner's views were in opposition to the later theories based on cognitive science, so although he has been widely revered for bringing a much-needed scientific approach to the study of human behavior, he has also been criticised for attempting to apply findings based largely on animal experiments to human behavior in real-life settings. Skinner's experiments were undertaken using the 'Skinner Box' which had levers for rats to press and discs that pigeons could peck, to deliver food. The results of the experiments were recorded on a cumulative recorder with a paper-covered drum. Skinner also invented the plastic crib used for babies in hospital, and a primitive teaching machine.

APPENDIX 2: Some initiatives and school systems that have influenced the world of early education

Forest Schools

www.forestschoolassociation.org
Forest Schools provide children (and some adults) with outdoor education in all weathers, mostly spent in woods and forests, and learning outdoor skills and woodland crafts, such as den building, outdoor cooking, whittling, with an emphasis on personal and social conditions and technical skills; the weather, the seasons and wildlife are major focuses. Children are encouraged to develop curiosity, independence, and problem solving approaches, and to work collaboratively, through cross-curricular topics covering many areas of learning. Most Forest School activities are provided as a part of the school week, although there are some outdoor schools where the children spend all day every day in the open air. Leaders are trained in the philosophy and in the activities, to ensure safety and enjoyment for all, and they ensure that there are high adult/pupil ratios. There are currently Forest Schools in Australia, Canada, New Zealand, the United States, Malaysia, Switzerland, Spain, Ireland and Germany as well as the UK. The government in Scotland has been particularly supportive of Forest Education and there are now several forest schools that operate all day every day.

Head Start

http://eclkc.ohs.acf.hhs.gov/hslc/hs
The Head Start programme was launched in 1965, and has now been established in the United States for several decades, enabling significant evaluation of its value for money. It is supported by the Office of Child Development in the Department of Health, Education

and Welfare to provide compensatory education for low-income pre-schoolers and their families, combined with health, nutrition and parent education. The aim is to foster stable family relationships, enhance child well-being and help them to develop strong cognitive skills. It has been one of the longest running programmes to support families and their children, with millions of children involved, and the production of the popular educational TV programme, Sesame Street. It has its supporters and its critics, but overall the evaluations have been positive.

High/Scope

http://www.highscope.org
The High/Scope Educational Research Foundation was established by David Weikart, and is an independent, non-profit organisation with headquarters in Ypsilanti, Michigan, that provides training, support and research in early childhood education. The best-known piece of research is The Perry Preschool Study, a long-term study into the effectiveness of the High/Scope Curriculum. This has acknowledged the benefit of pre-school education on the lives and future success of children who experience it. The organisation has outreach centres in the UK, Indonesia, Ireland, Mexico, South Africa, The Netherlands, Chile and many other countries. The High/Scope pre-school model includes curriculum guidance, assessment procedures, training and curriculum resources, and arranges conferences and training for teachers. The programme is particularly known for its conflict resolution strategies, which are considered to be among the most effective.

Montessori Schools

www.montessori.org.uk
Montessori schools have been established all over the world, to follow the approach first established by Maria Montessori. Features of these schools include Montessori trained teachers in every class, mixed age classes (often from 2–6), free choice from a range of options offered by the practitioners, a discovery model of education where children can follow their own interests and time during the day when the originally designed 'Montessori materials' are used. There are some schools that have adopted the Montessori name without the appropriate training for staff, or the use of the 'trademark' Montessori materials. This is because the Montessori name was never sufficiently protected by copyright law.

Reggio Emilia

www.reggiochildren.it

Reggio Emilia Preschools and Infant/Toddler Centres (Nidi or nests) are a feature of the town of Reggio Emilia. The schools were originally founded after the Second World War by parents with the support of Loris Malaguzzi (see page 189). They are internationally recognised as providing a high quality, child-centred creative education programme for children from babies to six years of age. The practice includes valuing the Hundred Languages of children – not just speaking and writing, but drawing, model making, painting, fabric work, pottery, singing etc. The Reggio Approach has been copied in many countries, with varying success, except in Sweden, where it has been implemented in a very careful and respectful way, which recognises the unique nature of each culture. The Reggio teachers say that their approach is like a living thing, which can only flourish if the conditions are right, and this implies that the schools are right for their time and place, but may not be suitable for universal implementation.

Te Whariki, Curriculum for New Zealand

www.education.govt.nz/assets/Documents/Early-Childhood/te-whariki.pdf

Te Whariki (usually translated as 'a mat for every child') is the New Zealand curriculum for the early years. It was implemented across the country from 1996, to bring together a wide range of existing early years provision. The curriculum has a commitment to the use of the Maori language and culture, which runs through the four curriculum principles:

- **Whakamana – Empowerment** – The early childhood curriculum empowers the child to learn and grow.
- **Kotahitanga – Holistic Development** – The early childhood curriculum reflects the holistic way children learn and grow.
- **Whānau Tangata – Family and Community** – The wider world of family and community is an integral part of the early childhood curriculum.
- **Ngā Hononga – Relationships** – Children learn through responsive and reciprocal relationships with people, places, and things.

The curriculum does not specify any specific subjects or specific knowledge, emphasising play, outdoor learning, and many of the features of an education within the home.

Waldorf Steiner schools

www.steinerwaldorf.org

The philosophy of the Waldorf/Steiner Schools is rooted in the philosophy of Rudolf Steiner, an Austrian philosopher and pedagogue whose practice emphasised the role of imagination in learning, striving to integrate the intellectual, practical, artistic and spiritual (but not religious) development of pupils. The approach to early education is experiential and hands-on, with an emphasis on creativity and play. Television and other electronic resources are discouraged, as they keep children inactive, and often contain unsuitable messages. Resources are made from natural materials such as wood or fabric, and the classroom is meant to replicate a home. There are over a thousand independent Waldorf schools (taking children from 3–18), about 2,000 kindergartens, and 646 centers for special education, located in 60 countries, which makes it one of the largest independent school systems in the world.

APPENDIX 3: Recent research projects into early education and childcare

The Carolina Abecedarian Project

abc.fpg.unc.edu/

The Carolina Abecedarian Project is included because of its focus on the benefits of early education for young children. Although the number of participants was smaller than the EPPE Project in England, it did focus on the inclusion of black children (98% of participants) – previous research had been criticised for its overwhelmingly white, middle class participation. The age of the children was also crucial. Most studies before had included children from the age of three, but the Abecedarian projects started from infancy (born between 1972 and 1977), and continued for five years. All the 111 infants involved were identified as 'high risk' based on maternal education, family income, and other factors. Of these, 57 were given high-quality intervention, consisting in part of educational games based on the latest in educational theory. The other 54 acted as a control group and the average starting age of participants was 4.4 months. The participants received child care for six to eight hours a day, five days a week. Educational activities were game-based and emphasised language. The control group was provided with nutritional supplements, support from social services and health care to ensure that these factors did not affect the outcomes of the experiment. The teacher-child ratio was low, ranging from 1:3 for infants to 1:6 at age five.

Follow up assessments at ages 3, 4, 5, 6.5, 8, 12, 15, 21, and 30, were made in cognitive function, academic skills, educational attainment, employment, parenthood and social adjustment.

From the results, the project concluded that high quality, educational child care from early infancy was of utmost importance. Other programs, such as the Head Start programme, have not had such marked success. It may be that elements such as the later start of the Perry Preschool research meant that children lost some ground compared with children in the Abecedarian program.

EPPE and EPPSE Effective Preschool, Primary & Secondary Education Project

www.ioe.ac.uk/research/4586.html

EPPE and EPPSE together constitute the first major study in the UK to focus on the effectiveness of early years provision. The project has followed children in a large scale, longitudinal study of more than 3,000 children, from preschool (age three) to post-compulsory education (age 16), considering the impact of a range of aspects of early education on attainment, progress and development.

The original phase of the project focused on identifying the features of high quality preschool provision, and how this might affect children's lives and educational attainment in the first stages of primary years that follow. Findings included:

- Preschool experience, compared to none, enhances children's all-round development

- Duration of attendance (in months) is important; an earlier start (under age three) was related to better intellectual development

- High quality preschooling is related to better intellectual and social-behavioural development

- Full time attendance led to no better gains for children than part-time provision

- Disadvantaged children benefit significantly from good quality preschool

- The beneficial effects of preschool remain evident at the end of Key Stage 1, although some outcomes were not as strong as they had been at five

- Specific pedagogical practices including interactions traditionally associate with the term 'teaching', and 'sustained shared thinking' were evident in more 'effective' settings and these were associated with more highly qualified staff

- Marital status, parent's socio-economic status and qualification levels related to child outcomes.

These benefits appear to have continued into secondary schools, where as well as improving outcomes in academic subjects, the findings of the 3–16 research concluded with the following statement in support of providing high quality preschool education for every child:

Finally the longitudinal nature of the rich EPPSE dataset allowed us to discover the long-term effects of pre-school experiences, especially those of high quality settings. Each student's preschool and early home learning environment created the 'platform' on which the marks of primary and secondary school are then etched.

(Effective pre-school, primary and secondary
education 3–14 project; EPPSE 3–14; DfE/London IoE, 2012)

HighScope and the Perry Preschool Project

www.highscope.org

This study has continued since 1962, but the original study was first evaluated in 1967 when the children left primary education. The Perry Project is one of many carried out by the HighScope research team, and studied the effect of preschool education on children from deprived families. Carried out at Ypsilanti, Michigan, and led by David Weikart, the project followed a group of 123 low-income African American three and four year olds, and collected information on them annually from ages three to 11, and again at ages 14, 15, 19, 27, and 40. Half of the group had preschool experience at a HighScope preschool, and the other half had no preschool experience.

The findings of the study were that participants with experience of child care achieved a higher level of academic success than the children with no preschool experience. Significant effect can only be achieved when the preschool is of a high quality, and the study lists the criteria for a high quality provision that will make a difference:

- *A preschool education program*
- *Run by teachers with bachelor's degrees and certification in education*
- *An adult child ratio of not more than 8 children to each adult*
- *Children living in low-income families*
- *Offering 2 school years at 3 and 4 years of age*
- *With daily classes of 2 ½ hours or more*
- *Using the HighScope educational model or a similar participatory education approach*
- *With teachers visiting families at least every 2 weeks.*

97% of the children were interviewed again at age 40 and it was found that the children with preschool experience were earning higher incomes, were more likely to own their own homes and were less likely to be on welfare or to have committed a crime. The outcomes of this research have been significant in promoting government investment in early education, which can be seen to have a positive effect on individuals and to be a cost-effective use of government money. HeadStart is one of the programmes currently funded by the United States government, but many states have researched and implemented their own versions of preschool education.

Investment in high quality preschool education has been seen to give children an advantage that lasts at least through their school years, and the Perry Preschool Project shows that the effect goes well beyond childhood and adolescence, influencing social and academic achievements throughout life.

Sound Foundations: A Review of Quality of Early Childhood Education

www.suttontrust.com/researcharchive/sound-foundations

Care for Children Under Three: Implications for Policy and Practice

This review of research evidence synthesises the current findings of research projects connected with children under three. The evidence has identified four key dimensions of good quality pedagogy for under-threes:

1 *stable relationships and interactions with sensitive and responsive adults*
2 *a focus on play-based activities and routines which allow children to take the lead in their own learning*
3 *support for communication and language*
4 *opportunities to move and be physically active.*

This review of the research evidence suggests five 'key conditions' for quality:

1 *Knowledgeable and capable practitioners, supported by strong leaders*
2 *A stable staff team with a low turnover*
3 *Effective staff deployment (e.g. favourable ratios, staff continuity)*
4 *Secure yet stimulating physical environments*
5 *Engaged and involved families.*

Within effective settings, practices that support the development of children under three identify the following key dimensions:

1 *play-based activities and routines which allow children to take the lead in their own learning*
2 *support for language and communication (through use of narrative, shared reading, informal conversations, song and rhymes)*
3 *opportunities to move and be physically active.*

The effect of early childcare on the early development of language and communication appears to have been positive:

● *The literature reviewed for this study generally identifies a cognitive advantage for children beginning non-maternal care between the ages of two and three.*

One of the most controversial aspects of very early childcare for children has been the possible effect on their sense of attachment, and that they may experience separation anxiety. Boys are often thought to be particularly subject to this. However, the report concludes:

> *After many years of controversy over the issue, the results of the most extensive study in the field (the NICHD study) did not show a main effect of early childcare or maternal employment on children's attachment security.*

The report concludes that simply providing additional places for two-year-olds (and particularly disadvantaged two-year-olds) will not be successful unless governments are prepared to invest in high quality provision, which will include more financial investment:

> *…a limited investment that fails to achieve quality will be a poor use of public money. It will not yield the expected gains.*

References

Addams, J, (1908) *The Public School and the Immigrant Child*. National Education Association of United States Journal, Washington DC

Association of Teachers and Lecturers, (2005) 'An intelligent look at Emotional Intelligence'. UK.

Athey, C. (1990) *Extending Thought in Young Children*. Sage Publications: London.

Baron-Cohen, S, (2013) 'Are geeky parents more likely to have autistic kids?' *Scientific American*.

Bodson, J. A., (1987) *The Later Works*.

Bruce, T. (2014) *Early Childhood*. Sage Publications: London.

Bruner, (1978) *Review of Children's Minds*.

Durant, W., (1967) The Story of Civilization, Volume 10: Rousseau and Revolution. Simon & Schuster.

Csikszentmihalyi, M., (2008) *Flow: The Psychology of Optimal Experience. Harper Collins: New York.*

Donaldson, M., (1978) *Children's Minds*. Harper Collins: London.

Dweck, C. (2007) *Mindset: The Psychology of Success*. Balantine Books.

Dweck, C. *Mindset: How You Can Fulfill Your Potential*. Constable & Robinson Limited; 2012.

Elkind, D. (2015) *Giants in the Nursery*. Redleaf Press: Minnesota.

Flavell, J. (1979) 'Metacognition and Cognitive Monitoring' in *American Psychologist* Vol 34, October 1979

Eysenck, H. J., (1971) *Race, Intelligence and Education*. Temple Smith: London

Eysenck, H. J., (1973) *The Inequality of Man*. Temple Smith: London.

Eysenck, H. J., (2000) *Intelligence: A New Look*. Transaction Publishers

Gardner, H., (2011) *Multiple Intelligences: The First Thirty Years*. Harvard Graduate School of Education.

Jarvis, P., (2014) *The McMillan Sisters and the Deptford Welfare Experiment; Bradford College.*

Knight, L. W., (2010) *Jane Adams: Spirit in Action*. W. W. Norton & Company, Inc.: New York.

OECD/EU, (2015) 'Indicators of Immigrant Integration' ; OECD

Public Health England, (2015) 'Promoting children and young people's emotional health and wellbeing.'

Sylva, K., et. al. (2004) 'The Effective Provision of Pre-School Education (EPPE) Project: Findings from pre-school to end of Key Stage 1'; Institute of Education, London

Malaguzzi, L, (2011) *The Hundred Languages of Children*. The Greenwood Press.

McMillan, M, (1919) *The Nursery School*. Bibliolife, London

Montessori, M. *(1916) The Montessori Method*. BN Publishing

Government Documentation

England

Development Matters in the Early Years Foundation Stage; Early Education; 2012

Early Years Pupil Premium and Funding for Two-year-olds; Department for Education; 2014

Effective Pre-school, Primary and Secondary Education 3–14 Project (EPPSE 3–14)
Final Report from the Key Stage 3 Phase: Influences on Students' Development From age 11 – 14; Sylva et al: Institute of Education, London; 2012

The Effective Provision of Pre-School Education (EPPE) Project; Sylva et al: Institute of Education, Surestart; 2014

English as an Additional Language (EAL) and educational achievement in England:
An analysis of the National Pupil Database; Professor Steve Strand; University of Oxford, Department of Education; Education Endowment Fund; 2015

Every Child a Talker: Guidance for Consultants and Early Language Lead Inclusion and Pupil Support; Department for Education; 2006

Inclusion Development Programme; Supporting children with Behavioural, Emotional and Social Difficulties: Guidance for practitioners in the Early Years Foundation Stage; Department for Education; 2010

Know how – The progress Check at Age Two'; Department for Education/National Children's Bureau; 2012

Letters and Sounds; Department for Education and Skills; 2007

Mental Health and Behaviour in Schools; Departmental advice for school staff; Department for Education; 2015

The Nursery School; Margaret McMillan; Dent; 1919 available as a free download from https://archive.org/details/nurseryschool00mcmiuoft

The Pupil Premium; Next Steps; Sutton Trust and Education Endowment Foundation; 2015

Read on Get on; The Save the Children Fund 2014

Statutory Framework for the Early Years Foundation Stage; Department for Education; 2014

Special Educational Needs and Disability: Code of Practice; Department for Education; / Department of Health; 2015

NORTHERN IRELAND

Creating a Curriculum for Excellence Part 1: 3–18 Curriculum; Perth and Kinross Council; 2004

Extended Early Years Special Educational Needs (SEN) Supplement; Northern Ireland Department of Education; 2012 (?)

The integration of newcomer children with interrupted education into Northern Ireland schools; Northern Ireland Strategic Migration Partnership; 2014

The Northern Ireland Curriculum Primary; CCEA; Northern Ireland; 2007

Thinking Skills and Personal Capabilities for Key Stages 1 and 2; CCEA; 2007

Understanding the Foundation Stage; CCEA; Northern Ireland; 2006

SCOTLAND

Building the Curriculum for Excellence; Smarter Scotland; Scottish Government; 2010

Building the Curriculum 1 (3–18); The contribution of the curriculum areas; Scottish Executive; 2006

Building the Curriculum 2 (3–18); Active learning in the early years; Scottish Executive; 2007

Children's development at the start of school in Scotland and the progress made during their first school year: An analysis of PIPS baseline and follow-up assessment data; University of York; 2016

Counting us in; Meeting the needs of children and young people newly arrived in Scotland; HMIE; 2009

Curriculum for Excellence through outdoor learning; Learning and Teaching Scotland; 2010

The Early Years Framework; The Scottish Government, 2008

Experiences and Outcomes, 3–18; Curriculum for Excellence; Learning and Teaching Scotland; (document not dated)

Focusing on Inclusion; Scottish executive; 2006

Framework Pre-birth to Three; Learning and Teaching Scotland, 2010

Literacy Commission; A Vision for Scotland: The Report and Final Recommendations of the Literacy Commission, Edinburgh: Scottish Parent Teacher Council; 2009

Read on Get on, Scotland; Save the Children Fund; 2014

The Reggio Emilia Approach to Early Education; Learning and Teaching Scotland; 2006

WALES

Foundation Phase child development assessment profile; Welsh Assembly Government; 2011

Foundation Phase Profile Handbook; Welsh Assembly Government; 2015

Foundation Phase Framework; Welsh Assembly Government; 2015

Inclusion and Pupil Support; Welsh Assembly Government; 2006

Personal and Social Development, Well-Being and Cultural Diversity; Welsh Assembly Government; 2008

Play/Active learning overview for 3 to 7-year-olds: Welsh Assembly Government: 2008

Play and early years: birth to seven years; PlayWales; 2013

Practical approaches to behaviour management in the classroom: a handbook for classroom teachers in primary schools; Welsh Assembly Government; 2012

SEN Code of Practice; Welsh Assembly Government; 2004

OTHER TITLES

Emotional Intelligence: Theory, Findings, and Implications; Salovey, Mayer, Caruso; Psychological Inquiry; 2004

An Intelligent Look at Emotional Intelligence; Association of Teachers and Lecturers; UK; 2005

Taking Reggio Emilia Home; Louise Boyd Cadwell; Teachers Clollege Press1997

Some Recent Articles and Reports on Brain Development and Early Learning

Children's Cognitive Development and Learning; Usha Goswami; Cambridge Primary Review. cprtrust.org.uk

The Early Development of 'Self Talk' and its Relationship to Early Learning Success; R Baker; *https://students.education.unimelb.edu.au/…/pub/…/1**SelfTalk**_RBaker.pd…*

Effective Pre-school, Primary and Secondary Education 3–14 Project (EPPSE 3–14) Final Report from the Key Stage 3 Phase: Influences on Students' Development From age 11 – 14; *K Sylva and P Sammons, University of Oxford; B Taggart and I Siraj, Institute of Education, University of London; E Melhuish, Birkbeck University of London and University of Oxford; 2012*

How neuroscience is affecting education: Report of teacher and parent surveys; Wellcome Trust; 2014. www.wellcome.ac.uk/stellent/groups/corporatesite/…/WTP055240.pdf

The Human Connectome, Mapping the human brain; http://www.humanconnectomeproject. org/

The implications of recent developments in neuroscience for research on teaching and learning; Sarah-Jayne Blakemore and Uta Frith; Institute of Cognitive Neuroscience; 2000. www.tlrp. org/pub/…/Neuroscience%20Commentary%20FINAL.pdf

Neuromyths in Education: Prevalence and Predictors of Misconceptions among Teachers; OECD; 2012

From Neurons to Neighborhoods: Committee on Integrating the Science of Early Childhood Development; Jack P. Shonkoff and Deborah A. Phillips, Editors; Committee on Integrating the Science of Early Childhood Development, Board on Children, Youth, and Families; 2000

How Babies Think; Alison Gopnik; Scientific American; 2010, www.alisongopnik.com/papers_alison/sciam-gopnik.pdf

Neuroscience and Education: Issues and Opportunities; A Commentary by the Teaching and Learning Research Programme; TLRP, Teaching and Learning Research Project; 2007. *www. tlrp.org/pub/…/Neuroscience%20Commentary%20FINAL.pdf*

Understanding the Brain: the Birth of a Learning Science. New insights on learning through cognitive and brain science; OECD (Organisation for Economic Co-operation and Development)/CERI (Centre for Educational Research and Innovation); 2008

Understanding the Brain; OECD/CERI; 2007. www.oecd.org/site/educeri21st/40554190.pdf

Index